From victory
to Vichy

MANCHESTER
1824

Manchester University Press

Cultural History of Modern War
Series editors

Ana Carden-Coyne, Peter Gatrell, Max Jones, Penny Summerfield and
Bertrand Taithe

Already published

Centre for the
Cultural History
of War

From victory to Vichy

Veterans in inter-war France

~

CHRIS MILLINGTON

Manchester University Press

Published by Manchester University Press
Altrincham Street, Manchester M1 7JA, UK
www.manchesteruniversitypress.co.uk

British Library Cataloguing-in-Publication Data is available

Library of Congress Cataloging-in-Publication Data is available

ISBN 978 1 5261 0659 9 *paperback*

First published by Manchester University Press in hardback 2012

This edition first published 2016

Printed by Lightning Source

For Alexandra

Contents

Acknowledgements

The practical and financial support of several institutions made this book possible. I thank the staff and students of the School of History, Archaeology and Religion at Cardiff University for providing the friendly, helpful and inspiring environment in which this project began and ended. I spent a stimulating year with the staff and students of Birkbeck, University of London. In particular, I enjoyed many discussions on inter-war France with the postgraduates whom I taught.

For financial aid at various stages of writing this book, I thank the Arts and Humanities Research Council, the British Academy Postdoctoral Fellowship scheme, the Cardiff School of History, Archaeology and Religion, the Institute of Historical Research, the Scouloudi Foundation and the Society for the Study of French History. I am grateful to the staff of the Archives nationales and the Bibliothèque nationale in Paris, the Centre des archives contemporaines at Fontainebleau, Sciences-Po, and the Arts and Social Studies library at Cardiff University for their help throughout my research. I thank too the staff at Manchester University Press for their assistance.

I thank the staff, members and president Hugues Dalleau of the Union nationale des combattants. I was granted unrestricted access to the association's archives and invited to many of the association's events and commemorations, and for this I am grateful. In particular I would like to thank Michel de Muizon, Marité Gaudefroy and Marité Massé, who were always ready to help and made my time at the UNC enjoyable. I thank Hugues de La Rocque for granting access to his grandfather's archives.

There are several people without whom this book would not have been completed. I am especially grateful to those who have read and commented on my work and helped me to develop my arguments in innumerable ways. Special thanks go to Kevin Passmore who provided excellent supervision, kind support and guidance throughout my research. I have enjoyed many conversations about my work with Caroline Campbell and I thank her for commenting on whatever I sent her. I thank Alison Carrol, Richard Hopkins, John Horne, Julian Jackson, Brian Jenkins, Samuel Kalman, Michelle Perkins, Martin Simpson, Jessica Wardhaugh and Louisa Zanoun for their advice and encouragement. David Uhrig deserves special mention for his hospitality, friendship and invaluable help with translations.

The most heartfelt thanks go to my family. I am indebted to my parents, Ron and Jean Millington, who have always offered me their unconditional love, support and generosity. I thank Rich Millington, with whom I have had many conversations about German history, and who, after reading and re-reading my work, hopefully found that French history could be interesting after all. Finally, I would like to thank Alexandra, who was there when it all began on our first day of university together, and quite a while before. Her support of me and this project has been unwavering throughout good times and moments of self-doubt. I am especially grateful for her patience during the long absences that research entails. She has provided help with my work and allowed me to think out loud on countless occasions, enduring many monologues on the history of French veterans in the process. For all these reasons and many more, it is to Alexandra that I dedicate this book.

A version of Chapter 2 was published as 'February 6, 1934: The veterans' riot', in *French Historical Studies*, vol. 33, issue 4, pp. 545–72. Copyright 2010, Society for French Historical Studies. Reprinted by kind permission of the publisher, Duke University Press.

Sections of this book were published in 'The French veterans and the Republic: The Union nationale des combattants and the Union fédérale, 1934-1938', *European History Quarterly*, vol. 42, issue 1. Copyright 2011. Reprinted by kind permission of the publisher, SAGE Publications.

List of abbreviations

ACJF	Association catholique de la jeunesse
AD	Alliance démocratique
AF	Action française
AGMG	Association générale des mutilés de la guerre
ARAC	Association républicaine des anciens combattants
CF	Croix de Feu
CGT	Confédération générale du travail
CIAMAC	Conférence internationale des associations de mutilés et anciens combattants
CNE	Conseil national économique
DRAC	Ligue des droits du religieux ancien combattant
FFCF	Fils et filles des Croix de Feu
FIDAC	Fédération interalliée des anciens combattants
FNC	Fédération nationale catholique
FNCR	Fédération nationale des combattants républicains
FOP	Fédération ouvrière et paysanne
FR	Fédération républicaine
GRP	Groupe de la région parisienne de l'UNC
JC	Jeunesses communistes
JOC	Jeunesse ouvrière chrétienne
JP	Jeunesses patriotes
JUF	Jeunes de l'UF
JUNC	Jeunes de l'UNC
LCF	Légion des combattants français
MSF	Mouvement social français des Croix de Feu
PDP	Parti démocrate populaire
PPF	Parti populaire français
PRNS	Parti républicain national et social

Abbreviations

PSF	Parti social français
SDC	Semaine du combattant
SF	Solidarité française
UF	Union fédérale
UNC	Union nationale des combattants
UNMR	Union nationale des mutilés et réformés
USF	Union sportive française
VN	Volontaires nationaux

Introduction

The *anciens combattants* and their associations

We vowed to each other not to be political and we practiced the only true politics. We made up our minds to do this from the moment it was clear that France no longer had an elite, the republic no longer had leaders, the people had lost faith, society [had lost] its conscience and the *patrie* was losing its soul ... We wanted to operate in France as a moral magistracy outside and above party quarrels ... Whether the problems were moral, political, social or economic, we searched for and found solutions, the same solutions that since 10 July 1940 are the substance of the 'National Revolution'. (Henri Pichot, *Les Combattants avaient raison* ... [Montluçon: Editions de la Maison du combattant, 1940], preface)

In September 1940, Henri Pichot's retrospective verdict on the inter-war years rang true for many French. From the victory of November 1918 to the founding of the Vichy regime in July 1940, an acute sense of national crisis pervaded France. Hopes for political renewal after the Great War were dashed as unstable coalition governments came and went. The dire economic predicament of the 1930s compounded the seeming impotence of democratic government. With 'decadent' France apparently in terminal decline and the faith of many in the parliamentary Third Republic undermined, hundreds of thousands of citizens joined right-wing extra-parliamentary groups known as leagues. The forces of the left confronted league members, verbally and physically, as an undeclared civil war broke out for the future of France.[1] When deputies voted to dissolve the regime after the disastrous collapse to Hitler's armies in June 1940, few were unhappy to see the end of the republic. Of course, there was nothing inevitable about France's defeat, but in 1940 many French found it relatively simple to locate the roots of the catastrophe in the troubled history of the now discredited republic.

Opposition to the Third Republic was not novel to the inter-war years. In the 1880s, General Georges Boulanger's movement for constitutional revision threatened to engage the masses in an anti-parliamentary cam-paign. The following decade, the flawed conviction for treason of Captain Alfred Dreyfus divided the nation between the largely republican Drey-fusards and the clericalist and right-wing anti-Dreyfusards. Nationalist intellectuals leant their weight to the cause against the regime. Maurice Barrès' theory of 'rootedness' in the land and Charles Maurras's depic-tion of the divorce between the *pays légal* (parliament) and the *pays réel* (the people) influenced the republic's enemies for decades.[2] Maurras's monarchist Action française (AF) movement presented the most strident challenge to the republic prior to the Great War.

Though the eruption of fighting in 1914 rallied the left and right to the regime in the spirit of the Sacred Union, the successful outcome of the war did not appease the republic's detractors for long. The victory of the Bloc national in 1919 may have placated conservatives but the agitation of organised labour spread the fear of communist revolution. Ephemeral parliamentary governments and the victory of the Cartel des gauches in 1924 revivified the right-wing enemies of the regime. Leagues such as Georges Valois's Faisceau, Antoine Rédier's Légion and Pierre Taittinger's Jeunesses patriotes (JP) espoused authoritarian plans to replace the ail-ing parliamentary regime, while the business and industrial elites took up the cause of Ernest Mercier's Redressement français.[3]

The republic weathered these storms yet during the 1930s it faced an unprecedented challenge. Parliamentary scandals, the onset of the glo-bal financial crisis and the instability of government coalitions spread anti-parliamentarianism beyond the preserve of extremist groups to the mainstream press and society at large. The riots of 6 February 1934, in which thousands of members of nationalist leagues and war veterans forced the centre-left government to resign, polarised French politics. Membership of the leagues rocketed. The exemplar of this growth was Colonel François de La Rocque's authoritarian Croix de Feu (CF). Its suc-cessor, the Parti social français (PSF), became the largest political group in French history. The extreme and parliamentary left joined forces in the Popular Front, alarmed at what they saw as the attempted 'fascist' coup of February 1934. The left's victory in the elections of May 1936 cemented the division of French politics.

The veterans of the Great War could not escape these developments. In 1920 there were 6.4 million war veterans in France. Approximately 3 mil-lion of these men would join a veterans' association during the inter-war years. Ex-servicemen's groups were not a new phenomenon in France. Veterans of the Franco-Prussian War had founded mutual aid societies that in several respects foreshadowed their successors. The groups offered a means to relive the fraternity of wartime and to commemorate the conflict and its battles. Associations also provided private welfare for veterans and widows.[4] The divergent experiences of both wars accounted for differences in the veterans' associations of the two conflicts. Veterans of 1871 were much fewer in number. Tainted by the defeat to Prussia, they were an unwelcome reminder of a past the nation wished to forget.[5] Conversely, the victorious Great War veteran, whether perceived as the living incarnation of order, moral authority and the nation, or a hero of the working class opposed to capitalist warmongers, was said to understand better than anyone else the interests of a nation for whom he had shed his blood. This 'veteran mystique' provided a convenient mobilising myth for an array of veteran and non-veteran groups. For the veterans' associations, the shared experience of the war lay at the heart of their claim to a common identity. It made the veterans a potentially powerful political force.[6]

This ostensible unity did not translate into a unified association. Veterans' groups came to reflect the political loyalties of their founders and members. The two largest associations were the centre-left Union fédérale (UF) and the conservative Union nationale des combattants (UNC). Of the 3 million veterans who belonged to an association, the UF and the UNC represented a sizeable portion, with around 900,000 members each. Other than these two heavyweight associations, many more existed, such as the right-wing Association générale des mutilés de la guerre (AGMG) and the communist Association républicaine des anciens combattants (ARAC). Few groups possessed the support and resources available to the UF and the UNC.[7] The smaller associations could conceivably redress the balance through the Confédération nationale des anciens combattants et victimes de la guerre, a veterans' forum founded in November 1927. Yet the potency of the Confédération largely depended on the sporadic enthusiasm of the UF and the UNC for this inter-associational body.[8]

Founded at Lyon in February 1918, the UF was a federation of departmental veteran and war-wounded (*mutilés*) associations. Formed on the initiative of autonomous provincial groups, it maintained a democratic organisation and structure. Recruitment was not restricted to those who had seen active service during the war. Though less successful than the UNC in recruiting members in the immediate post-war years, the UF overtook its competitor in the 1930s, claiming more than 1 million members in 1939.[9] It was strongest in the south-east and the Nivernais as well as other areas where personalities dominated such as Pichot, the UF's most prominent figure, in the Loiret. A primary school teacher, Pichot was wounded in 1914 and subsequently captured by the Germans. Having returned to France, he co-founded the Mutilés du Loiret group in December 1916 and two years later entered the executive committee of the UF. Intermittently president of the national association until May 1934, when he took up the post permanently, Pichot founded and edited the UF's three major national publications: *La France mutilée*, the *Cahiers de l'UF* and *Notre France*. The association also produced its own version of the *Journal des mutilés et réformés*, the only veterans' newspaper available at newsstands. With a significant number of civil servants present in its leadership, the UF leant towards the radical party. It supported the centre-left Cartel governments of 1924–26 and 1932–34 and in May 1936, the UF gave its backing to the newly elected Popular Front.

The UNC was founded in Paris on 11 November 1918 as an association for ex-soldiers. The idea of Father Daniel Brottier while still in the trenches, the association received a grant of 100,000 francs from prime minister Georges Clemenceau to aid its founding. General Léon Durand became the UNC's first president and, with Brottier, formulated the UNC's 'united as at the front' motto. The association's leadership was predominantly bourgeois. With a smaller proportion of leaders from the liberal professions than the UF, the UNC had more former officers, industrialists and representatives of commercial interests among its principal members than its rival. This conservative complexion found favour with the army, the Church and business. The networks of these influential backers, along with the UNC's national weekly newspaper, *La Voix du combattant*, allowed the association to spread quickly throughout France, especially in traditionally conservative areas.[10] From a total of 6,000 members in 1919, the UNC grew to count 300,000 followers in 1923. By 1929, it had approximately 392,000 members. At the end of the inter-war period this number had more than doubled to 900,000 members.[11]

The UF and the UNC were divided on foreign and domestic policy. In foreign matters the UF supported the League of Nations and Aristide Briand's ideas on the international organisation of peace. The association favoured rapprochement with Germany and to this end the UF was instrumental in founding the Conférence internationale des associations de mutilés et anciens combattants (CIAMAC) in 1925. The UNC continued to regard Germany with suspicion and it distrusted the League of Nations. Instead of collective security, the association preferred to maintain wartime alliances through bodies such as the Fédération interalliée des anciens combattants (FIDAC), founded in 1920 with the UNC's first secretary general Charles Bertrand as president. Only in 1931 did the UNC come round to a *briandiste* position though old misgivings remained.[12]

In domestic politics, during the 1920s the UF and the UNC fought several campaigns for the improvement of veterans' state financial benefits. The associations did not shy away from other issues. In July 1926, for example, the Mellon-Bérenger agreement between France and the US failed to prioritise the issue of reparations over that of war debt repayments. If Germany defaulted, France would go on paying. Through a public display of discontent, the associations aimed to force a change in policy. On 11 July 1926, veterans from many groups protested on the streets of Paris. Conservatives in the movement perhaps hoped to topple the ruling majority too.[13] It would not be the last time that some veterans took to the streets with a political goal in mind.

The 1930s saw the associations, and especially the UNC, become increasingly involved in politics. Under the presidencies of Henri Rossignol (July 1926–February 1934), Georges Lebecq (February 1934–December 1935) and Jean Goy (December 1935–August 1940) the UNC persistently moved in a more political direction. The association supported rightist governments and reviled left-wing administrations. It participated in the riot of 6 February 1934 during which its members cooperated with leaguers and fought police. The UF's preference for the radicals led it to decry the involvement of its rival in the fall of Edouard Daladier's government the following day. The subsequent polarisation of French politics affected the associations. The UNC founded youth and non-combatant auxiliaries that allowed it to go further in its political action while preserving an apolitical facade. It grew closer to the nationalist leagues. After the elections of May 1936, in contrast to the UF's support for Léon Blum's Popular Front government, the UNC sought to become the centre of an anti-Popular Front alliance that included elements of the extreme right. Its newspaper regularly attacked the left and flatly accused Blum of supplanting the republic with a soviet regime.

Though sometimes bitter, the differences between the UF and the UNC were not irreconcilable and there were sporadic periods of cooperation. The associations made common cause when both felt that the well-being of their members, or the nation, was under threat. A united campaign of all veterans' associations twice succeeded in forcing the government to accept their pension claims. In spring 1934, with the support of the UF, the UNC's programme on state reform became the Confédération's official manifesto on the issue. Finally, the UF and the UNC concluded the inter-war years in close collaboration with each other. In March 1938, as industrial disputes paralysed the French economy and Hitler's violations of the Treaty of Versailles multiplied, the UF and the UNC turned to authoritarian plans for reform of the state. They launched a joint campaign for a government of public safety, which would operate without the machinery of parliamentary democracy. The UF and the UNC, like all combatants' associations, were subsumed into Vichy's Légion française des combattants in August 1940.

'Being' a veteran

In spite of the diverse and fractured nature of the veterans' movement, all associations shared a discursive construction of reality, a 'veterans' world' based on common reference points: the 'combatant spirit' and the 'trench fraternity'. These touchstones had their opposites: the 'politician (or party) spirit' and 'politics'. Each was evoked or denounced at will and all were attributed values and behaviours. It is difficult to discern whether veterans internalised this discursive reality. They were subject to a multitude of cultural, political and social influences. The discourse of the veterans' associations, however preponderant within the movement, was but one of these influences.

Nonetheless, veterans from all associations reproduced in speeches and writings the same broad themes. The combatant spirit and the trench fraternity were intimately linked. The latter gave birth to the former and consequently influenced its characteristics. The much eulogised and mythologised trench fraternity was a classless society. Men had fought united, shoulder-to-shoulder with no regard for military rank.[14] Through their bravery and self-sacrifice, measured in their muscles and their courage, the martyrs and saints of the front proved themselves as men.[15] Veterans learnt the virtuous lesson of the war and returned home regenerated and impregnated with morality and selflessness.[16] The veterans' associations thus claimed this egalitarian and moral heritage.

Discussion of the combatant spirit depicted veterans in an overwhelmingly positive light. The trench experience gifted veterans a common soul, transforming them into a homogeneous mass that would spread the combatant faith.[17] Physically and morally, the veterans were the most healthy, stable and sure elite.[18] They possessed many righteous qualities including sincerity, honesty, probity, dignity and justice.[19] They were patriotic too. Having fought and bled for France the veterans thought and acted 'en français' and were apostles of the Fatherland.[20] The veterans

alone were thus capable of bringing about recovery, rally, reform, resurrection, renovation and rejuvenation.[21] Bringing a burst of vigour to
France, the veterans' programme was supple, open, flexible and uniquely
realistic.[22] Their work would be constructive, expressed as building a new
order, a cathedral, or city.[23]

Politicians and politics represented the antitheses of the veterans'
values. Politicians engaged in mad battles with political rivals; their influence was divisive.[24] 'Intellectually colour-blind' to the ideas of other
parties and serving exclusively political ends, politicians' incompetence and
idleness paralysed the country.[25] Parliamentarians left France to fate and had
little clue about proper government.[26] Suspicion, trickery and criminality
surrounded the political classes. These false gods hid behind masks and
hidden forces.[27] Their hoodwinking was intoxicating and the veterans
feared being duped and domesticated.[28] At their most violent, veterans
described politicians as thieves, liars, murderers, bastards and swine.[29]

Further themes characterised veteran discourse on politics and politicians. Some of these themes bore the mark of the wartime experience.
Veterans accused politicians of being in league with war profiteers and
shirkers. Deputies were said to have waited out the war tranquilly in
their armchairs.[30] The shirker was an inferior category of man, created by
God with the scraps left over from Adam: stringy muscles, flabby flesh,
flat feet, organs without vigour, a hare's heart and navel juice.[31] Medi-
cal terms provided a vivid means of attack too. Politics was an infection
and a virus.[32] Governments were beset with the rottenness and the gangrene of parties and scandals. All politicians could offer as a remedy were
ointments.[33] Conversely, the veterans would amputate, remove tumours,
clean and disinfect, and perform surgery on the regime.[34]

The contrast between 'words' and 'action' was a well-worn tactic in
veteran discourse. Politicians specialised in snivelling and demoralising
speeches and excelled at useless chitchat.[35] They were not men of action
but pen-pushers and lovers of fine words.[36] Though veterans were not
averse to speechmaking, when they pronounced on subjects their words
were described as stirring, cutting, logical, clear, simple and understood
by all classes.[37] Ultimately, though, veterans favoured action over words.
Their action was coded in gender terms to qualify them further as the
solely capable saviours of France. Acts were male while words were female.[38] Manliness characterised the veteran, from his 'programme of
virility' to his 'virile guts', there was nothing feminine about him. Meanwhile the politician practised an emasculated parliamentarianism that
had left France sterile.[39]

Though the division between veterans and politicians appears straight-forward, certain ambiguities existed in the veterans' conception of the world. The war experience was not always described as regenerative. The conflict had also left veterans with poor, emptied, worn-out, wounded and painful bodies. Maimed and disabled, they sank into rest and docility at the end of the war.[40] Veterans were a martyred youth, broken and disillusioned, consumed with melancholy, rage and disgust.[41] Veterans' involvement in politics was also ambiguous. Most associations claimed to be apolitical. If the veterans admitted at all to undertaking political action (which they often termed 'civic' action), the admission came with a qualification: they practised politics in the 'elevated' sense of the word.[42] Their politics was outside and above the parties; it was new, hardy and independent.[43] Conversely, 'politician politics' was politics in the vulgar sense of the word and 'pure' politics.[44] One could not escape the fact, though, that some veterans belonged to political parties. Opinion in the associations was divided on this matter. In some cases, it was felt useful to spread the combatant spirit within the parties. Infiltration of this kind would improve the quality of parties and politicians. Politics was therefore a duty.[45] Yet others believed that politics (with all its negative connotations) was incompatible with being a veteran. If veterans remained in parties they would be 'officially castrated'.[46] In this case, the combatant spirit was weaker than politics.

The quality of 'being' a veteran itself was not objective. Of course, in the first instance this title depended on one's war record: if one had served as a soldier, one was a veteran. Yet in this respect the veteran community was not egalitarian because, for some associations, there was a hierarchy of wartime experience: the UF admitted war victims as well as veterans, while for the UNC the only true combatant was the one who had risked his life in the trenches.[47] The latter claimed that not only did pensioned non-combatants have different interests to veterans, they had neither the same 'spirit' nor mentality.[48] Status as a veteran depended too upon one's post-war conduct as much as one's army service. Pichot wrote: 'To have fought does not suffice … to remain a combatant; one must continue to serve the country … if not, one is no more than a glorious memory, a respectable past … a dead man on leave … The [veterans'] Association created the civic and social combatant … [it] gave him a reason for being … an isolated combatant has no purpose.'[49] The UNC agreed: the veteran who rejected civic action was a neutral, a eunuch and a beggar.[50] The status of 'veteran' could be withdrawn at will. The UNC denounced the veterans who had stood against its president, Lebecq, when he ran as a candidate in the May 1935 Parisian municipal elections. These men were no longer veterans but 'vile politicians'.[51] Such men, deemed unworthy of the title, were chased from the 'veteran family'.[52]

United with his former comrades through the pseudo-spiritual bond of the combatant spirit, an ex-serviceman's morality was beyond reproach, forged in the egalitarian society of the trenches where men readily gave their lives for their comrades and for the *patrie*. A patriotic and moral force, the veterans would restore France after the catastrophe of the war because, after all, only they knew how. Standing in their way, the veterans alleged, were the elected men of the republic. The veterans' historical legitimacy, based on the war experience, trumped the democratic authority of parliamentarians. Self-interested politicians had waited out the war in the comfort of the Chamber; they could not understand the notion of self-sacrifice. Corrupted by the pursuit of power, parliamentarians looked after only their personal interest. Deputies and parties practised 'politics', a term which implied the worst moral and political practices. Conversely, veterans' associations undertook 'civic action' or 'good' politics in the national interest. It was upon this opposition that the veterans staked their claim to the leadership of France.

'Defining' the veterans

Antoine Prost's *Les anciens combattants et la société française, 1914–1939* (1977) dominates the historiography of the French veterans' movement.[53] Prost demonstrates the importance of the veterans in French society, from their national campaigns that sought to influence government policy on a multitude of issues, to the activity of veterans in the daily associational life of rural French communes. Unlike in Germany and Italy, the French veterans' associations entrenched the social classes most susceptible to fascism within democratic organisations. Hence Prost asserts that despite their inherent antiparliamentarianism, the ex-servicemen's associations were integral to a French inter-war democratic political culture. Accordingly, veterans' bombastic rhetoric counted for little. It was disconnected from reality, full of stereotypes and allegories designed to rouse the enthusiasm of members but contained little seriousness. Although one can read their discourse as fascist, and some 'fascistic' veteran leaders envisaged the creation of a mass movement for 'proto-Vichyite' (*vichyssoise avant l'heure*) state and social reform, the republicanism of provincial veterans meant they did not (and could not) launch a coup.[54] Ordinary veterans may have expressed support for the dangerous ideas of their leaders, yet they did so out of esteem and friendship. They 'knew' that such ideas were not serious. Inherently republican in their aims, methods and 'spontaneous reactions', veterans constituted 'one of the major obstacles to the development of fascism in France'.[55]

Nonetheless, extremist groups laid claim to the symbolic value of the veteran and sought to represent the constituency.[56] Ex-servicemen were the founders and main clientele of extreme right-wing movements that desired an end to the republic. The Faisceau, founded in 1924, sought to attract veterans to a project for their 'Combatant state'. The same year, veterans figured among the founders and leaders of the JP. The CF was created in 1927 as an organisation for decorated veterans and continued to appeal to the veterans throughout its existence. On the extreme left, the ARAC no more sought to shore up the bourgeois regime than did its opponents on the anti-republican extreme right. These groups demonstrate that a sector of the veterans' movement was attracted to extreme and often violent politics. However, regardless of the leagues' claims to represent the veterans, historians largely consider extremist groups unrepresentative of the veterans' movement. Certainly, as Prost points out, it would be wrong to judge the mass of veterans on the practices of the leagues.[57] In any case, he argues that the veterans' movement perceived extreme right-wing groups as a 'foreign body', something different and otherworldly.[58]

The influence of Prost's conclusions is evident in the work of other scholars. Stéphane Audoin-Rouzeau and Annette Becker claim that, unlike in Germany and Italy, once the material demands of the French veterans were satisfied they faded into the background. Robert Soucy admits that the UNC leadership flirted with fascism but that the general membership remained aloof to extremism. Albert Kéchichian states that the UNC and UF were more representative of the veterans' movement than the CF. While arguing that the UNC was important to the growth of the CF, Kevin Passmore supports Prost's conclusion that most veterans were loath to follow the political designs of their leaders. Samuel Kalman questions Prost's conclusion on the benignity of veteran rhetoric but makes no assertion on the extent of its influence on ordinary veterans.[59]

With the benefit of hindsight, one *can* dismiss veteran discourse as 'incantatory'. After all, the veterans did not take power. Yet this judgement rests on a dubious approach to the issue. Firstly, neither the UF nor the UNC encouraged their members to take power violently. True enough, many times the associations warned that they would 'sweep' the republic clean but their intentions remained ambiguous. It is therefore a mistake to designate veteran discourse as unserious because the associations did not seize power; it is not clear that they intended to do so. Secondly, as Michel Dobry argues, the only way to distinguish 'pseudo-revolutionary' from 'authentic revolutionary' language is by reference to the fact that in the former case the revolution did not happen.[60] One should not read backwards from the fact in an attempt to discern the serious from the unserious.

If one accepts the incantatory function of veteran discourse one must also accept that contemporaries understood it as such too, a point that is difficult to examine forensically. One cannot judge how audiences perceived veteran discourse. Did they simply enjoy the showmanship of the speechmaker or the flamboyancy of the author? Or did they read more into such expressions? Would a veteran at the time, living through a period of crisis and upheaval, have appreciated the benign nature of these calls to action? On occasion veterans heeded their leaders' call to action, such as on the night of 6 February 1934 when several thousand UNC veterans took part in the street violence that brought down the elected government. This point is especially pertinent given that veteran discourse *was not* disconnected from political reality. Certainly, groups often condemned politicians and parties en masse but this was not always the case. Particularly after May 1936, when the left came in for venomous criticism, the UNC was not afraid to single out politicians and parties in its acrimonious campaign against the Popular Front.

At first sight much appears to depend on the political definition one assigns to the veterans' movement. But to define the essence or nature of the veterans' associations is also erroneous. Working from a definition, one classifies examples of discourse and action as either revelatory of the true identity of the group or contrary to the group's 'true' nature. This attempt at classification can hinder the study of a group if one seeks to define an 'essence' or 'nature'.[61] This book does not classify the veterans' associations under examination. It understands that rather than being governed by an inherent nature, the UF and the UNC adapted their tactics and discourse according to immediate political context. Certainly, both associations subscribed to certain political traditions, yet they also reacted to dynamic situations in which rhetoric and action were subject to myriad internal and external influences.

Though rejecting classifications, this work nevertheless represents an attack on what Dobry has termed the 'immunity thesis' or the 'orthodox school of French historiography' according to William Irvine and Robert Soucy.[62] Developed in the 1950s and 1960s, under the influence of the resistance-centric history of the Vichy years and the totalitarian model that sought to compare fascist and communist regimes in order to discredit the latter, the immunity thesis pertains to the long implantation of democracy in France and the nation's subsequent 'allergy' to fascism.[63] Any fascist groups that did exist were marginal, insignificant and simply copied foreign fascism. As Michel Winock writes: 'The historiography of contemporary France has long diagnosed our national allergy to fascism. That import product may have had a few fans – but far fewer than the yo-yo or the Charleston.'[64] According to this logic, the veterans' movement was essential to the edification and maintenance of a democratic culture. Veteran anti-parliamentarianism merely expressed a legitimate dissatisfaction with a regime that no longer functioned. The associations' true convictions lay in their ideas on a democratic reform of the state, which foreshadowed the Fourth and Fifth Republics.[65]

Since the 1980s, the immunity thesis has come under attack.[66] Scholars such as Irvine, Soucy and Kevin Passmore stress that fascism was a significant force in France on the level of ideas and political movements. Moreover, the argument for the existence of a common political culture is problematic. However widely a group may publicise its doctrine or ideology, the internalisation of such a culture on an individual level, that is to say for 'ordinary' citizens, is subjective. Each person has prejudices and preconceptions that would make them more or less receptive to one idea or another. One cannot credit a whole nation with the same fundamental political values.[67]

In the case of the veterans, their virulent antiparliamentarianism was greater than a marginal phenomenon in the movement.[68] In branding parliament as incompetent and corrupt, the veterans depicted government as acting contrary to the will of the nation. Though the veterans did not declare their aversion to the Third Republic as a regime, they denied legitimacy to its component parts – its institutions – and their content – parliamentarians. It is difficult to ascertain how (or indeed if) the veterans undermined the perceived legitimacy of the republic in the minds of French citizens. Contemporaries held diverse conceptions of the republic, which often entailed ideas on what the republic *should be*. Nevertheless, one must question to what extent the veterans' violent criticism of the institutions and personnel of the Third Republic constituted an attack on the regime itself and the bearing this has on the conclusion that the UF and the UNC reinforced the French commitment to republican democracy.

The culture of war thesis

Developments in the historiography of the Great War inform the approach of this book.[69] In particular, recent French historiography has centred on the motivations behind the continued participation of soldiers and civilians in the conflict: what sustained the commitment of men and women at the front and the rear as the war worsened and conditions became ever more dire? Two answers, structured in a crude dichotomy, have been proposed: people were either *coerced* into the war, or they *consented* to it. Neither term is wholly satisfactory.[70]

Nevertheless, historians' attempts to determine the motivation of ordinary citizens and soldiers have proved fruitful in the investigation of the 'culture' of the war. The culture of war thesis concerns the conceptual framework (or frameworks) by which soldiers and civilians interpreted and made sense of the experience. Research has shown that Allied soldiers and civilians synthesised patriotic and religious elements to construct (and reconstruct) the war as one fought in defence of Western civilisation against Asian barbarism. Furthermore, the internalisation of scientific and racial thinking led the French to believe themselves a superior race, while Germany was the incarnation of barbarity.[71] As early as 4 August 1914, *Le Matin* described the conflict as 'a holy war of civilisation against barbarity'. The French media ascribed racial characteristics to the enemy, such as 'square heads, sack-like bodies' and a smell like a rabbit hutch, rancid fat and stale beer. Scholarly articles stated and restated these 'scientific findings'.[72] Visceral hatred of the enemy thus sustained the nation long after the illusions of a short war had disappeared. Cultures of war are useful to our understanding of the war experience in so far as they comprise the ideas, values and concepts for which the French persuaded themselves that they were fighting, and why they persuaded themselves to keep fighting.

Cultures such as these survived the end of hostilities. In France, the uncertain international and domestic circumstances following the war meant that the conceptual framework and vocabulary of the culture of war remained in place. Until the conclusion of the Paris peace conference, the prospect of renewed hostilities with Germany remained real. Even once the peace treaties were agreed, suspicion of the 'Boche' remained as France's former enemy appeared unwilling to recognise its guilt and accept punishment. Simultaneously, the culture of war acquired a new target: the revolutionary left. In the closing years of the conflict, a minority on the left had supported a negotiated peace with Germany.

Conservatives accused these 'traitors' of working for the enemy. When the Bolsheviks came to power in Russia and denounced the war, it was easy for the right to believe that the revolutionary left was in fact working for German ends. Post-war industrial unrest coincided with the peace negotiations, leading conservatives to associate the Bolshevik with the German, both of whose chicanery appeared coordinated and blatant. In sum, France had demobilised militarily and economically but 'cultural demobilisation', to borrow John Horne's term, remained elusive.[73]

Only in the mid-1920s did a more conciliatory atmosphere pervade France. This created favourable conditions for the demobilisation of wartime representations, values and mentalities to begin in earnest on a national scale. By 1924, France had come to terms with the process of mourning. Most local and national sites of commemoration had been established and the reconstruction of the 2.5 million hectares of devastated land in the north-east was well advanced. The 'internal enemies' of wartime were rehabilitated, including soldiers who had been executed during the war and politicians such as Joseph Caillaux who had been suspected of harbouring sympathies for a negotiated peace. The conciliatory foreign policy of the Cartel further facilitated the demobilisation of the war culture. Foreign minister Briand led a significant departure from the Bloc national's *poincariste* intransigence. In 1925 he concluded the Locarno Pact with Germany and in 1926 he negotiated Germany's entry to the League of Nations. The German wartime 'brute' was now humanised. He became a civilised comrade in the common struggle against the threat of war.[74] Yet the slow process of cultural demobilisation was neither linear nor complete. For some French, the German would remain the Boche. The veterans' movement demonstrates the complexities of France's metaphorical exit from the war. While the UF was prepared to consider reconciliation with the Germans long before cultural demobilisation took hold in France more generally, the UNC reluctantly accepted *briandisme* only in 1931.

Cultural demobilisation may have brought the right into the *briandiste* fold yet it did not affect conservatives' conception of communism. The communist remained an enemy of France and Western civilisation. The Soviet Union was a barbaric state that sought to extend its influence within France. Between 1924 and 1926, when the rehabilitation of the German was under way, the right's fear of the left worsened. The return of Raymond Poincaré to the premiership in July 1926 reassured conservatives and their fear of revolution receded. Poincaré kept Briand at the Foreign Office and reconciliation with Germany continued. However, though a right-wing government had now opted for reconciliation with Germany, cultural demobilisation did little to weaken the culture of war's association with the revolutionary left. In 1926, the threat from communism may have abated but the culture of war survived, ready to be employed the next time the revolutionary left challenged the right.

This challenge came in summer 1936. In May, the French had elected their first socialist prime minister, Léon Blum. His Popular Front government ruled with the ministerial participation of the socialists and radicals and the support of the communists. When in July 1936, the communists pressed for French intervention in the Spanish Civil War, the right took fright. Intervention, the right alleged, would lead to civil war in France and possibly a general war in Europe, to the sole benefit of the Soviet Union. Once again, the communist barbarian seemed to threaten European peace for the profit of an enemy of Western civilisation. This time though, communists were part of the governing coalition. It was not long before the culture of war was transposed onto the whole of the Popular Front, which was now alleged to be in the pay of Moscow.

The connection between the veterans and the culture of war may seem obvious. Yet just as the war gave rise to a multiplicity of experiences there was no unitary experience of the post-war, especially in the organisationally and politically diverse veterans' movement. Given the nationalism inherent to the war culture it is unsurprising that it persisted most strongly in right-wing associations. This attachment to the right was further reinforced by the subsequent association of the culture with anti-communism. Certainly, nationalism and anti-communism were not alien to the left but, in the context of this book, the left-leaning UF experienced the broader process of cultural demobilisation. Though the UNC came to accept *briandisme* its anti-communism, influenced by the war culture, remained. Little can be drawn from this regarding the brutalisation of French soldiers on a personal level. The persistence of the culture of war hints at a more general brutalisation of French politics yet it is beyond the scope of this study to trace a direct relationship between the culture of war and France's nationalist leagues in the same way that George Mosse demonstrated the importance of the 'Myth of the War Experience' to political violence in inter-war Germany. Rather, the culture of war remained a weapon in the arsenal of the right, suited to particular purposes and circumstances.

This book does not claim to offer a comprehensive history of the veterans' movement. Rather it seeks to reassess the political history of the UF and the UNC in inter-war France. The following chapter traces the trajectory of both associations from the end of the war until the close of 1933. This period saw the development of characteristics and behaviours in the veterans' movement in general and the UF and the UNC in particular. Generally, though diverse, the multitude of veterans' associations showed the ability to unite in a common cause, such as the campaigns for pensions in 1924 and 1932. The UF established itself as firmly supportive of the parliamentary regime though its criticism of parliamentarians remained sharp. The UNC's attachment to parliamentary government was revealed to be conditional. When the right was in power, the association was more or less content. Under left-wing governments, the UNC allied with violent anti-parliamentary leagues. However, its members were split between those who favoured such action and others who remained anxious about political involvement. This split was a lasting feature of the UNC.

Chapter 2 re-examines the role of the UNC in the riots of 6 February 1934. Important to an understanding of the Third Republic and its decline, the night opened a virtual French civil war that would not end until the Liberation a decade later. The riot has been the keystone of the immunity thesis for decades. While the chapter does not argue that the veterans attempted a coup it does offer a more nuanced interpretation than previous accounts and it affirms further the UNC's conditional support for the regime. On the night, though the association claimed to march peacefully and in protest against government corruption, its veterans collaborated with leaguers and engaged in violence against the police.

Chapter 3 concerns the movement for state reform of spring and summer 1934. With reformism gaining unprecedented popularity, the UF and the UNC undertook a vigorous campaign for an authoritarian reform of the republic. Though united, the associations' motives differed starkly. Having lost faith in the parliamentary system following the February riot, the UF turned to constitutional revision to restore authority to the republic. With the conservative Gaston Doumergue now in power, the UNC placed its confidence in parliament and the new government. The association hoped that Doumergue would reform republican institutions according to its authoritarian programme. The veterans' campaign culminated in the 8 July ultimatum in which the Confédération threatened to topple the government if the veterans' demands were not met.

Chapter 4 investigates the veterans' links with the extreme right. Based on the success of the CF, the UNC launched its own league-style auxiliary. The Action combattante group found support among some local sections and marked an escalation in UNC political tactics. Furthermore, UNC veterans collaborated with extreme right-wing leagues at a local and national level. They joined these groups and patronised their meetings for political purposes. Cooperation with leagues that desired an end to the Third Republic further demonstrates the detachment of some UNC veterans from the regime. This course of action was not uncomplicated. Moderates in the UNC rejected the leagues and disapproved of activists' association with these groups, especially the CF.

Chapter 5 explores the role of youth and young people in the discourse and activities of the UF and the UNC. Each association used the concept of youth as a political weapon to cast doubt on the competence of incumbent parliamentarians and further reinforce the veterans' own perceived legitimacy. Both associations founded a youth group. The Jeunes de l'UF (JUF) and the Jeunes de l'UNC (JUNC) were diverse entities. In general, they offered members sporting, leisure and cultural pursuits. The JUF was concerned with the social and material situation of French youth. Its interest in politics was not great. On the other hand, the JUNC engaged in political action. It encouraged its members to work with the leagues and it did not shy away from demands for authoritarian government.

Chapter 6 looks at the UF and the UNC's actions during the reign of the Popular Front governments after May 1936. With the left once again in power, the UF expressed optimism. It had always been supportive of the radicals and it was heartened to see the government take account of the France's largest labour union the Confédération générale du travail (CGT) in its strategy too. This optimism would not last and by 1938 disillusionment gripped the UF. Conversely, the UNC's hostility to the Popular Front was constant and relentless. Accusing the government of subjugation to Moscow, the UNC feared that the left would drag France into a communist-sponsored war. The culture of war, still attached to the revolutionary left, resurfaced in the association's attacks on the coalition. By March 1938, both associations were displeased with the leftist alliance. Prompted by persistent ministerial instability and worrying developments in international politics, the UF and the UNC united in a campaign to restore authority to France. The 'public safety' government would operate without the machinery of parliamentary democracy. With the parliamentary parties 'on ice', a government of veterans and 'national' figures would work unhindered towards French recovery. Both associations developed an ever closer relationship that in part foreshadowed Vichy's unified veterans' Legion.

Though the UF and the UNC did not explicitly demand an end to the republican regime, they decried incessantly the practices and inefficiencies of the parliamentary system and the conduct and alleged self-interest of parliamentarians. Their attacks targeted successive administrations of left and right, ministers and ministries and the electoral system. The associations' depiction of the government as in opposition to a subjective 'national' interest eventually came to encompass the regime. As a result, the veterans' plans for state reform would not have left the institutions of the Third Republic intact. In casting doubt on the capability of republican institutions and parliamentarians to represent the national interest and in posing themselves as the true representatives of these, the veterans undermined the perceived legitimacy of the regime.

The outbreak of the Second World War and the establishment of the Vichy regime meant that the veterans no longer needed to establish their own government of national and moral union. Ostensibly concerned for the efficiency of the republic, the veterans came to define effective government as a strong authoritarian regime under a military personality with scant regard for parliamentary mores. The UF and the UNC exposed their members to these authoritarian ideas. In doing so, they prepared the ground for the Vichy regime. However, while it may be tempting to assume a direct and uncomplicated trajectory from the Great War to Vichy, such a retrospective analysis obscures the complexities of the period. The veterans may have felt vindicated in 1940, but this book shows that their political history was neither linear nor uncomplicated.

Notes

1 Julian Jackson, *France: The Dark Years 1940–1944* (Oxford: Oxford University Press, 2001), p. 65; Robert O. Paxton, *Vichy France: Old Guard and New Order* (New York: Knopf & Random House, 1972), p. 243.

2 Samuel Kalman, *The Extreme Right in Interwar France: The Faisceau and the Croix de Feu* (Aldershot: Ashgate, 2008), p. 14.

3 François Monnet, *Refaire la République: André Tardieu, une dérive réactionnaire, 1876–1945* (Paris: Fayard, 1993), pp. 201–2. Kalman, *The Extreme Right* examines the Faisceau in the 1920s. On the JP in the 1920s see volumes I and II of Jean Philippet, *Le Temps des Ligues: Pierre Taittinger et les Jeunesses Patriotes*, 5 vols (Lille: Atelier national de reproduction de thèses, 2000). Robert Soucy, *French Fascism: The First Wave* (New Haven, CT and London: Yale University Press, 1986) looks briefly at the Légion and the AF and in depth at the JP and the Faisceau. On Ernest Mercier and the Redressement français see Richard F. Kuisel, *Ernest Mercier: French Technocrat* (Berkeley, CA: University of California Press, 1967).

4 Bertrand Taithe, *Defeated Flesh: Welfare, Warfare and the Making of Modern France* (Manchester: Manchester University Press, 1999), pp. 197–205;

Introduction

Karine Varley, *Under the Shadow of Defeat: The War of 1870–1871 in French Memory* (Basingstoke and New York: Palgrave Macmillan, 2008), pp. 126–7.

5 Taithe, *Defeated Flesh*, p. 181.

6 Richard Bessel, 'The "front generation" and the politics of Weimar Germany', in Mark Roseman (ed.), *Generations in Conflict: Youth Revolt and Generation Formation in Germany, 1770–1968* (Cambridge and New York: Cambridge University Press, 1995), pp.121–2.

7 Antoine Prost, *Les Anciens Combattants et la société française, 1914–1939*, 3 vols (Paris: Presses de la Fondation nationale des Sciences politiques, 1977), I, pp. 83–6.

8 *Ibid.*, pp. 110–11 and p. 124.

9 Elliot Pennell Fagerberg, *The 'Anciens Combattants' and French Foreign Policy* (Geneva: Graduate Institute of International Studies, 1966), p. 30.

10 Prost, *Les Anciens Combattants*, I, p. 59.

11 Fagerberg, *The 'Anciens Combattants' and French Foreign Policy*, pp. 42–3.

12 Prost, *Les Anciens Combattants*, I, p. 139.

13 *Ibid.*, p. 100.

14 P. Galland, 'Une formule creuse', *La Voix du combattant* (hereafter *VC*) (21 July 1934); L. Renard, 'Les Jeunes et nous', *Le Combattant du Poitou* (31 June 1933); H. Arbeletche, 'La Roue tourne', *VC* (18 August 1934). In all references to press articles, the author is cited where known.

15 F. Jouet, 'Le pain! la paix! la liberté! et notre droit', *L'Union fédérale du Gard* (April 1936); 'Groupe de Bourgogne et Franche-Comté', *VC* (31 December 1938); R. Dorgelès, 'S'ils avaient gardé l'âme d'antan', *VC* (7 April 1934).

16 H. Pichot, 'UF1918–1934', *Les Cahiers de l'UF* (hereafter *CUF*) (1 January 1934); P. Delore, 'Pensées d'automne', *Le Combattant du centre* (December 1933); 'L'heure des Anciens Combattants', *L'UNC de Paris* (22 February 1934).

17 P. Galland, 'Union pour le Salut', *VC* (5 December 1936); A. Linville, 'Les AC et la vie publique', *Journal des mutilés et réformés* (hereafter *JM*) (27 May 1934); Vincent, 'La foi combattante', *VC* (14 August 1937).

18 J. Fourcade-Chourry, 'Jeunes et Anciens ont des obligations mutuelles', *VC* (25 February 1939).

19 Vincent, 'La peur de vivre', *VC* (30 July 1934); H. Arbeletche, 'La Roue tourne', *VC* (18 August 1934).

20 A. Goudaert, 'La tâche d'aujourd'hui et de demain', *VC* (17 November 1934); H. Arbeletche, 'La Roue tourne', *VC* (18 August 1934); H. Isaac, 'Ce que doit être notre tâche', *VC* (6 November 1937).

21 Patay, 'Debout les survivants!' *Le Combattant d'Ille-et-Vilaine* (15 October 1934); H. Pichot, 'L'Esprit Combattant', *CUF* (1–15 September 1934); H. Pichot, 'Le gouvernement du 11 novembre 1934', *CUF* (15 November 1934).

22 Archives nationales, Paris (hereafter AN) F7/12954, 'Les institutions

parlementaires attaquées par divers groupements d'anciens combattants', 20 February 1926; Y. Fouéré, 'Doctrine et programme', *Notre France* (hereafter *NF*) (June 1936).

23 P. Delore, 'Eléments de rénovation', *VC* (21 July 1934); A. Goudaert, 'Ayons confiance … en nous', *VC* (12 January 1935); G. Dubray, 'L'esprit combattant dans la renaissance française', *VC* (10 October 1936).

24 H. Pichot, 'Pour une autorité républicaine: Que fera l'Union fédérale?', *CUF* (1 March 1934); 'Rassemblement', *VC* (11 November 1936).

25 H. Aubert, 'Le Français cafardeux', *VC* (20 November 1937); R. Dulys, 'Le devoir militaire', *VC* (20 April 1935); Hoffmann, 'Les Anciens Combattants et la politique', *VC* (12 January 1935); 'L'Esprit du Parti', *VC* (8 January 1938); 'Principales allocutions: Henri Pichot', *CUF* (10–25 April 1939); 'Le Trait', *L'UNC de Normandie* (March 1934).

26 H. Rossignol, 'Nous ne ratifierons pas', *VC* (3 July 1926); P. Galland, 'Et nous avons péché aussi', *VC* (12 June 1926).

27 G. de Cromières, 'Pays d'esclave', *Le Combattant du centre* (October 1936); 'Après la Manifestation de l'UNC à la salle Wagram à Paris', *Le Combattant du centre* (November 1933); G. de Cromières, 'Hier et demain', *Le Combattant du centre* (August 1936).

28 H. Aubert, 'C'est notre faute', *VC* (27 November 1937); P. Delore, 'Sauvegarder et affirmer l'esprit combattant', *VC* (25 September 1937); A. Linville, 'L'action s'engage', *JM* (22 October 1933); H. Aubert, 'L'esprit combattant. Vit-il encore?' *VC* (11 April 1925).

29 G. de Cromières, 'Vérité', *Le Combattant du centre* (March 1934); A. Godon, 'Menteur, Lâche, Assassin', *L'Echo montmartrois* (February 1934); A. Linville, 'La situation', *JM* (14 February 1934).

30 'Ce qu'est le Nazisme', *VC* (30 December 1933).

31 'L'embusqué', *Le Mutilé et combattant de la Haute-Loire* (March 1935).

32 D. Tritsch, 'Où il est question de microbe', *VC* (29 July 1933); H. Arbeletche, 'Redressment, Rénovation', *Le Poilu basque* (November 1933).

33 P. Galland, 'Ambassadeurs de la justice' (10 March 1934); H. Pichot, 'Billet 1939', *NF* (January 1939); H. Aubert, 'Examen de conscience', *VC* (7 July 1934).

34 D. Tritsch, 'Où il est question de microbe', *VC* (29 July 1933); P. Galland, 'La Révolution dans l'ordre', *VC* (21 April 1934); H. Aubert, 'En écoutant le Président Doumergue', *VC* (29 September 1934).

35 H. Aubert, 'Sous le signe de l'espérance', *VC* (2 January 1937); Vimal, 'Demain', *Le Combattant d'Ille-et-Vilaine* (11 November 1933).

36 G. Vandewalle, 'Les Coupables', *Le Créneau* (May 1934).

37 Patay, 'Notre nouveau Président Général', *Le Combattant d'Ille-et-Vilaine* (15 December 1935); G. Brissac, 'Avec Henri Pichot au congrès de Meurthe-et-Garonne', *NF* (March 1938).

38 H. Aubert, 'Pour que ça aille bien', *VC* (2 February 1935).

39   R. Dulys, 'Le devoir militaire', *VC* (20 April 1935); Bordachar, 'Plaidoyer pour les Jeunes … et contre nous', *VC* (21 January 1933); H. Rossignol, 'Lettre d'un militant', *VC* (13 February 1926); H. Pichot, 'L'âme des Jeunes', *La Revue des Vivants* (October 1927); L. Schaepelynck, 'Les Raisons d'une Action Nationale des Anciens Combattant', *VC* (1 September 1928).

40   F. Jouet, 'Le pain! la paix! la liberté! et notre droit', *L'Union fédérale du Gard* (April 1936); AN, F7/12954, 'Les institutions parlementaires attaquées par divers groupements d'anciens combattants', 20 February 1926; H. Aubert, 'C'est notre faute', *VC* (27 November 1937).

41   R. Marin, 'Avec ceux qui en sont revenus', *VC* (27 October 1934); P. Galland, 'Chant pour l'UNC, à Georges Lebecq', *Le Combattant du centre* (October 1934); H. Aubert, 'Le Français cafardeux', *VC* (20 November 1937).

42   A. Parmentier, 'Le 6 Février 1934', *Le Front* (January–February 1934).

43   Tapin, 'Rivollet au Ministère des Pensions', *Le Béquillard meusienne* (March 1934); H. Pichot, 'La politique', *La France Mutilée* (hereafter *FM*) (10 June 1923); P. Guillermou, 'La politique et les Anciens Combattants', *Après le combat* (December 1934).

44   H. Pichot, 'Des Hommes de Fer!' *NF* (May 1939); A. Parmentier, 'Le 6 Février 1934', *Le Front* (January–February 1934); J. Bonnefoi. 'Les Anciens Combattant et la Politique', *Le Front* (March 1931).

45   J. Pintout, 'La Politique', *Le Combattant creusois* (February 1934); J. Pintout, 'Après le 8 juillet', *Le Combattant creusois* (September 1934).

46   E. Lacquièze, 'Les AC et la politique', *VC* (21 April 1928).

47   'Combattant? Ils veulent tous l'avoir été', *VC* (3 April 1926).

48   H. Isaac, 'Retour de Nice', *VC* (17 April 1926).

49   H. Pichot, 'Combattants', *Après le combat* (November–December 1933).

50   E. Scharpf, 'Encore les neutres!', *VC* (20 April 1933).

51   'Ignobles procédés', *VC* (18 May 1935).

52   L. Vandewalle, 'Le Sang a coulé', *Le Créneau* (February 1934).

53   See also Lynette Shaw, 'The anciens combattants and the events of February 1934', *European Studies Review*, 5 (1975), 299–311. Shaw's article was published in 1975, the same year as Serge Berstein, *Le 6 février* (Paris: Gallimard, 1975), which includes an examination of the UNC's role on 6 February 1934; Jean-Noël Jeanneney, 'Les anciens combattants: Fascistes ou démocrates?', *Histoire*, 1 (1978), 86–8; Robert Soucy, 'France: Veteran politics between the wars', in Stephen R. Ward (ed.), *The War Generation: Veterans of the First World War* (Port Washington, NY and London: Kennikat Press, 1975), pp. 59–103; Lyn Gorman, 'The anciens combattants and appeasement: From Munich to war', *War and Society*, 10 (1992), 73–89. Recent works on aspects of the veterans' movement include Sophie Delaporte, *Gueules cassées de la Grande Guerre* (Paris: Viénot, 2004); Martin Hurcombe, 'Raising the dead: Visual representations of the combatant's body in inter-war France', *Journal of War and Culture Studies* 1 (2008), 159–74; Rebecca Scales, 'Radio

broadcasting, disabled veterans, and the politics of national recovery in inter-war France', *French Historical Studies*, 31 (2008), 643–78.

54 Prost, *Les Anciens Combattants*, I, pp. 164–5.

55 *Ibid.*, III, p. 217.

56 For an analysis of the extreme right that covers both decades of the inter-war period see Soucy, *The First Wave* on the JP and the Faisceau, while Soucy's *French Fascism: The Second Wave* (New Haven, CT and London: Yale University Press, 1995) examines the Solidarité Française, CF/PSF and the Parti populaire français. On the CF/PSF see Gareth Adrian Howlett, 'The Croix de Feu, Parti Social Français and Colonel de La Rocque' (Ph.D. dissertation, Nuffield College, Oxford University, 1986); William D. Irvine, 'Fascism in France: The strange case of the Croix de Feu', *Journal of Modern History*, 63 (1991), 271–95; Kalman, *The Extreme Right*; Sean Kennedy, *Reconciling France Against Democracy: The Croix de Feu and the Parti Social Français, 1929–1945* (Montreal and London: McGill-Queen's University Press, 2007); Cheryl Koos, 'Fascism, fatherhood, and the family in interwar France: The case of Antoine Rédier and the Légion', *Journal of Family History*, 24 (1999), 317–29; Didier Leschi, 'L'étrange cas La Rocque', in Michel Dobry (ed.), *Le Mythe de l'allergie française au fascisme* (Paris: Albin Michel, 2003), pp. 155–94; Kevin Passmore, 'Boy-scouting for grown-ups? Paramilitarism in the Croix de Feu and the Parti Social Français', *French Historical Studies*, 19 (1995), 527–57; 'The Croix de Feu: Bonapartism, national populism or fascism?', *French History*, 9 (1995), 93–123; '"Planting the tricolour in the citadels of communism": Women's social action in the Croix de Feu and Parti Social Français', *Journal of Modern History*, 71 (1999), 814–52; John Rymell, 'Militants and Militancy in the Croix de Feu and Parti Social Français: Patterns of Political Experience on the French Far Right (1933–1939)'(Ph.D. dissertation, University of East Anglia, 1990). On the Faisceau see Allen Douglas, 'Violence and Fascism: The case of the Faisceau', *Journal of Contemporary History*, 4 (1984), 689–712. On smaller groups in the 1920s and 1930s that contained some veteran elements see Robert O. Paxton, *French Peasant Fascism: Henry Dorgères's Greenshirts and the Crisis of French Agriculture, 1929–39* (New York and Oxford: Oxford University Press, 1997); Philippet, *Le Temps des Ligues*.

57 Prost, *Les Anciens Combattants*, I, p. 119.

58 *Ibid.*, I, p. 173; III, p. 179.

59 Stéphane Audoin-Rouzeau and Annette Becker, *14–18: Understanding the Great War* (London: Profile, 2002), p. 232; Kalman, *The Extreme Right*, note 123, p. 47; Albert Kéchichian, *Les Croix de Feu à l'âge des fascismes* (Seyssel: Champ Vallon, 2006), p. 33; Kevin Passmore, *From Liberalism to Fascism: The Right in a French Province, 1928–1939* (Cambridge: Cambridge University Press, 1997), p. 223; Soucy, *The Second Wave*, pp. 29–30.

60 Michel Dobry, 'February 1934 and the discovery of French society's allergy to the 'Fascist Revolution', in Brian Jenkins (ed.), *France in the Era of Fascism*

(New York: Berghahn, 2005), p. 134. Dobry's chapter is a translation of the article 'Février 1934 et la découverte de l'allergie de la société française à la "Révolution fasciste", *Revue française de sociologie*, XXX (1989), 511–33.

61 Michel Dobry, 'La thèse immunitaire face aux fascismes. Pour une critique de la logique classificatoire', in Dobry (ed.), *Le Mythe de l'allergie française au fascisme*, p. 5.

62 Irvine, 'Fascism in France', 294; Soucy, *The Second Wave*, p. 6.

63 Brian Jenkins, 'Contextualising the immunity thesis', in Jenkins (ed.), *France in the Era of Fascism*, p. 6.

64 Michel Winock, *Nationalisme, antisémitisme et fascisme en France* (Paris: Editions du Seuil, 2004), p. 195.

65 Prost, *Les Anciens Combattants*, III, p. 219.

66 See the collection of essays in Dobry (ed.), *Le Mythe de l'allergie française au fascisme* especially Dobry, 'La thèse immunitaire'; Irvine, 'Fascism in France'; Passmore, *From Liberalism to Fascism*; 'The Croix de Feu'; Robert Soucy, 'French fascism and the Croix de Feu: A dissenting interpretation', *Journal of Contemporary History* 26 (1991), 159–88; *The Second Wave*; 'Fascism in France: Problematising the immunity thesis', in Jenkins (ed.), *France in the Era of Fascism*, pp. 65–104.

67 Kevin Passmore, 'The construction of crisis in interwar France', in Jenkins (ed.), *France in the Era of Fascism*, p. 164.

68 Leschi concurs. 'L'étrange cas La Rocque', pp. 155–94.

69 Audoin-Rouzeau and Becker, *14–18*, pp. 94–159; Annette Becker, *La Guerre et la foi* (Paris: Armand Colin, 1994); John Horne, 'Remobilizing for "total war": France and Britain, 1917–1918', in John Horne (ed.), *State, Society and Mobilization in Europe during the First World War* (Cambridge and New York: Cambridge University Press, 1997), pp. 195–212; Alan Kramer, *Dynamic of Destruction: Culture and Mass Killing in the First World War* (Oxford: Oxford University Press, 2007), pp. 175–80; George L. Mosse, *Fallen Soldiers: Reshaping the Memory of the World Wars* (New York: Oxford University Press, 1990), p. 32; Leonard V. Smith, *The Embattled Self: French Soldiers' Testimony of the Great War* (Ithaca, NY: Cornell University Press, 2007), pp. 62–75. For a critique of the culture of war thesis see Rémy Cazals, '1914–1918: Chercher encore', *Le Mouvement Social*, 199 (2002), 107–13; Antonio Gibelli, 'Le refus, la distance, le consentement', *Le Mouvement Social*, 199 (2002), 113–19; M. Isnenghi, 'Un livre problématique et inquiet', *Le Mouvement Social*, 199 (2002), 103–7; Antoine Prost, 'La guerre de 1914 n'est pas perdue', *Le Mouvement Social*, 199 (2002), 95–102; 'Les limites de la brutalisation: Tuer sur le front occidental, 1914–1918', *Vingtième Siècle*, 81 (2004), 5–20. A recent and stimulating discussion of the controversy over coercion versus consent is to be found in Jay Winter (ed.), *The Legacy of the Great War: Ninety Years On* (Columbia and London: University of Missouri Press, 2009), pp. 91–123.

70 *Ibid.*, p. 107.
71 Audoin-Rouzeau and Becker, *14–18*, p. 143; Annette Becker, 'From war to war: A few myths, 1914–1942', in Valerie Holman and Debra Kelly (eds), *France at War in the Twentieth Century: Propaganda, Myth and Metaphor* (Oxford: Berghahn, 2000), p. 19.
72 Kramer, *Dynamic of Destruction*, p. 183.
73 John Horne, 'Demobilizing the mind: France and legacy of the Great War, 1919–1939', *French History and Civilization*, 2 (2009), 101–7; John Horne, 'Introduction', in John Horne (ed.), *14–18 Aujourd'hui-Today-Heute: Démobilisations culturelles après la Grande guerre* (Paris: Editions Noesis, 2002), pp. 45–53; John Horne, 'Locarno et la politique de démobilisation culturelle: 1925–1930', in *ibid.*, p. 77.
74 *Ibid.*, p. 77.

1

The Union fédérale and the Union nationale des combattants: 1918–33

Following the Armistice, the return of soldiers, living and dead, presented a huge administrative challenge to the French authorities. Approximately 8 million men served during the war. By November 1918, more than 1.3 million men had been killed and 5 million remained under arms. The process of demobilisation lasted eighteen months. Though it was a remarkable feat to return this large quantity of men home in this short space of time, for soldiers and their families the experience of demobilisation often felt protracted. Demobilised by age rather than according to military unit, younger men saw their wartime 'family' shrink as older comrades returned home first. Boredom and frustration exacerbated the sense of injustice felt by those left behind.[1] For families not lucky enough to welcome home a soldier, the return of bodies from the front, though authorised in July 1920, did not begin until summer 1922. Six hundred thousand men were never found, their bodies lost in the destruction of the battlefield. Provincial monuments to the dead and the interment of an unidentified *poilu* under the Arc de Triomphe in Paris on 11 November 1920 provided a place of mourning for the many families who lacked a graveside to visit.[2]

Once demobilised, many ex-soldiers found it difficult to settle back into their former lives. There were physical and emotional challenges. The war left more than a million disabled and an unknown number experienced psychological trauma. Economic realities proved harsh. War pensions were derisory and the government was slow to address the complexities of the welfare system.[3] Post-war employment could be difficult to obtain. While the government required employers to return demobilised soldiers to their former jobs, these men had to present a written request within two weeks of demobilisation. Many missed the deadline. Only in 1923 did a law guarantee employment to the war-wounded.[4] Employers could be reluctant to take back ex-employees where younger men had filled the posts vacated by soldiers. Worse still, wrote Charles Bertrand of the UNC, demobilised soldiers could find their jobs occupied by foreign labour or women who were neither widows nor the wives of combatants.[5] Returning soldiers feared working women's challenge to male authority. Some worried they would return to a home in which they took second place to their breadwinner wife. Unemployment and a sense of uselessness, coupled with the disability and injury inflicted at the front, amounted for some to a loss of social status and virility.[6]

In addition to personal hardship, soldiers returned to a nation wracked by insecurity. Fighting had ceased in November 1918 but France was not yet secure. The German regime had fallen to revolution rather than invasion and the country's armies and territory remained intact. This period of uncertainty came to an end only with the conclusion of the Treaty of Versailles on 28 June 1919. With much of the French population unable to forgive their neighbours across the Rhine, a harsh treaty was preferable to rapprochement. Despite the severe terms of the peace, which required 132 billion marks in reparations payments, Germany still appeared threatening. Its industrial potential remained great while France's richest industrial areas had been devastated. The German population continued to dwarf that of France while the huge human losses of the war exacerbated French fears of demographic decline. Germany might once again become strong enough to wage war on its Western neighbour, albeit at some unknown point in the future. The belief in the barbarian of wartime persisted.

France seemed barely more secure at home. A feeling of domestic insecurity owed in part to exterior factors. As revolution gripped Russia and then Germany, French conservatives feared the development of bolshevism in their own country. Some on the right believed that the revolutionary left desired peace at any price, even if this meant capitulation to Germany. The presence of a pro-Bolshevik minority in the CGT aggravated conservative anxieties. In December 1917, the CGT conference at Clermont-Ferrand had unanimously condemned the *Union sacrée* and given its support to the Bolshevik revolution in Russia. Reporting on the CGT's decision, the conservative daily *Le Temps* accused the labour union of prioritising the Workers' International over the cause of victory, to the benefit of 'Prussian militarism' and 'German imperialism'.[7] *Le Figaro* perceived a weakening of the 'national character' of the CGT as its revolutionary and pacifist minority threatened to bring about 'a Russian peace'.[8] Such rhetoric chimed with the campaign of the Union des grandes associations contre la propagande ennemie, a government-sponsored body that organised meetings and produced propaganda designed to counter claims for a negotiated peace and weed out defeatists.[9]

With the conceptual framework of the culture of war still lingering in French minds, the threats of Germany and bolshevism were conflated. The conservative press located the roots of Marxism in Prussian militarism: the Bolshevik and the German sought to sabotage the peace. Like German Kultur, Russian bolshevism threatened to reduce France and Europe to a 'primitive state'.[10] Conservative suspicions were apparently confirmed when communist-backed industrial unrest and civil disorder throughout the first six months of 1919 coincided with the peace conference. In April 1919, French sailors in the Black Sea mutinied. That same month, the government halted demobilisation when talks with the central powers deteriorated.[11] On May Day, despite the fact that the government had granted collective bargaining and an eight-hour day to the labour movement, workers defied a ban on demonstrations and took to the streets of Paris. One demonstrator died in clashes with the police. Prime Minister Georges Clemenceau managed to head off the threat of a general strike with further concessions yet fear of revolution nevertheless filled the hearts of French conservatives.

The dual concern for the enforcement of the treaty and the prospect of left-wing revolution informed the legislative election campaign of November 1919. Clemenceau framed the poll as a choice between bolshevism and France. Speaking in Strasbourg on 5 November, he denounced the 'bloody dictatorship of Russian anarchy' that 'bolshevist socialism' wished to install in the country.[12] Though this rhetoric chimed with the concerns of many veterans, left-wing radicalism attracted some ex-servicemen. The ARAC, founded in July 1917 by Henri Barbusse, Paul-Vaillant Couturier and Raymond Lefebvre, and the Fédération ouvrière et paysanne (FOP), which was founded in June 1919, spoke to a growing extreme left-wing tendency among the war disabled and veterans.[13]

As the elections approached, a group of veterans' associations resolved to make felt the influence of the burgeoning ex-servicemen's movement. By this time a united veterans' party was out of the question. The idea was rejected at the UF's congress at Orléans in April 1919, opposed by those who wished to see the veterans' movement remain 'apolitical' and by groups that already had clearly defined political objectives, such as the ARAC.[14] Instead, five associations - the Ligues des combattants volontaires, the Ligue des chefs de sections, the Camarades de combat, the UF and the UNC - agreed a pact that expressed loyalty to the republican constitution and rejected bolshevism, revolution and violent attempts on power.[15] The signatories of the pact asked members to vote for their comrades and reject politicians who had not served during the war. Jean Binet-Valmer, founder of the Ligue des chefs de section, called for the election of 'new men, renewed men, transformed, metamorphosed by the great ordeal [of the war]'. The UNC's Bertrand, who stood for election, expressed a similar desire to see veterans in parliament. He demanded that an unspecified number of seats be reserved for ex-servicemen.[16] Bertrand's campaign was perfectly in tune with the contemporary pre-occupations of the right. His decision to run for office stemmed from a desire to 'spare France the horrors of bolshevism and ensure the moral and material recovery of [the] country'.[17]

The Bloc national, 1919–24

In November 1919, the electorate returned a conservative majority to the Chamber under the auspices of the 'Bloc national'. Many veterans were elected to the so-called 'Sky Blue' Chamber, thus named for the blue dress uniforms of a large proportion of deputies. Twenty-three *mutilés* and 220 holders of the *Croix de Guerre* were elected, accounting for roughly 40 per cent of the 616 available seats.[18] Nevertheless, André Linville, editor of the popular *Journal des mutilés et réformés*, expressed disappointment; too many politicians had won seats. He believed that veterans had turned their back on the elections.[19] Of all the veterans' associations, the UNC contributed most to this renewal of the parliamentary elite. *La Voix du combattant* boasted forty-four elected candidates (including Bertrand) of which thirty-six became deputies for the first time, though many new-comers to parliament usually had some previous political experience.[20]

Former socialist Alexandre Millerand took charge of the first Bloc national government in January 1920. Industrial unrest and German recalcitrance continued to preoccupy the nation. The CGT's influence had grown since the end of the war, buoyed by the concessions won from Clemenceau in 1919. Its revolutionary minority had nurtured the discontent of the working class and unemployed veterans. In February 1920, a dispute on the railways provoked strikes in mines, docks and construction yards throughout France. The CGT, under pressure from its revolutionary minority, backed the strike wave. Trade unionists and socialists increasingly spoke of revolution. A general strike on May Day ended in violence between strikers and the police. Meanwhile, in Germany the Kapp putsch in March 1920 demonstrated the refusal of some on the right to accept the reduction in the size of the armed forces stipulated in the treaty. Linville warned that the failed coup had revealed Prussia's lust for revenge. If Germany was still weak, this would not be the case for long.[21]

The UF and UNC's reactions to the strikes differed. In both cases, the political character of each association influenced its conduct. The UF was in a difficult position. The association sympathised with the plight of the working class yet its preference for the radical party, which had moved closer to the governing coalition, left the UF unable to criticise openly the government. Moreover, the diversity of opinion in the association meant that any political pronouncements would likely split the membership. Its policy on the strike was therefore ambiguous.[22]

The UNC did not hide its hostility to the strikers. The association had not always been so explicit about its opposition to industrial action. During the unrest of June 1919, a UNC poster made conciliatory overtures to workers. While it expressed support for the 'professional' demands of strikers, the association nevertheless warned against a general strike that could wipe out the 'five years of sacrifice' since 1914. In the name of the war dead, the nation and humanity, the UNC implored workers not to disarm France 'faced with an enemy of whom we know the *energy and the treacherousness*'.[23] Like the right, the UNC perceived the hand of Germany and international communism at work in the labour dispute. By the time of the railway workers' strike in 1920, the UNC's opposition had hardened. Hubert Aubert claimed that at the moment when the country needed to regain its strength in order to disarm Germany, strikers had effectively re-opened the wounds of the war.[24]

Conservatives organised replacement labour in groups known as civic unions.[25] The first such union appeared in Lyon under the direction of Jules Millevoye.[26] The *lyonnais* union provided a model for other blackleg labour formations, which took similar advantage of bourgeois enthusiasm to combat the strikes.[27] Following consultation with prefects, minister of the interior Théodore Steeg granted legal status to the unions on 20 April 1920, referring to them as an 'auxiliary police'.[28] By mid-May the civic unions had spread throughout France.[29]

Right-wing veterans' groups supported the civic unions. Binet-Valmer put his members at the service of the government.[30] Given the bourgeois nature of the UNC's cadres and membership, it is unsurprising that its veterans responded in a similar fashion.[31] The UNC's Humbert Isaac and six other members were on the provisional committee of Millevoye's pioneering union and they remained members.[32] Nationally, the UNC asked its members to lend the government 'the assistance of [their] intelligence and [their] arms' to ensure the continued function of public services.[33] Several provincial groups echoed this request.[34] The UNC's support for the unions was not wholly disinterested. In March 1920, Bertrand received a donation of 100,000 francs from the railway companies in return for the UNC's help in anti-strike action.[35] He later claimed that a warning about the revolutionary nature of the strikes from Steeg had further prompted the UNC's call to action.[36]

In spite of their participation in the civic unions, conservative veterans did not single-handedly break the strike wave. Millevoye's first union depended largely on students from local *écoles* and *lycées* rather than on ex-servicemen.[37] The UNC was relatively undeveloped in some departments. In these areas, its presence was therefore not strong enough to make a contribution to the unions. Nonetheless, the experience of the civic unions marked an important stage in the activism of conservative veterans. It demonstrated that some UNC veterans were willing to act when they perceived the nation to be under threat from the left. Though the civic unions were not political formations, their anti-leftist, bourgeois complexion was evident.

In the early 1920s, the UF and the UNC were divided too on foreign policy. In line with the Bloc's policy on the enforcement of the treaty, the conservative UNC rejected collective security, rapprochement with Germany and relations with German veterans. Accordingly, the association expressed scant confidence in the League of Nations and Wilsonian ideas. Instead, it supported the foreign policy of prime minister Raymond Poincaré, prime minister since January 1922. Poincaré's foreign policy aimed to keep Germany at bay through the strict application of the treaty and the payment of reparations.[38] In November 1920, the UNC founded the FIDAC for ex-servicemen of former allied nations only. Bertrand assumed the presidency.[39]

The UF was more receptive than its rival to meeting France's former enemies. In September 1921, UF delegates attended a meeting of the International Labour Organisation at which German and Austrian veterans were present.[40] The UF combined this cautious conciliation with a preference for the international arbitration of peace embodied in the League of Nations. Despite these tentative steps, the UF was relatively quiet on international issues in the early 1920s. Having expressed confidence in the failed ideas of US President Woodrow Wilson and unable to fully endorse the *poincariste* position, the UF remained tight-lipped on international issues for the time being.

When in January 1923 Germany defaulted on reparations payments and France occupied the Ruhr, the veterans' associations largely responded according to their prior positions. The UNC supported the action. Bertrand described the French incursion as a simple application of the treaty rather than a military adventure, while Aubert demanded that Germany pay France its due and desist from making empty promises.[41] Cartoons in *La Voix du combattant* pictured Germany as a fat woman, ostensibly overwhelmed by poverty yet evidently richer than she was prepared to admit.[42] The UNC requested readers send food parcels to the 'poilus' of the Ruhr, the comparison with Great War soldiers evident.[43] The UF's reaction to the occupation of the Ruhr was mixed. Pichot's response was unequivocally *poincariste*, yet UF director Paul Vaillant feared that the risk of another war was too great to justify military intervention.[44] The association's provincial sections mirrored this division.[45]

Though differences over domestic and foreign policy often characterised the relationship of the two largest associations at this time, the approach of legislative elections in 1924 provided once more an opportunity for cooperation. Each with several hundred thousand members, the UF and the UNC were aware of the potential influence they wielded at election time. In 1923, the UNC's Ernest Pezet gave voice to similar wishes in his report on veterans and 'public life'. Pezet described the moment as the veterans' 'realisation' (*prise de conscience*) that they had a 'civic duty' to undertake. Far from the politics of parties, the veterans would demand a 'national' politics, and effect a civic action. Pichot agreed with Pezet. Civic intervention was not just a matter of conscience for the veterans' associations: either they enter the electoral campaign or they would cease to exist.[46] Twelve combatant associations, including the UF and the UNC, drew up a manifesto of demands. In the main concerned with material concessions, the final point of the manifesto called for respect of the treaties, the payment of reparations and the reinforcement of international organisations such as the League of Nations. The manifesto was sent to the provincial sections of the signatory associations. The closing of the Bloc national era thus saw the veterans' associations determined to take a more active role in national life.

The Cartel des gauches, 1924–26

By the elections in May 1924, the Bloc national government had lost much of its popularity. The election of many ex-servicemen to the Chamber in 1919 had raised hopes beyond the confines to the veterans' movement that the combatant spirit would infuse new life into parliamentary politics. Yet the first post-war parliamentary experience proved unable to bring about national renovation. Disillusioned, an important number of the 326 newly-elected deputies either did not complete their term or did not stand for re-election.[47] Poincaré's tough stance on Germany and the Ruhr occupation may have temporarily sated the nationalist demand to 'make the Boche pay' yet it was a lengthy and costly enterprise. The prime minister, vulnerable to accusations of bellicosity, faced a revitalised left in the radical and socialist coalition, the 'Cartel des gauches'. Furthermore, a burgeoning economic crisis brought on by a large budget deficit precipitated the collapse of the Franc in January 1924. With the cost of living on the rise, veterans, many of whom relied on fixed incomes to survive, were hit particularly hard. In May 1924, the Cartel triumphed and radical Edouard Herriot assumed the premiership. Faithful to their policy of non-participation in a bourgeois government, socialists refused to take up portfolios. Soon after the election Millerand, president of the republic since September 1920, resigned. The right had quit government completely.

In principle, the UF supported the Cartel. Prior to the election, the radicals had made overtures to the association in an attempt to secure its support.[48] Following the second round of the election, Pichot declared the UF to be the 'home of the Cartel' and made clear the association's willingness to work with the coalition, if elected.[49] The UNC was less enthusiastic about the new government. Though it claimed sixty elected deputies, compared to forty-four in 1919, the left-wing complexion of the government was not to the liking of some UNC veterans. Bertrand resigned from the UNC's leadership when the executive committee decided to invite the Cartel's minister of labour Justin Godard to the national congress at Périgueux that year.[50]

The associations were divided too over *cartelliste* foreign policy. With the process of cultural demobilisation under way, the new government's relations with Germany marked a significant departure from the Bloc's *poincariste* intransigence. French troops withdrew from the Ruhr in August 1925. The reduction of reparations set out in the Dawes Plan was accepted. In 1925 Aristide Briand agreed the Locarno Pact with Germany and the following year, he facilitated Germany's entry to the League of Nations. The UF was heartened. It had favoured rapprochement with German veterans long before 1924. Once caught between the failure of Wilsonian peacemaking and a half-hearted acceptance of *poincarisme*, the UF now found a third way: *briandisme*.[51] In September 1925, the association invited German veterans to a conference in Geneva. A resounding success, the conference took place again the following year and led to the foundation of the CIAMAC.[52] In October 1925, Pichot declared himself a 'locarniste'.[53] The pact, he claimed, marked the transition from a period of hostility to one of collaboration and mutual comprehension that would benefit Europe.[54]

The right was aghast. The withdrawal of French forces from the Ruhr showed a weakness that would only encourage German *revanchisme*. The Cartel's willingness to reduce reparations, and thus cede the spoils of the victory, was tantamount to treachery. In December 1924, former minister of war André Maginot branded the government the 'gravedigger of French prestige'. He accused the Cartel of betraying the victory and the veterans. The government had shown 'unforgiveable weakness' in yielding to communist demands. A country, Maginot concluded, could die from coalitions such as the Cartel.[55] The Cartel's conciliatory foreign policy was unacceptable to the UNC, which remained intransigent in its attitude to Germany. It condemned the UF's meeting with German veterans and refused to attend the Geneva conferences in September 1925.[56] In spite of Locarno and Germany's admittance to the League of Nations, the UNC desired proof of German good faith. Words were not enough to wipe out the memory of five years of war.[57] Nevertheless, concerned that the UF's vigour in international relations would trump the work of FIDAC, the UNC organised its own meeting with German veterans in Luxemburg in July 1927, though it remained steadfastly suspicious of German motives.[58]

Cultural demobilisation may well have affected France's relationship with Germany after 1925. Subsequent conservative governments retained Briand at the foreign ministry, even after Poincaré returned as prime minister in July 1926. In this sense, the culture of war, which had represented the conflict as a struggle between Western civilisation and German barbarism was indeed demobilised, despite certain pockets of resistance. Yet in another respect the war culture persisted. Attached by conservatives to the left in the period of industrial and civil unrest during 1918–20, the process of cultural demobilisation did little to weaken this link.

On 23 November 1924, the ashes of socialist Jean Jaurès were interred in the Panthéon. The leaders of the Cartel led a cortege to the republican temple where an official ceremony took place. Conservative commentators noted the worryingly revolutionary character of the day.[59] Groups of communist counter-demonstrators had followed the official procession. The UNC's Aubert denounced these 'unruly' and 'sexually forward' bands.[60] *Le Matin* reported that Jaurès' coffin was surrounded by ten flags: eight of them red, one the sky blue of the Masonic Grand Loge de France, and a sole tricolour.[61] The spectacle deepened the right's anxiety. Had not German socialist Breitscheild joined the Cartel delegation? Had not *cartelliste* ministers consorted publicly with revolutionaries? Not only did the Cartel threaten the hard-won fruits of the victory, according to the right, it appeared to be in league with the revolutionary left and Germany too.

When the government withdrew its ambassador to the Vatican and pledged to extend the secular laws to Alsace and Lorraine, Catholics joined nationalists in their opposition to the Cartel. The Catholic and nationalist right united in the fear that revolution was imminent. In response to the perceived threat from the left, political groups known as leagues were founded. Informed by the experience of the civic unions and foreign paramilitary movements, the leagues became the right's front-line defence against communism. All were hostile to the Cartel government and in some cases the republican regime. Catholic activists joined General de Castelnau's Fédération nationale catholique (FNC) while the moderate and parliamentary right patronised Millerand's Ligue républicaine nationale. The two most important nationalist leagues of the mid-1920s were the Faisceau and the JP. Both relied in part on veterans. Georges Valois's Faisceau, founded on Armistice Day 1924 as a veterans' association, was avowedly fascist. With up to 60,000 members it was the largest of the leagues during the 1920s. Valois threatened to mobilise his veteran-dominated paramilitary legions to destroy the republic. His message to ex-servicemen was clear: the Faisceau alone would return to France a 'politics of victory'.[62] Taittinger's JP, launched in December 1924, drew little distinction between the radicals, the socialists and the communists. Taittinger blamed the Cartel and parliamentarianism for preparing the way for a socialist dictatorship.[63] Incidents of communist violence appeared to signal the beginning of a bloody insurrection, particularly the deaths of four JP members at the hands of the communists at the rue Damrémont in Paris during April 1925.[64] Its paramilitary 'centuries' were ready to defend France from the threat of leftist insurrection.[65] The JP's 'Iron Brigade' was reserved for the best men. It recruited only veterans who had seen active service during the war.[66]

League initiatives also emanated from within the combatants' movement. In 1925, the UNC's Jean Goy founded the Front républicain with the financial aid of Ernest Mercier. Goy became a fervent activist in the

UNC, eventually rising to the association's presidency in 1935. An industrialist and a deputy, Goy's personal and political life would end ingloriously under Vichy: a collaborator and founding member of Marcel Déat's Rassemblement national populaire, Goy's funeral in 1944 was attended by an SS platoon. In 1924, Goy was joined in the Front républicain's leadership by fellow UNC activists Bertrand, Victor Beauregard and Aubertin, as well as JP leaguers.[67] UNC member Jacques Péricard founded the Ligue des droits du religieux ancien combattant (DRAC). Péricard was an intractable anti-communist. During the strikes of 1920 he had colourfully suggested drowning all communists at the bottom of a river, as one would 'a litter of wolves or stinking beasts'.[68] Such rhetoric was not unique to Péricard. At a meeting of the DRAC in June 1925, a Reverend Zimmerman told the audience: 'Faced with Herriot and his gang as during the war, I will shout to whoever will want to hear: "Everyone to the firing posts and give them a burst!"' The audience, which included AF and JP members, gave Zimmerman an enthusiastic ovation.[69] Zimmerman's association of the left with the wartime enemy was plain.

As the largest conservative veterans' association, the UNC engaged in the right's campaign against the left. In December 1924, the UNC voted a motion promising to 'block the way of communism'. The motion reminded members that they were 'activists of victorious France'. As such, they had the association's permission to take all necessary measures to counteract the revolutionary threat.[70] That same month the UNC joined an alliance of anti-communist groups, which included the FNC and the JP.[71] In May 1926, police reported that the JP was assured the aid of UNC veterans 'if the need [arose]'.[72] It is likely that this 'need' would come at the time of communist revolution. What action did the UNC envisage in such an event? André Colleau, at the time editor of *La Voix du combattant*, proclaimed the UNC's willingness to join nationalist groups in the street should communist insurrection threaten public order.[73] Isaac reassured members that the government was not blind to the communist threat. A moderate in the UNC, Isaac was an engineer and son of Auguste Isaac, minister in the Millerand government of 1920. He briefly took over the presidency of the UNC following Bertrand's resignation in 1925. Isaac's case demonstrates that even in circumstances when the conservative activists of the UNC held sway, such as when the left was in power, more conventional republican voices were still strong in the association. Isaac steadfastly rejected collaboration with political leagues and his reputation for honesty stood him in good stead with the UNC's members. In January 1925, despite his request for faith in the government,

Isaac wrote that anti-communist 'citizens' groups', composed mainly of veterans, were still necessary. They would fight communism with the police, or alone, if the police were found lacking. Veterans were particularly qualified for this task: 'The energy that vanquished the Boche [would] vanquish the domestic enemy as well'.[74] Though this warning was ambiguous, given his rebuff of the leagues it is unlikely Isaac meant that veterans should take up paramilitary violence. Other veterans were less ambiguous in their statements. Aubert promised that when the communists came armed with rifles, machine guns and bombs, the veterans would be ready for them. After all, they had defeated similarly armed and disciplined young men seven years earlier.[75]

Some UNC veterans patronised the leagues. Bertrand led by example. On 18 December 1924, he was nominated to the leadership committee of the Ligue des patriotes, the JP's parent organisation.[76] Provincial UNC veterans attended JP gatherings.[77] A police informer reported that veterans composed the 'main body' of 'fascist' organisations.[78] It is improbable that these veterans joined paramilitary groups to defend veterans' rights. UNC veterans, for example, belonged already to an association that had proved successful in this area. Rather, some conservative veterans joined the leagues for political reasons. Certainly, they had joined the civic unions in 1920. Yet those groups were state-sponsored formations and ostensibly apolitical. In the mid-1920s, the leagues of the 'first wave of French fascism' were different. While veterans may have had multiple motivations, they joined leagues that were avowedly political and openly hostile to the incumbent government, if not the parliamentary republic itself.

Some veterans remained unsure about collaboration with the leagues. In the Nord, police reported that an unnamed local veterans' association had been approached to join an anti-communist league. Discussion of the issue provoked the resignation of several members.[79] This conflict between activists and those reluctant to join the leagues was not unique to the Nord.[80] The UF accused the Front républicain of being a political group that had appropriated the veteran mystique.[81] Led by Freemason A.J. Fonteny, the Fédération nationale des combattants républicains (FNCR) persistently condemned the UNC as a reactionary organisation.[82] Within the UNC, Isaac reassured members reluctant to join anticommunist groups that they could just as easily use existing UNC structures for the same purpose.[83]

In other respects, the emergence of the leagues coincided with a period of unity in the combatants' movement. With the cost of living rising, the veterans launched a campaign for an increase in combatants' pensions under the direction of the movement's entente committee, an inter-associational council that included the UF and the UNC. The combatants' press drove the campaign, which became known as the 'battle for pensions'.[84] On Armistice Day 1924, 40,000 veterans took to the streets of Paris to demand the revaluation of pensions. Throughout November and December the language of the combatants' press sharpened in the face of Herriot's reluctance to grant the requested increase. Provincial veterans held meetings across France. Using the vocabulary of military conflict, the combatants' press counted down the time until 'H hour' and thus lent a certain ambiguity to the veterans' campaign. Equally, Pichot announced that the day of reckoning was nigh, while Amédée Chivot asked readers of the *Journal des mutilés* to prepare themselves for the coming assault.[85] Would the combatant associations turn to violence if thwarted? When in January 1925, the government agreed to increase pensions to a level still short of the veterans' demands, the battle intensified. On 7 February, the *Journal des mutilés* set out plans for a 'monster' demonstration in Paris. The combatants' 'D-day' would mobilise the whole movement.[86] Simultaneously, *La Voix du combattant* declared the battle against the government under way: 'Now, it's the struggle … On D Day, at H Hour, the movement, under order, will be unleashed … it is not about attacking the government, if it puts up no resistance. It is about breaking obstacles wherever we encounter them. Government, Chamber, Senate.'[87] Under such severe pressure, the government agreed in full to the veterans' demands.

Divisions did not hinder common action when it involved ostensibly apolitical issues. The veterans' movement would unite again in the campaign against the Washington Accords on the repayment of war debts in 1926. The Accords, agreed between France and the US, stipulated that in the event that Germany defaulted on reparation payments, France would continue to meet its debt payments to the US. This requirement infuriated the veterans' associations and, furthermore, came at a time of effervescence in the movement. The Bloc national had failed to stabilise both parliamentary government and the economy. Now the Cartel was proving just as ineffective. Since Herriot's resignation on 10 April 1925, five administrations had governed France. Veteran contempt for the 'clowns' of the 'Folies Bourbon' grew.[88] The UF bemoaned parliamentary incompetence that had made government an 'impossibility'.[89] Gaston Rogé recommended forming a veterans' party, which would 'relegate to secondary importance parliamentary and governmental preoccupations'.[90] Chivot condemned 'politicking' for having weakened France since the victory.[91] New UNC president Henri Rossignol railed against the 'bunch of bawlers' in the Chamber.[92] France, according to UNC vice-president Galland, was in the hands of 'mediocre men and old survivors of a jaded generation'.[93]

In the campaign against the Accords, the UF and the UNC's opposition differed in degree. Maurice Randoux, president of the UF, was careful not to challenge the authority of parliament. He feared that if the Chamber rejected the Accords and subsequently suffered American financial re-taliation, the country would blame the veterans for having forced par-liament's hand. Nevertheless he called the agreement unjust.[94] The UNC was incandescent with rage. It railed against 'the ruin of our victory' at the hands of parliamentarians. France was on the brink of catastrophe.[95] UNC official Schaepelynck denounced the 'ungrateful nation' and the men who had resolved to 'impoverish' and 'annihilate' the veterans.[96] The Accords were a 'death sentence' for France and the UNC's national con-gress at Arras decided to obstruct ratification 'by all means'.[97]

The entente committee organised a protest march in Paris for 11 July 1926. The route of the march took the veterans to the Tomb of the Unknown Soldier and on to the Place des Etats-Unis. The press reported that between 15,000 and 34,000 veterans took part.[98] The UF, the UNC and many other veterans sections marched together.[99] George Valois led a contingent of blue-shirted Légions while Maurice Pujo headed a group of AF veterans.[100] Upon reaching the Place des Etats-Unis, Jean Goy and other members of the UNC's executive committee laid a plaque at the foot of the statue of Washington. Upon the plaque, a message in French and English asked the American people to reconsider the question of inter-allied debts. The press roundly applauded the dignity and calmness of marchers. It described the moving sight of disabled veterans in their 'little cars' at the head of the column. Police believed that the presence of the *mutilés* was intended to hamper and deter their intervention.[101]

The two years of Cartel government proved a tumultuous time for the UF and the UNC. It was a time of sporadic unity. Political differences *could* be left aside in favour of a united campaign, usually concerning veterans' rights or against a perceived injustice, as in July 1926. Yet the reign of the Cartel saw the politics of each association come to the fore. The UF was freed from the difficult position that the radicals' participation in the Bloc national and the general desire for vengeance after the war had placed it. The cultural demobilisation of the Cartel era left the UF free to preach conciliation with Germany. Certainly, the association joined the battle for pensions and opposed the Washington Accords. At times its discourse hinted at a wholesale renovation of the regime and the installation of veterans in power. Nonetheless, the UF's centre-left proclivity restrained overt political opposition to the Cartel.

The UNC perceived multiple threats from the Cartel. Herriot's reluctance to satisfy the veterans' pension demands rankled conservative veterans. Pensions were considered a moral right granted by a grateful nation in recognition of the wartime sacrifice. The Cartel's obstinacy was therefore interpreted as an affront to the survivors of the war. The battle for pensions coincided with worrying political developments. The government's foreign policy, according to the UNC, had undermined France's strength in relation to its former enemy and allies. The Cartel placed too much trust in the good nature of the German, while enforcement of the treaty fell by the wayside. The Washington Accords left France indebted to the US whether Germany paid (or in the UNC's opinion 'chose' to pay) or not. Outraged veterans claimed that France had loosened its grip on its enemy and was menaced with financial enslavement to its ally.

Domestically, the left-wing character of the government was unacceptable. Its alleged pandering to the revolutionary left made communist dictatorship seem likely to some conservative veterans. Drawing on the language of the war culture, Isaac condemned the extreme left, whose 'new religion' had deified Lenin and sought to undo French civilisation and security.[102] The convergence of the multiple elements of the Cartel's 'campaign' against the veterans and the gains of the victory, to the profit of the Boche and the Bolshevik, prompted some UNC veterans to join the leagues. In this way, the persistence of the culture of war detached some members of the right from the republic. But this detachment was conditional and not necessarily permanent or all-encompassing. It depended on circumstance. The culture of war was a discourse available to conservatives when they considered the 'national' interest under threat. Of course, definition of this national interest was subjective. The solution for some lay in violent extreme right-wing groups that expressed scant sentimentalism for the Third Republic.

Deceptive unity: 1927–31

On 23 July 1926, the *cartelliste* majority effectively abdicated and recalled former prime minister Poincaré to government. The leftist coalition had been unable to solve the parliamentary and economic crisis. Poincaré's return reassured conservatives. He was a man of authority who as president of the republic had appointed Clemenceau to lead the government in 1917. Poincaré's administration seemed to offer the competent and strong 'national' leadership that the right demanded. The prime minister took over the ministry of finance and stabilised the rapidly falling franc at one-fifth of its pre-war value. The markets were cheered and confidence returned to the economy. The fall of the Cartel and harsher repression of communist activism under the Paris prefect of police Jean Chiappe meant that the fear of revolution now receded. In foreign policy, France found a renewed confidence in its foreign standing. Poincaré retained Briand at the foreign ministry. France's position in relation to Germany strengthened with the construction of the Maginot line fortifications and the completion of German disarmament. With the left split, Poincaré's Union nationale triumphed in the legislative elections of April 1928.

The final years of the 1920s saw important developments in the combatants' movement. Associations welcomed an unprecedented influx of members. The creation of the 'combatant's card', granted by the government from June 1927 to the war-wounded and those men who had spent at least three months in a fighting unit, presented an effective recruitment tool. Possession of the card entitled the bearer to certain benefits. To join an association therefore allowed a veteran to defend his pension rights and contribute to campaigns for the extension of these rights.[103] At the same time, the veterans' associations began to define themselves in terms of their generation. The notion of the 'generation of fire' took hold and reinforced the sense of collective identity among the combatants' associations.[104] The movement grew to approximately 3 million members.

A new desire for inter-associational unity gripped a section of the veterans' world. Pichot addressed the issue in June 1926. He suggested a 'single front' of veterans' associations, which would render more efficient collective campaigns. Backed by Linville and the unparalleled influence of the *Journal des mutilés,* he called for the meeting of a 'Congress of Congresses' that would act as a national assembly of the veterans' associations.[105] The UNC was unenthusiastic about the idea.[106] It feared that an inter-associational body, which would speak for the veterans as a whole, would in reality fall under the tutelage of the centre-left and *briandiste* UF.[107] Undeterred by this opposition, in November 1927, Pichot and Linville organised the 'Estates General of Wounded France' at Versailles. Six hundred and thirty-five delegates from veterans' associations (including the UNC) were present. Attendees decided to found the veterans' Confédération, which was officially launched in March 1928.

The Confédération's aim was to develop common programmes for the veterans' movement and efficiently channel the associations' energies into the cause of civic action. The UF's Randoux became the body's first secretary general and, though the UNC still had reservations about the project, Rossignol was appointed adjunct secretary general.[108]

The Confédération led a troubled existence. Its relative importance in the combatants' movement waxed and waned with the enthusiasm of the UF and the UNC. When both associations perceived some usefulness in supporting it, the Confédération offered a united front for the veterans' movement. But the body was frequently a source of disunity due to the divergent politics of its two largest members. The Confédération's first major crisis is indicative of this. When Rossignol replaced Randoux as secretary general in January 1929, the UF refused to sit on the Confédération's executive committee and ignored the forum for the rest of the year, displeased by the influence of conservatives such as Rossignol in the leadership.

The direction in which Rossignol took the Confédération continued to irk the UF. His first campaign as secretary general targeted the war debt agreements. It denounced French enslavement to 'Germano-American' finance.[109] On 23 June 1929, the Confédération organised another street demonstration against the Washington Accords, whose ratification the government continued to defer. The planned itinerary of the march was to take the veterans to the Place de la Concorde and onto the ministry of finance. Unlike the previous protest of July 1926, this time the veterans would target two political destinations. For this reason, the government forbade this route and the veterans instead marched to a meeting at the Salle Wagram. The Confédération's adjunct secretary Edmond Bloch of the AGMG reassured his comrades that there was no need for disappointment. The day was just the beginning and marked the rallying of troops before the attack.[110] The UF condemned the move as 'thoughtless' and 'impulsive'. It refused to take part because Rossignol and Bloch had recently attended a meeting of the AF that had condemned as traitors those deputies who voted for ratification or abstained from the ballot.[111] Some UNC veterans continued to associate with the leagues.[112]

The UF's patience with the Confédération finally ran out in November 1929. Rossignol and Bloch had steered the organisation to the brink of anti-*briandisme*. Both men had condemned the premature evacuation of the Rhineland and the new agreement on reparations set out in the Young Plan.[113] When the Confédération next met, UF delegates managed to push through a text that implicitly endorsed Briand's foreign policy.

Rossignol and Bloch resigned, the former claiming that the *briandistes* had 'killed' the Confédération.[114] Georges Rivollet, secretary general of the Union nationale des mutilés et réformés (UNMR), succeeded the UNC president as secretary general. Rossignol and Pichot publicly criticised each other and relations between the UF and the UNC cooled.[115]

With the UF once again sitting on its executive committee, the Confédération issued a statement endorsing the government's foreign policy in June 1931.[116] It was supported by all member associations including the previously anti-*briandiste* UNC and AGMG. Prost attributes this reversal to the veterans' tireless efforts to formulate a common policy. Furthermore, the large Nazi vote in September 1930 and a worryingly vengeful Stahlhelm and Nazi party presence in Coblenz and Breslau forced the UNC to recognise that the stubborn enforcement of the peace terms would likely bring about conflict with a rapidly strengthening Germany.[117] Nevertheless, old prejudices persisted. The UNC warned against the persistent influence of Prussian militarism that was evident in the increasingly hierarchical, authoritarian and disciplinarian nature of Germany society. Germany had not been 'morally disarmed'.[118] The UNC therefore ensured that FIDAC did not expand to admit ex-enemy veterans.[119]

The return of the Cartel, 1932–33

In the elections of May 1932, the socialists and the radicals won a majority in the Chamber. The parties had become close following the radical congress at Angers in November 1928, which had forced radical ministers to withdraw from the Union nationale government. As in 1924, Herriot became prime minister of a socialist-backed radical government. He inherited a precarious financial situation. France had initially escaped the worst effects of the American stock market crash in October 1929. Yet by 1931, with a moratorium on German reparations in effect but the system of inter-allied debt repayments still in place, the Great Depression began to bite in France. Unemployment crept up as industrial production declined and farm prices collapsed. The Cartel's deflationary policy did little to ease joblessness and government instability worsened. Herriot resigned in December following the Chamber's refusal to endorse the next instalment of debt payments to the US. The fall of five governments in the following fourteen months nourished anti-parliamentarian sentiment.

The second *cartelliste* administration did much to upset veteran opinion. In September 1932, the government attempted to revise war pension entitlement. With their material benefits menaced, the veterans' associations launched the second 'battle for pensions'. An unprecedented unity characterised the campaign. Meetings witnessed UNC speakers share stages with ARAC spokesmen.[120] The Confédération distributed a text to local sections, which members signed and then presented to their members of parliament. Under pressure from veteran constituents, deputies several times rejected the government's proposal.[121]

The onset of the economic crisis and the change of government in 1932 gave rise to a new impulse for political activism within some associations. This activism centred on the reform of the republican state. These projects will be discussed in Chapter 3. Suffice it to say here that the Confédération's meeting of 11–12 March 1933 saw Robert Monnier call for a constituent assembly to revise the constitution.[122] Neither partial reform of the institutions would be sufficient nor could reform be left in the hands of parliament. The entire edifice of the regime needed an overhaul.[123] The UF was suspicious of institutional reform and the potential threat it posed to the republic. Although Pichot admitted that the words 'authority' and 'republic' were not always complementary, his association expressed support for the parliamentary regime and disavowed reform projects. Improvement of the regime should come from within parliament under pressure from public opinion.[124]

Conversely, the UNC was receptive to constitutional revision. In 1932, with the centre-left returned to power, the value of the parliamentary regime once again diminished in the opinion of some conservative veterans. As in 1924, the government had tried to limit expenditure on veteran pensions, so threatening those men who deserved most respect in France. Parliamentary instability, evidenced in the rapid succession of radical administrations, further devalued the system. The accession of Hitler to power in January 1933 and his contempt for the peace treaty deepened the UNC's concerns. Doubting the potency of the League of Nations following the Japanese invasion of Manchuria, the association urged France to remain vigilant.[125] Yet the country could not confront Germany if government instability persisted. Throughout 1933, the UNC therefore called for a 'formidable sweeping' and 'a serious cleaning' of parliament in order to correct its deficiencies.[126] Aubert wrote, 'There is a civic Marne to win. The ship is adrift; we must return order to the house.'[127] The constitution would need to be revised.[128]

In October 1933, the UNC reached a seminal moment in its existence. The association convened a meeting at the Salle Wagram in Paris. At the meeting, the association launched the 'Wagram manifesto', a programme for 'civic action' that promised to 'liberate' France from the 'intolerable tyranny' of the parties.[129] The text of the manifesto and subsequent commentaries were of a disquieting tone. Rossignol wrote that the veterans would, when H hour sounded, leave their trench and commence the attack.[130] Police suggested that UNC meetings may erupt into street action directed at the Chamber of Deputies. In this event, they foresaw clashes between the security services and protesting veterans.[131] Some within the UNC's executive committee expressed concern at the likely reception of the manifesto.[132] Péricard defended the UNC in the pages of *L'Ouest-Eclair*. He stated pointedly that the UNC was not entering 'politics' in the 'pejorative sense of the word', that is, the politics of parties. But, he admitted, no question was free from politics.[133] The Wagram meeting coincided with agitation in sections of the veterans' movement.[134] Once again Linville launched a 'battle' in the pages of the *Journal des mutilés*, this time in favour of amputees' rights. He threatened a street demonstration if parliament refused to yield.[135] Newly founded groups on the extreme right such as the Solidarité française and the *francistes* targeted the meetings of ex-servicemen to distribute propaganda and encourage them into political action.[136]

Conclusion

By 1934, the veterans' associations were well established throughout France. The UF and the UNC's memberships were roughly equal; the former's was larger with 900,000 members compared to the UNC's 835,000.[137] They had been successful as pressure groups and vastly improved the state financial entitlement granted to ex-servicemen. Their campaigns had helped to solidify a collective identity as the generation of fire. This identity was useful when common interests were at stake yet it receded when political differences surfaced. The veterans' movement did not possess a single political character. The UF preferred centre-left radical governments. Under conservative administrations it continued to back the parliamentary regime, shunning revisionist projects in favour of reform from within parliament. Its foreign policy was *briandiste*. The UF experienced cultural demobilisation before the process spread more widely in France, by which time it could pursue openly its policy towards Germany. The Confédération's text of June 1931 perhaps points to the preponderance of the UF in the combatants' movement at that time. Yet the residue of wartime attitudes and language remained. The association joined in the 'battle for pensions' campaigns, which used wartime vocabulary and seemed to threaten violent action. Cultural demobilisation did not affect the UNC until June 1931. Even then, the association's acceptance of relations with Germany came with some reluctance.

The UNC was conservative and supported like-minded governments. Under particular conditions, notably when the left appeared threatening, hard-line conservatives came to the fore. They vigorously opposed the *cartelliste* governments and allied with the leagues. Yet the UNC was not monolithic. Moderate members continued to be heard in the association. The resignation of Bertrand in May 1924 showed that moderate republicans could still make their weight felt even at times of apparent conservative dominance in the UNC. Dependent on circumstance, each faction could make advances or suffer reversals in their negotiations for the control of association policy. This conflict would characterise the internal dynamics of the associations throughout the 1930s.

Significantly, though cultural demobilisation may have partially rehabilitated the German, it did not detach the culture of war from the revolutionary left. The right's anticommunism may have receded following Poincaré's return in 1926 yet it remained embedded within the reworked conceptual framework of the war culture. This discourse was ready to be (re-)mobilised at times when the 'national' interest appeared threatened by the Bolshevik, the uncivilised enemy. Though there was no straightforward transmutation of the culture of war into the leagues, in instances when the right came to associate the incumbent government with communism the lingering influence of the culture on post-war mentalities and discourse detached some conservative veterans from the republic and prompted them to join extreme right-wing anti-republican leagues. Five months after the Wagram meeting, in February 1934, UNC veterans joined the leagues on the streets of Paris in a riot that brought down the radical government of Edouard Daladier. After so many threats, it appeared that the veterans had made good on their promise to attack those in power.

Notes

1 Bruno Cabanes, *La Victoire endeuillée. La sortie de guerre des soldats français 1918–1920* (Paris: Seuil, 2004), pp. 312–34; Prost, *Les Anciens Combattants*, I, pp. 48–9.

2 Cabanes, *La Victorie endeuillée*, note 50, p. 484; Bruno Cabanes, 'Les vivants et les morts: La France au sortir de la Grande guerre', in Stéphane Audoin-Rouzeau and Christophe Prochasson (eds), *Sortir de la grande guerre: Le*

monde et l'après 1918 (Paris: Tallandier, 2008), p. 35; Antoine Prost, 'Les monuments aux morts', in Pierre Nora (ed.), *Les Lieux de mémoire* (Paris: Gallimard, 1984), I, pp. 195–225.

3 Prost, *Les Anciens Combattants*, I, pp. 8–18.

4 Cabanes, 'Les vivants et les morts', p. 30.

5 C. Bertrand, 'Notre tâche', *VC* (27 July 1919).

6 Cabanes, 'Les vivants et les morts', p. 30; Laura Levine Frader, *Breadwinners and Citizens: Gender in the making of the French Social Model* (Durham and London: Duke University Press, 2008), p. 17; Mary-Louise Roberts, *Civilization without Sexes: Reconstructing Gender in Postwar France, 1917–1927* (Chicago: Chicago University Press, 1994), p. 60.

7 'Une faillite', *Le Temps* (26 December 1917).

8 A. Capus, 'La CGT', *Le Figaro* (27 December 1917).

9 Horne, 'Remobilizing for "total war"', pp. 198–207; Benjamin Martin, *France and the Après Guerre, 1918–1924* (Louisiana State University Press: Baton Rouge, LA, 1999), pp. 8–9.

10 'Bulletin du jour. Le coût du bolchévisme', *Le Temps* (6 November 1919).

11 Cabanes, *La Victoire endeuillée*, p. 320.

12 'Le discours de M. Clemenceau', *Le Temps* (6 November 1919).

13 Prost, *Les Anciens Combattants*, I, p. 38.

14 *Ibid.*, pp. 62–7.

15 'Aux combattants de la France', *VC* (21 September 1919).

16 J. Binet-Valmer, 'Les anciens combattants en vue des prochaines elections se sont mis d'accord pour une action commune', *Le Petit Parisien* (9 September 1919).

17 'Communiqué', *VC* (2 November 1919).

18 Gilles Le Béguec, 'L'entrée au Palais Bourbon: Les filières privilégiées d'accès à la fonction parlementaire 1919–1939' (Ph.D. dissertation, Université de Paris X-Nanterre, 1989), p. 333.

19 A. Linville, 'Quleques réflexions au lendemain d'un Scrutin', *JM* (22 November 1919).

20 'Les Membres de l'UNC à la Chambre', *VC* (14 December 1919); Le Béguec, 'L'entrée au Palais Bourbon', pp. 350 and 355.

21 A. Linville, 'La Situation', *JM* (20 March 1920).

22 Prost, *Les Anciens Combattants*, I, p. 75.

23 'Notre Appel aux Travailleurs. Les commentaires de la Presse', *VC* (13 July 1919), italics in the original.

24 H. Aubert quoted in J. Hap, 'Les Paysans contre les Grèves', *VC* (23 May 1920).

25 On the civic unions see Adrian Jones, 'The French railway strikes of January–May 1920', *French Historical Studies* 12 (1982), 508–40; Annie Kriegel, *La Grève des cheminots 1920* (Paris: Armand Colin, 1988), pp. 109–12.

26 AN, F7/14608, 'Le Ministre de l'Intérieur à messieurs les préfets', 8 March

1920; 'Le préfet du Rhône à Monsieur le Ministre de l'Intérieur', 13 March 1920; J. Bastide, 'L'Union Civique Parisienne', *L'Echo de Paris* (28 April 1920).

27 AN, F7/13015, 'Le préfet de la Savoie à Monsieur le Ministre de l'Intérieur', 3 April 1920; 'Le préfet de la Haute-Savoie à Monsieur le Ministre de l'Intérieur', 9 April 1920.

28 AN, F7/14608, 'Décret du 30 avril 1920', 30 April 1920.

29 'Les volontaires', *Le Temps* (14 May 1920).

30 AN, F7/14608, letter from Binet-Valmer to the Minister of the Interior, 26 February 1920.

31 Prost, *Les Anciens Combattants*, II, pp. 128–9 and 157; AN, F7/14608, 'Le préfet de la Haute-Marne à Monsieur le Ministre de l'Intérieur', 13 March 1920, Annexe 3; 'Le préfet du Cher à Monsieur le Ministre de l'Intérieur', 18 March 1920.

32 AN, F7/14608, 'Union Civique', undated.

33 C. Bertrand, 'L'UNC et la grève des cheminots', VC (7 March 1920).

34 'Le grève des cheminots et les groupes régionaux de l'UNC. En Alsace', VC (14 March 1920); 'A travers nos sections. Région parisienne: 16e arrondissement', VC (11 April 1920); 'A travers nos sections. Corrèze: Vernon', VC (25 April 1920).

35 Kriegel, *La Grève des cheminots*, p. 111.

36 C. Bertrand, 'Réponse de Charles Bertrand', VC (25 June 1922).

37 AN, F7/14608, 'Le préfet du Rhône à Monsieur le Ministre de l'Intérieur', 13 March 1920.

38 C. Tisseyre, R.M. d'Avigneau and C. Bertrand, 'L'UNC et la Paix', VC (3 December 1922).

39 Prost, *Les Anciens Combattants*, I, pp. 74–5

40 *Ibid.*, pp. 75–6; R. Cassin, 'La Réunion de Genève', FM (25 September 1921).

41 H. Aubert, 'Le pays attends', VC (7 January 1923); C. Bertrand, 'Justice, réparation: Un même mot sous deux vocables, dont ne peut se passer l'Humanité', VC (14 January 1923).

42 'L'Or du Reich', VC (28 January 1923).

43 'Pour les Poilus de la Ruhr', VC (11 March 1923).

44 H. Pichot, 'Pour aboutir à la Paix'; P. Vaillant, 'Contre la prochaine "Dernière des Guerres"', FM (2 February 1923).

45 Prost, *Les Anciens Combattants*, I, p. 90.

46 E. Pezet, 'Les Combattants et la Vie Publique', VC (May 1923); H. Pichot, 'De Clermont à Vichy par Marseille', FM (3 June 1923); H. Pichot, 'La politique', FM (10 June 1923); Pichot, *Les Combattants avaient rasion ...*, pp. 41–51.

47 Le Béguec, 'L'entrée au Palais-Bourbon', pp. 376–98.

48 AN, F7/12952, 'Chez les radicaux', 6 December 1923.

49 H. Pichot, 'La Chambre du 11 Mai et le Ministère du 1 Juin', *FM* (18 May 1924).

50 Prost, *Les Anciens Combattants*, I, p. 99; 'Une retraite. Charles Bertrand quitte la présidence active de l'UNC', *VC* (11 April 1925).

51 H. Pichot, 'Mort le protocol, vive le pacte!', *FM* (15 March 1925).

52 Prost, *Les Anciens Combattants*, I, pp. 104–5.

53 H. Pichot, 'Le sentier de la paix', *JM* (24 October 1925).

54 H. Pichot, 'Aprés Locarno. La Bonne Girouette', *JM* (12 December 1925).

55 '"La politique du cartel des Gauches conduit à la Révolution ou à la Dictature" dit M. Maginot', *L'Echo de Paris* (22 December 1924).

56 V. Beaureagrd, 'Un grave incident chez les combattants français', *VC* (3 October 1925).

57 H. Rossignol, 'Les deux méthodes', *VC* (18 September 1926); J. Hap, 'Après Locarno', *VC* (24 October 1925); P. Galland, 'Après Locarno: Les Allemands et Nous', *VC* (5 December 1925).

58 Prost, *Les Anciens Combattants*, I, p. 107.

59 Soucy, *The First Wave*, p. 54.

60 H. Aubert, 'En attendant …', *VC* (20 December 1924).

61 'Les cendres de Jaurès au Panthéon', *Le Matin* (24 November 1924); 'Une interpellation sur la manifestation communiste à l'occasion du transfert de Jaurès au Panthéon', *Le Matin* (26 November 1924).

62 Kalman, *The Extreme Right*, p. 5; AN, F7/13006, 'Le commissaire spécial à M. Le Directeur de la Sûreté Générale', 12 November 1925; AN, F7/13208, 'Le Commissaire Central à M. le Directeur de la Sûreté Générale', 21 November 1925; 'Faisceau Notes', 13 December 1927; 'Un grand movement national. Les Légions veulent donner à la France la politque de la victoire', *Paris-Centre* (21 August 1925).

63 Soucy, *The First Wave*, p. 63.

64 Philippet, *Le Temps des Ligues*, I, p. 221.

65 Soucy, *The First Wave*, pp. 39–87.

66 AN, F7/13233, 'Les Jeunesses Patriotes', 7 March 1925; AN, F7/13232, 'Les Jeunesses Patriotes', May 1925.

67 'Le Front Républicain', *Le Poilu républicain* (15 August 1926); AN, F7/13233, 'Le commissaire spécial à Monsieur le préfet de la Loire-Inférieure', 13 July 1926.

68 J. Péricard, 'Le bolchévisme', *VC* (20 June 1920).

69 AN, F7/13228, 'Réunion privée organisée par le comité de la Ligue des Droit du religieux ancien combattant [sic]', 3 June 1926.

70 'Mot d'ordre', *VC* (20 December 1924).

71 Philippet, *Le Temps des Ligues*, I, p. 77; AN, F7/13231, 'Liste des associations et ligues plus ou moins adhérents aux fédérations de Castelnau et de Millerand', undated.

72 AN, F7/13232, 'L'opposition', 20 May 1926.

73 A. Colleau, 'Revues d'effectifs', *VC* (19 November 1924).

74 H. Isaac, 'Danger communiste', *VC* (3 January 1925).

75 H. Aubert, 'En attendant …', *VC* (3 January 1925).

76 'Une importante réunion du Comité directeur de la Ligue des Patriotes', *L'Echo de Paris* (19 December 1924).

77 For example see, 'Le courier des ligueurs: Auxerre', *Le National* (24 January 1926) and Fagerberg, *The 'Anciens Combattants' and French Foreign Policy*, p. 46.

78 AN, F7/12954, untitled document, 26 January 1926.

79 AN, F7/13006, 'Le Préfet du Nord à Monsieur le Ministre de l'Intérieur', 1 September 1925.

80 AN, F7/13208, 'Le Préfet de la Meuse à Monsieur le Ministre de l'Intérieur', 29 May 1926.

81 P. Brousmiche, 'Considérons la fin', *FM* (4 July 1926).

82 Prost, *Les Anciens Combattants*, I, p. 89; 'Les Combattants Républicains de la Meuse acclament le programme de la FNCR', *Le Poilu républicain* (10 July 1926).

83 H. Isaac, 'Guerre civile ou progrès social', *VC* (7 February 1925).

84 Prost, *Les Anciens Combattants*, I, pp. 94–7.

85 'La bataille pour les pensions. Entre nous', *JM* (25 October 1924); H. Pichot, 'Dans l'attente de l'Heure H. La vie est chère. Il faut payer', *JM* (27 September 1924); A. Chivot, 'Dans l'attente de l'Heure H. Profitons des leçons du passé', *JM* (27 September 1924).

86 'La mobilisation de la France meutrie', *JM* (7 February 1925).

87 'La mobilisation de la France meutrie', *VC* (7 February 1925).

88 'Notre Opinion', *Le Mutilé du Centre* (25 January 1926); AN, F7/12954, 'Les institutions parlementaires attaquées par divers groupements d'anciens combattants', 20 February 1926.

89 *Ibid.*

90 *Ibid.*

91 *Ibid.*

92 H. Rossignol, 'Lettre d'un militant', *VC* (13 February 1926).

93 P. Galland, 'Et nous avons péché aussi', *VC* (12 June 1926).

94 M. Randoux, 'La manifestation du 11 juillet', *FM* (4 July 1926); H. Pichot, 'Les dettes interalliées: Pieds et poings liés', *JM* (15 May 1925)

95 P. Galland, 'Vers Waterloo', *VC* (8 May 1926); H. Rossignol, 'Nous ne ratifierons pas', *VC* (3 July 1926).

96 L. Schaepelynck, 'La réaction contre la Victoire: La nation ingrate', *VC* (5 June 1926).

97 'Deux discours. Deux actes. Toast de Jean Goy', *VC* (22 May 1926); 'Les dettes interalliées et les Anciens Combattants', *JM* (12 June 1936).

98 *Le Petit Journal* reported the lower number and *JM* reported the higher. *Le Figaro* estimated that 20,000 veterans were present: 'Les Anciens

Combattants ont défilé avec dignité et dans le calme', *Le Petit Journal* (12 July 1926); 'La Grandiose Manifestation du 11 juillet', *JM* (17 July 1926); S. Arbellot, 'La Manifestation des Anciens Combattants', *Le Figaro* (12 July 1926).

99 See 'Organisation de la manifestation', *JM* (11 July 1926) for a full list of associations present.

100 S. Arbellot, 'La Manifestation des Anciens Combattants', *Le Figaro* (12 July 1926).

101 AN, F7/12954, 'Au sujet de la manifestation des Anciens Combattants contre les Accords de Washington', 8 July 1926.

102 H. Isaac, 'Guerre civile ou progrès social', *VC* (7 February 1925).

103 Prost, *Les Anciens Combattants*, II, p. 39.

104 Bruno Cabanes, '"Génération du feu": Aux origines d'une notion,' *Revue historique*, 641 (2007), 150.

105 H. Pichot, 'Le front unique', *JM* (12 June 1926); H. Pichot, 'Le Congrès des Congrès', *JM* (21 August 1926).

106 H. Rossignol, 'Le Front Unique. Oui, mais pourquoi?', *VC* (9 October 1926).

107 Prost, *Les Anciens Combattants*, I, p. 109.

108 H. Aubert, 'L'Entente est faite. Mais sur quoi?', *VC* (19 November 1927).

109 'Alerte', *VC* (8 June 1929).

110 'Le Meeting de la Salle Wagram: Discours d'Edmond Bloch', *VC* (29 June 1928).

111 'Le refus de l'esclavage', *Action française* (22 June 1926).

112 AN, F7/13234, 'Le Commissaire Central de Police à Monsieur le Directeur de la Sûreté Générale', 16 June 1927; 'Le préfet d'Ille-et-Vilaine à Monsieur le Ministre de l'Intérieur', 13 July 1927.

113 H. Rossignol, 'Faillite', *VC* (29 June 1928); 'Le Meeting de la Salle Wagram: Discours d'Edmond Bloch', *VC* (26 October 1928).

114 H. Rossignol, 'Pourquoi le Bureau de la Confédération a démissionné le 24 Novembre', *VC* (30 November 1928).

115 'A propos de la démission du bureau de la Confédération', *JM* (12 August 1929).

116 'La Résolution sur la Paix', *VC*, 27 June 1931.

117 Prost, *Les Anciens Combattants*, I, p. 139.

118 Fortis, 'A quoi tiennent les déceptions que nous vaut notre politique extérieure en matiére franco-allemande', *VC* (4 July 1931).

119 Smogorzewski, 'La FIDAC et la CIAMAC', *VC* (21 January 1933).

120 AN, F7/13316, 'Meeting de protestation organisé par le Comité d'Entente des Associations d'Anciens Combattants', 6 December 1932.

121 Prost, *Les Anciens Combattants*, I, pp. 152–3.

122 A . Colleau, 'De quoi demain sera-t-il fait?', *VC* (4 February 1933).

123 AN, F7/13316, 'Anciens combattants (divers)', 1 December 1932.

124   H. Pichot, 'Autorité ou Républque?', *CUF* (1 February 1933); P. Patou, 'L'ordre républicain', *CUF* (15 February 1933); H. Pichot, 'République', *CUF* (1 March 1933); G. Rogé, 'La réforme de la constitution ou le voyage inutile', *CUF* (15 July 1933).

125   See for example 'La mentalité d'Outre-Rhin', *VC* (1 April 1933); P. Galland, 'Le Reichsbund a parlé', *VC* (15 April 1933); E. Lacquièze, 'Le monde en folie', *VC* (25 March 1933).

126   H. Aubert, 'Propos divers', *VC* (15 April 1933); H. Aubert, 'Dans l'attente des jours à venir', *VC* (15 July 1933).

127   AN, F7/13317, 'AC', 11 October 1933.

128   'A la Sorbonne: La réforme de la constitution', *VC* (28 January 1933).

129   Police estimated that 3,500 veterans attended, AN, F7/13317, 'Réunion organisé par l'Union Nationale des Combattants, Salle Wagram, le 15 octobre', undated.

130   H. Rossignol, 'Parallèle de départ', *VC* (21 October 1933).

131   AN, F7/13317, 'AC', 21 October 1933.

132   Archives of the UNC (heareafter UNC), Paris, minutes of the executive committee (hereafter EC), 14 October 1933.

133   'L'UNC et les problèmes actuels', *L'Ouest-Eclair* (16 October 1933).

134   See for example, AN, F7/13317, 'Réunion organisée par la Comité d'entente des Associations Ivryennes d'anciens combattants et victimes de la Guerre', 14 October 1933 and 'Le Ministre des pensions à Monsieur le Ministre de l'Intérieur', 19 November 1933.

135   A. Linville, 'L'action s'engage', *JM* (22 October 1933); 'La situation', *JM* (29 October 1933).

136   AN, F7/13317, 'Réunion organisée par l'Union Nationale des Combattants, Salle Wagram, le 15 octobre', undated; Prost, *Les Anciens Combattants*, I, p. 153.

137   *Ibid.*, II, p. 65.

2

6 February 1934: The veterans' riot

In 1933, the failure of successive radical governments to find a solution to the deepening economic crisis sharpened hostility to the regime. When leading figures in the radical party were implicated in the schemes of the fraudster Alexandre Stavisky, the right-wing press and extra-parliamentary leagues sensed a scandal. They alleged that leading radicals, including Georges Pressard, the brother-in-law of premier Camille Chautemps, had repeatedly helped Stavisky escape justice. After his most recent swindle involving the Bayonne Municipal Pawnshop came to the attention of the police, Stavisky fled. At Chamonix on 9 January 1934, surrounded by police, he took his own life. The right and the left alleged that the forces of order had silenced Stavisky before he could make potentially damaging revelations. Throughout January, Chautemps's persistent refusal to open an inquiry into the scandal exacerbated the situation. Contempt for parliamentarians grew as acrimony and intolerance filled the air. Citizens booed and whistled newsreel footage of politicians and daubed graffiti on the walls of the Chamber and Senate. Some café owners displayed signs stating that deputies would not be welcome in their establishment. The leagues took to the street in protest.[1]

A further financial scandal brought down the Chautemps administration on 28 January. The new government under Edouard Daladier set about reorganising the departments compromised in the Stavisky affair. Jean Chiappe, prefect of the Paris police, was the most contentious casualty of this reshuffle. The right held Chiappe in high regard for his heavy-handed treatment of communists, while the left had long condemned the prefect's leniency toward the nationalist leagues. Unsurprisingly, the left-wing press welcomed Daladier's decision. The conservative dailies denounced Chiappe's transfer to a backwater job in Morocco as a concession to the socialists whose support, they alleged, Daladier was trying to win.[2] On 5 February, right-wing Parisian municipal councillors produced a poster inviting Parisians to protest. The council included several leaders of the extreme right and veterans' associations including Georges Lebecq, newly-elected president of the UNC. Following a month of agitation, the leagues and the UNC called a demonstration for 6 February.

That night, thousands of leaguers and veterans took to the streets to protest against the 'corruption' of government. The mood of demonstrators at the Place de la Concorde, the centre of the protest, soon turned ugly. A riot ensued. At the height of the violence, police fired on protesters, killing thirteen and wounding six.[3] Hundreds more were injured. In the aftermath of the riot the government resigned, despite having survived three votes of confidence during the disturbances. Former French president Gaston Doumergue succeeded Daladier. A conservative, Doumergue formed a national union administration. The violence had succeeded in reversing the parliamentary mandate and installing a right-wing prime minister.

In the months that followed, the conflict between the left and right split France. The language of civil war permeated France as each day the partisan press spat its venom into the political arena. Violence was not confined to the press as partisan factions mobilised; perhaps fifty people died in political violence between 1934 and 1938. Radicals, socialists and communists founded the Popular Front coalition in response to the attempted 'fascist' coup of February 1934. The left-wing alliance enjoyed electoral success in May 1936. Meanwhile, extreme right-wing leagues attracted thousands of men and women into mass organisations that sought the removal of the democratic and parliamentary republic.

Historians have spilled much ink over the intentions of the rioters on 6 February 1934.[4] Since René Rémond's *La Droite en France* (1954) argued that the events of 6 February were little more than a street demonstration that went wrong, the orthodox school of thought has held that the rioters' failure to overthrow the republic demonstrated their lack of serious intent.[5] Serge Berstein claims that the lack of coordination between the nationalist leagues and the absence of a plan to invade the Chamber show that the riot was not an attempted coup. The heterogeneity of the groups involved underlines the disjointed nature of the protest.[6] Michel Winock distinguishes two distinct elements in the riot: violently intransigent anti-republicans and more moderate demonstrators. Moderates were representative of the mainstream public opinion. They were content to air their grievances against the inefficiencies of parliament and remained separate from illegal actions.[7] In a judgement that has implications for the broader history of the period, proponents of the orthodox school claim that the rioters' failure proved the French nation's deep commitment to democracy and its 'allergy' or 'immunity' to fascism. The riot is thus taken as an allegory of 1930s politics. The leagues' noisy opposition to the regime drowned out the voices of moderation. The political confrontation of the 1930s was thus largely 'artificial' (*l'affrontement simulé*). In reality, the French were deeply committed to democracy.[8]

Since the early 1990s, research has undermined the immunity thesis and, with it, the orthodox interpretation of the February 1934 riot.[9] Though the principal actors in the riot – the AF, the CF, the taxpayers' group the Fédération des contribuables de la Seine, the Groupe de la région parisienne (GRP) of the UNC, the JP and the SF - were ostensibly a diverse bunch, there were no rigid boundaries between them. They shared common ideas, an anti-democratic attitude and their memberships often overlapped.[10] The CF, the JP, the AF and the UNC had, for example, supported the *contribuables* campaign in 1932 and 1933.[11] In 1934, organisational divisions did not prevent collaboration between groups before, during and after the riot. Activists of the AF and the *contribuables* worked together on 9 January, as did members of the JP and the SF on 11 January. On 23 January a call to demonstrate saw the names of the AF, the JP and the *contribuables* on the same poster. On the night of the riot nationalist associations collaborated in large provincial cities such as Lille and Lyon.[12] Collusion between nationalists should not be discounted simply because it was not perceived as successful; informal cooperation was the norm.

Prominent members of the UNC had contact with leaders of the JP prior to the riot and publicly associated their names with these men. The Parisian municipal council included Lebecq and Jean Ferrandi, president of the UNC colonial section and the Association nationale des officiers combattants. JP leader Taittinger was also a member of the council and a deputy in the Seine. His name appeared alongside UNC vice-president Jean Goy and those of twenty-eight other deputies in an open letter of protest to minister of the interior Eugène Frot. This was turned into a poster and displayed around Paris on the night of 5 February. An unsigned poster that emanated from the municipal council called on the people of Paris to demonstrate on 6 February. According to Pierre Pellissier, it is likely that Lebecq and Ferrandi were involved in the poster's production.[13]

Were these men part of a plan to establish a provisional government? CF leader colonel de La Rocque thought so. Speaking to Daladier while both were prisoners of the Germans in 1944, La Rocque claimed that Lebecq, Taittinger and AF leader Maurras among others were in the process of planning a coup when Chiappe lost his post. Deciding to bring their action forward, the leagues and the UNC moved against the government. La Rocque, with one eye on the post-war period, may have been intent on blaming others for weakening the republic. Daladier, also looking to his post-war political career, may have wanted to discredit La Rocque. However, Daladier noted that La Rocque refused to involve himself in the plan. If Daladier fabricated the meeting then he would have had more to gain by implicating the colonel. Perhaps La Rocque's story was true. In support of this hypothesis is the fact that on the afternoon of 6 February an unnamed municipal councillor offered the AF's Maxime Réal del Sarte a place in a new government. This suggests that the plan was still in gestation and supports La Rocque's claim that the plotters had brought their action forward following the fall of Chiappe.[14]

Whatever the ultimate intentions of the rioting groups, as Michel Dobry argues, it is dubious at best to use the outcome of events to presume the intentions of those involved. The failure of rioters to enter the Chamber and their apparent satisfaction with the subsequent government of Gaston Doumergue does not prove that another, more extreme intent did not exist. The leagues' failure to take power on one night should not reduce the threat they posed to the Republic throughout the decade. After all neither the German Nazis nor the Italian Fascists violently seized control of the state. Hitler and Mussolini combined a campaign of violence with more conventional engagement in political competition. In France, it was the leagues' lack of parliamentary representation that hampered their ability to influence the formation of governments and left them unable to capitalise on the fall of Daladier.[15]

The veteran contingent

Veteran participation in the riot was not representative of the movement in general. The UNC's GRP made up the biggest proportion of the veteran delegation. Contrary to the association's claim that 30,000 members turned out, the police estimated that of the approximately 8,000 marchers about 5,000 were genuine UNC members, the remainder being from the CF – remnants of the group's march had crossed the Pont Alexandre III to join the UNC – and onlookers.[16] Paul Chopine, at the time head of the CF's shock troops, the *dispos*, witnessed the mixing of CF and UNC members at the Cours la Reine.[17] UNC veterans, marching in orderly ranks, medals worn proudly, preceded by flags and banners, perhaps made a great impression on observers. The presence of the UNC attracted people to the protest, including veterans of other groups and those who attended in an individual capacity. One eyewitness came to the riot in response to a telephone call from his friend who told him that the government had fired on ex-servicemen.[18]

Veterans from several other associations joined the UNC. The communist ARAC and several regimental associations such as the Légionnaires décorés au péril de leur vie were also involved. The ARAC's aims were different to those of the UNC. Communist newspaper, *L'Humanité* claimed that its veterans' group would protest against the regime while the UNC would march in solidarity with Chiappe.[19] The CF was no longer the exclusive preserve of veterans and the other leagues present on the night were not in the majority made up of former soldiers, though each possessed a veteran wing. Contrary to this relatively minor involvement, after the riot the right propagated the myth that *only* veterans had rioted in order to vilify the government. It depicted the government as heir to the barbarous adversary of the Great War and equated the victims with the war dead. Consequently the image of the riot as a veterans' protest violently and bloodily put down entered the popular imagination.

To the extent that the right portrayed the UNC's march as a peaceful protest, immunity thesis historians have largely reproduced this representation. Antoine Prost depicts the UNC column as staging a kind of 'protest within a protest'. The march remained separate from the riot on the Place de la Concorde as well as from the charges made toward the barricaded bridge and the clashes that left police and protesters dead and injured. On reaching the Place de la Concorde, the column turned away from the Chamber and toward the Madeleine, which Prost claims proved the UNC's respect for republican legality. Its involvement was 'a demonstration within a demonstration, an original episode which spoke for itself, juxtaposed to the scenes of the riot as if it were entirely alien to them'.[20] According to Berstein, for evidence of this separateness one need look no further than the fact that no UNC members suffered gunshot wounds or were shot dead. UNC president Georges Lebecq cited the same reason as 'proof' that UNC members did not riot.[21] However, with fewer than twenty people suffering gunshot wounds that night, this criterion for participation in the riot disqualifies the majority of people on the Place de la Concorde from being rioters. Conversely, bystanders who were shot must logically be considered rioters. Certainly, the UNC did not encourage its members to engage in violence yet its discourse frequently implied a solution to parliamentary corruption that was far from peaceable. The UNC was not unique in this. During the 1930s, a climate of civil war reigned in France as political groups used violent discourse and military tropes in their discourse. Threats of violence were not without consequence. The period between 6 February 1934 and 30 November 1938 saw seventy-five people killed in political violence.[22]

While veterans had long rejected electoral participation, preferring to lobby deputies through letter-writing campaigns, the UNC did not extol the might of the pen over the sword. It cast the association's struggle against politicians in the language of military engagement. The veterans' task was framed as similar to the one they had faced in wartime, situating the conflict with politicians on the metaphorical battlefield rather than in the recognised institutions of democratic representation. The UNC divided France into two opposing trenches, those of the forces of good (veterans) and the forces of evil (politicians).[23] The trenches confronted each other across a 'civic Marne'. The veterans would 'fire the first shots' and 'take the trenches of the interior'.[24] After the riot, UNC executive member Aimé Goudaert inscribed the 'battle' of February into history alongside other instances of French heroism at the Marne and Verdun.[25]

Employing terms such as 'battle', 'march', 'ranks', 'mission' and the wartime battle cry *'en avant!'*, UNC veterans compared their civic action to military duty.[26] The association regularly made reference to a forthcoming 'D-Day' and 'H-hour' in which its 'merciless war' against politicians would be settled once and for all. UNC veterans often stated that they would 'sweep' (*balayer*) the politicians from power and that they possessed the 'brooms' to 'pitilessly restore order to the house'.[27] In January 1934, president of the UNC's Ardennes group Schmitt warned that the electorate was sick and tired of the profiteers and buffoons in power. Political debauchery may well cause a crisis of regime and in this event the veterans would be ready to 'sweep' the house.[28] On 6 February 1934, the UNC claimed its veterans had not carried arms but 'moral brooms'.[29] Extreme right-wing groups made similar use of this metaphor.[30] In military terms, the verb *balayer* implied armed action. It meant 'to drive away the enemy' or described the broad range of fire of a machine gun.[31] This ambiguous term contained an aggressive meaning that the UNC did not hesitate to express explicitly in other ways

Both reflecting and contributing to the violent atmosphere in French politics, UNC discourse on politics was not moderate. In imposing the imagery of the war onto political conflict, the association presented French society as divided between the veteran-led 'honest' elements and the anti-national and decadent political classes. In doing so, the UNC questioned parliament's claim to represent the national interest. It did not call for violent action but its use of military metaphors portrayed violence as a possible and effective solution. When the UNC urged the taking of the enemy trench this did not mean via an electoral campaign but through an extra-parliamentary route to power.

The road to February 1934

Within the veterans' movement, the Stavisky affair came after two years of simmering discontent over the monetary sacrifices asked of the veterans and demands for state reform. The UF was growing short on patience. In November 1933, the association's council attacked the disorder and corruption in parliament. It warned that if the government did not act, the republic itself would be threatened.[32] As for the UNC, the Stavisky 'scandal of scandals' only confirmed what it had long believed: France risked death if the decay within government was allowed to continue. The time had come to remove the *république des camarades*.[33] In spite of the association's moralising, the UNC's own president Rossignol was embroiled in Stavisky's shadowy dealing. Facing the threat of substantial provincial resignations if he remained in office, Rossignol resigned the presidency on 3 February 1934 though he remained an executive member.[34]

Georges Lebecq, president of the UNC's Parisian group, agreed to become interim national president until the national congress in May. Lebecq, a small businessman and activist in the Parti démocrate populaire, represented a right-wing fascistic tendency in the UNC. After the riot, his preference for political activism would entail collaboration with the extreme right. In a movement as large as the UNC, though, a variety of political loyalties co-existed. Unanimity was hard to come by within the executive committee. The first choice for Rossignol's replacement had been Isaac, a moderate less inclined to political activism. Yet in February 1934, he refused the presidency and endorsed Lebecq's candidature.[35]

Originally, the UNC planned to demonstrate on 4 February. This demonstration would demand the punishment of the 'Stavisky majority' in the Chamber.[36] The planned itinerary of the march would see the veterans meet at the Clemenceau statue on the Avenue des Champs-Elysées and then move toward the Place de la Concorde. In previous public displays, the veterans had marched in the opposite direction toward the tomb of the Unknown Soldier. On 11 July 1926, the march ended at the Place des Etats-Unis, which though politically symbolic in the context of the agreement on inter-allied war debts, did not implicate the French state. On 4 February, the demonstration would have a decidedly political terminus. Lebecq postponed these plans when Chiappe threatened to resign if the march went ahead. The prefect of police warned that troublemakers would likely hijack the march and in this event Chiappe could not send his men against veterans. Lebecq informed the UNC's executive committee of the postponement at a meeting on 3 February. Nine of the twelve members of the GRP's executive committee disagreed with the decision to call off the protest.[37]

Despite the deferment, 150 UNC activists gathered in front of the statue of Clemenceau on 4 February at the scheduled meeting time of 3 p.m. Once informed of the deal between Lebecq and Chiappe, some members of the crowd criticised the leadership for this decision. Cries of 'Long live Chiappe!', 'Long live Hitler!' and 'Down with the ministry of the interior!' were overheard by police. Joined by members of suburban sections, the group of three hundred veterans, under the orders of Hubert Aubert, marched to the Arc de Triomphe, where security forces dispersed the troop.[38]

The removal of Chiappe changed the situation. Lebecq revived the idea of a demonstration against the government at a meeting of the GRP in Courbevoie. The veterans in attendance approved. UNC members at Châtenay-Malabry voted a similar motion. The executive committee of the GRP fixed the date of the new demonstration for the evening of Tuesday 6 February. Lebecq neither consulted the authorities nor the national executive committee.[39] For the second scheduled march the meeting time of 8.30 p.m. was much later and this coincided with the plans of the leagues. However, the later hour may simply be attributed to the fact that a maximum number of members would be able to attend on a weekday evening rather than in the afternoon during business hours.

The UNC's second call to protest implicitly called the veterans to insurgence against not only the Stavisky majority but also the Daladier government. It condemned the premier's *vite et fort* brand of justice. It railed against the 'Judas kiss' of Frot, who warmly shook Chiappe's hand when the prefect had persuaded Lebecq to call off the first march, before delivering him to the 'vengeance of the socialist party'. The UNC called all veterans, not just its members, to protest against 'the clan of sycophants', 'political brokers', and 'the ballot paper merchants' in government.[40] Goy was confident that the police would not act against the veterans. Nevertheless, he promised, UNC members would respond with force if provoked.[41] At a meeting of the Parisian municipal council and the president of the republic, Goy warned that even though the UNC would not send its members against better-armed adversaries, they might make hostages of those responsible for any bloodshed.[42]

Before the postponed march of 4 February, Lebecq set out the aims of the action in *La Voix du combattant*. UNC street demonstrations up to that point had concerned the defence of the veterans' material rights and issues of foreign policy. The aim now was to protest against the alleged parliamentary dishonesty at the heart of the Stavisky affair and the politicians who had subsequently attempted to cover up their crime. A mass demonstration of the UNC's strength would cow the government into meeting the association's demands on the punishment of political corruption. The UNC neither called for the overthrow of the republic, like the AF, nor did it advocate a 'national revolution' as the JP did.

Nevertheless, the UNC cannot be defined as essentially 'republican' for the term itself is contested. In one sense the UNC opposed what it termed the '*République des camarades*' and the 'Stavisky majority', labels used to vilify the radical government. The UNC associated this 'republic' with wastage, fraud, corruption and cronyism.[43] This was nothing new. Historically both left and right had focused on the return of 'competence' to government. Depending on the political colours of the incumbent regime, all groups laid claim to competence in government or alleged a lack thereof.[44] Immediately before the riot this alleged lack of competence was compounded by apparent evidence of corruption. According to the UNC, the *République des camarades* was also the republic of Stavisky, of the *métèques*, in which the 'swindlers [were] legion'.[45] Editor of *La Voix du combattant*, Aubert gave the UNC's backing for the words of Henri Béraud in *Gringoire*:

> Is that the Republic? Come on! Is that the Republic, this stinking mix of sharks, beggars, croupiers, corrupt officials, traffickers of influence and shady ministers? This regime, the continual comings and goings of business dinners and commissions of inquiry? The temple of laws, this caravanserai the antechambers of which are cluttered with blackmailers, flashy foreigners and swindlers, where the look of a man beyond reproach searches instinctively every wrist for the mark of handcuffs.[46]

This tactic, therefore, precluded any mention of an attack on the republic for the *République des camarades* was different to the UNC's conception of the 'republic'. Throughout the 1930s, the UNC asserted that the 'true' republic, the 'virtuous', 'honest' republic 'of our dreams', 'of tomorrow', 'of the combatants' was not to be confused with the current 'guests of the Chamber of Deputies'.[47] The UNC argued that the republic would remain the best form of government only if the 'antiquated and outdated' constitution was 'profoundly altered'.[48] Pichot's discourse was similar. He claimed that the veterans were republicans '1934-style', compared to the republicans '1900-style' in parliament.[49] In this way, veteran discourse was symptomatic of a more general detachment of pluralism and democracy from republicanism, by which it was believed that enemies who claimed to be republican were disingenuous.[50]

The UNC's plan for national renovation thus went beyond the removal of Daladier. The installation of Doumergue and the change of coalition was a minimum requirement rather than an end in itself. UNC vice-president Goy stated that the change of government was but the first step of the revolution.[51] He believed that the new government was a temporary administration that would enact the 'necessary' reform.[52] Some UNC provincial sections declared their readiness for further action, suggesting that they did not believe the UNC was finished. A group in the Côtes-du-Nord warned its members to remain alert and prepared to intervene directly in the affairs of the country if needed.[53] In the Finistère, the UNC's *Le Poilu* advised the veterans not to rest on the laurels of their victory.[54] UNC vice-president Paul Galland claimed the 'abscess had been lanced' and the new government, imposed by the veterans, would now begin the purification of parliamentary mores and the process of reform. The veterans intended to be at the heart of and to direct this reform. He twice claimed that the association's action was a warning shot and that the French were awaiting the combatants' next move.[55] The veterans of the UNC hoped that a new administration would reform the republic according to its authoritarian programme. If not, then the association was prepared for action. In this context, the February march was a dummy run for 'D-Day' and 'H-Hour'.[56]

A protest within a protest?

Given the significance attached by some scholars to the 'moderate' participants in the riot – that they reflected the 'true' mood of the French - the role of the UNC on February 1934 requires careful consideration. A close examination of the veterans' march allows one to deconstruct the orthodox historiography. The UNC's march was not separate to the rest of the riot. As the column advanced towards the Place de la Concorde, turned away from the Chamber and then returned towards the riot (albeit significantly reduced in number) the cortege gained and lost numerous members, leaguers and bystanders. The main body of the demonstration set out at 8.30 p.m. yet some small groups of UNC and CF members were reportedly moving towards the Place de la Concorde as early as 7.15 p.m.[57] At 7.30 p.m. police officer Max Gurney was involved in a confrontation at the barricades with a group that contained members of both groups. Blows were exchanged.[58] Victor Broissiat, police inspector of Paris's tenth district, reported a confrontation with UNC veterans who had advanced to the north end of the Pont de la Concorde. The veterans refused to retreat until a fire hose dispersed them. This incident took place at 'about 8 p.m.'[59] The report of Laurence, commander of police group 135, supports Broissiat's statement. He claimed that the veterans arrived on the square at about 8 p.m., over thirty minutes prior to the arrival of the main body of the UNC. An hour later, the veterans were completely mixed up with the other demonstrators and put pressure on the police cordon.[60]

This observation uncovers a further flaw in the belief that the UNC was able to maintain itself as a discrete group. Photographs from the night show members dressed in suits and overcoats, the only distinguishing feature being the war medals pinned to their chests, medals that some lost on the night. At the height of the riot, it would have been difficult to distinguish who was a genuine veteran and who was not. Though some of the leagues wore distinctive clothing, an eyewitness stated that there were many men dressed 'as everyone else' on the square at 7.20 p.m.[61] Perhaps one could make out veterans from troublemakers by the advanced age of the former, yet even respectable old bourgeois men helped younger rioters uproot benches and reinforce barricades.[62] To add to the confusion, several UNC flags were allegedly stolen and used by rioters on the Place de la Concorde to disguise their true allegiance. It is possible that UNC members took part in violence and lost their flags themselves. Lebecq congratulated flag-bearers who had not hesitated to use their flagpoles as weapons.[63] An accurate identification of the provenance of rioters is therefore problematic.

At approximately 8.30 p.m. Lebecq, joined by a group of Parisian municipal councillors, led the UNC procession from its meeting place at the Cours la Reine. Upon the UNC's entry to the Place de la Concorde police saluted the veterans.[64] This lends weight to the argument that the UNC had a calming effect on the riot. Many policemen were veterans and this may have stayed their hand. The UNC claimed that as they reached the square *agents provocateurs* cried for the veterans to advance on the Chamber. But the procession turned away as its aims were not political.[65]

It appeared that the plan was not to invade the Chamber and install a government of veterans.

Upon reaching the Place de la Concorde, Lebecq and the leadership hesitated. It is difficult to deduce the intentions of the UNC. The fluid character of any riot means plans may be abandoned, adapted or spontaneously formed according to the immediate situation. In the absence of a premeditated plan, one may only speculate at what point unfolding events dictated the direction of the column. The *Bulletin de l'UNC*'s account of the riot claimed that the plan was always to march toward the Elysée palace for an audience with the president. Yet on 8 February the GRP stated that this course of action was decided upon only when police began firing on protesters.[66] UNC member Jacques Péricard hinted that the UNC veterans had always planned to cross the bridge albeit with the 'strength of their chests' alone.[67] Lebecq's statements to the commission of inquiry told a different story. The column's change of direction towards the Elysée was a spontaneous move as passage to the Madeleine was blocked by a police barricade. Lebecq admitted that some UNC members did demand an advance on the Chamber as the 'contagion' spread by the *agents provocateurs* took hold. Marching with the UNC, councillor Charles Roëland recounted that when he heard calls to move towards the Chamber he joined in as this course of action seemed a rational one.[68] Some veterans may have shared this view. A unanimous opinion cannot be ascribed to a group of several thousand people. The entire UNC column thus did not turn toward the rue Royale on the orders of Lebecq. A large number followed Lebecq but others, reportedly veterans of the Légionnaires décorés au péril de leur vie joined by AF leaguers, turned toward the bridge and the violence resumed. Preceded by a tricolour flag, these men shouted insults and launched a hail of projectiles at the police.[69]

The bulk of the UNC column proceeded toward the rue Royale and away from the Chamber. As the veterans entered the street a police manoeuvre angered some. Superintendent Siron and fifty officers had received orders to occupy pavements on both sides of the street. He ordered his officers to do this just as the UNC column passed by. Le Clère alleges that Lebecq had always planned to go to the Elysée if the bridge to the Chamber could not be crossed. Siron's action, which caused some veterans to believe that the police were attempting to infiltrate their ranks, provided the justification to employ this secondary plan.[70] The UNC claimed that its procession attempted to reach the Madeleine but, its passage blocked by a barricade, the column split and part of it was forced into the rue du Faubourg Saint-Honoré. Witnesses disputed the existence of this barricade. Lebecq claimed that the only way to take the column was to the left as the barricade prevented a move northward. To turn right would have led back to the Place de la Concorde. This was not true. A rightward turn would have taken the column into the rue Saint-Honoré. Only another turn to the right along the rue Saint-Florentin would have led the UNC back toward the riot. Furthermore, the advance of the majority of the column toward the Madeleine supports the statements of witnesses who claimed that there was no such barricade.[71]

Now split in two, Lebecq led a smaller column in the direction of the president's residence. This column broke through three police barricades, forcing officers to retreat, and set a car alight outside the British embassy. Only when the veterans found themselves within 20 metres of the palace did mounted police and officers on foot manage to halt their progress. Brutalised by police, the demonstrators had transformed into a group of indignant and vengeful veterans. A witness overheard some veterans planning to return with their rifles the next day.[72]

The UNC claimed that it did not want violence but it nevertheless forcefully overcame three police barricades. Several reports attest to veteran violence against the authorities. Police reacted to this aggression. Truncheon blows, sabre cuts and pistol whippings injured fifty-three members of the UNC.[73] On the rue du Faubourg Saint-Honoré, a confrontation with the police saw Lebecq struck on the head with a rifle butt and Goy injured. According to Chopine, the CF's hardened shock troops, the *dispos*, joined the UNC at the rue du Faubourg Saint-Honoré. Although one cannot corroborate Chopine's opinion, he wondered if this cooperation had not been pre-planned to give the UNC formation a more combative edge.[74] Violence also took place among UNC members themselves. A UNC vice-president who refused to fight with the forces of order was beaten by other veterans. He requested that the police protect him from his comrades.[75]

At about 10 p.m. the contingent of veterans that had advanced towards the Madeleine about-faced and headed back toward the riot. Police reported, too, that 2,000 veterans were heading to the Place de la Concorde, shouting 'String up Daladier' and inviting people to join them. The police now found it impossible to distinguish veterans from youths mixed up in the crowd. Blind and disabled veterans preceded younger rioters and leaguers.[76] Enraged by the treatment of their comrades on the rue du Faubourg Saint-Honoré, the returning veterans exerted pressure on the bridge over the Seine. Witnesses and police claimed that this was the most critical moment of the night.[77]

Police noted various further disturbances involving veterans. At 10.20 p.m., 3,000 UNC members purportedly paraded in front of the Clemenceau statue and then proceeded in the direction of the riot. At 11 p.m. a reportedly 5,000-strong mixed group of UNC and Croix de Feu members descended the Champs Elysées to cries of 'To the Chamber, Daladier murderer!'[78] At 11.15 p.m., a group of veterans left the Place de la Concorde and made their way down the Champs-Elysées to the Tomb of the Unknown Soldier. However, upon passing the gates to the Elysée's gardens they halted and only a cavalry charge dispersed them.[79] At 12.35 a.m., police reported murmurings among the small groups of veterans and the AF's *camelots du roi* roaming the streets: the next day they would bring down the prime minister and the minister of the interior.[80]

No clear picture of the UNC's actions and involvement in the riot can be drawn. While the leadership attempted to exercise control over the column and its members, agreeing on a specific time and place to meet, it could not control everyone. The UNC's march was not a protest within a protest. The fact that no UNC members were shot does not prove their separateness to the riot. The procession did not exist within a bubble, through which leaguers entered to corrupt veterans but out of which veterans could not exit. Political groups infiltrated the ranks of the cortege and incited some to militant action. Some UNC members sought out violent action among the political leagues present. Others broke police barricades and attacked officers out of anger. They put pressure on the police barricade on the Pont de la Concorde and were involved in the ensuing violence.

Reaction from local UNC sections

At 11.15 p.m. on 6 February Daladier issued a statement in which he condemned political leagues and armed gangs for attempting a coup. He also recognised that the veterans had 'refused to associate with professional agitators'.[81] Reaction from the veteran community was mixed. The left of the movement, most notably the ARAC and the FNCR, condemned the UNC's involvement. In the Dordogne, UNC activist Boucher requested help from the national executive committee in fending off the attacks of the FOP.[82] Even the AGMG, usually close to the UNC, did not wholeheartedly back the action. The Confédération expressed reservations. It had warned its members against rowdy demonstrations prior to 6 February.

The UF issued a statement distancing itself (*se désolidariser*) from street battles led by groups 'outside of the movement and the combatant spirit'. Provincial sections were split. Some UF sections regretted veteran involvement on the night and demanded that the veterans concern themselves with material demands alone. The UF's section in the Deux-Sèvres supported the national association's motion, as did the *creusois* section.[83] In the Loiret UF members were divided not only over the involvement of the UNC but also the reaction of their national leadership. The section in Tigy alleged that an activist minority in the UF, out of touch with ordinary members, had written and published the statement of disassociation. It claimed that the use of the word *désolidariser* had angered its members and the local population, as it appeared that the UF had abandoned its former comrades-in-arms. The section went so far as to regret its membership of the UF if decisions were to be imposed from above. UF comrades in Jouy-le-Potier aired the same dissatisfaction. At Epieds UF veterans expressed their solidarity with and sympathy for the UNC, the CF and the people of Paris.

Discontent among UF sections in the Loiret caused departmental president Perdoux and Pichot to clarify the association's position. Pichot admitted that the wording of the statement was unclear and open to interpretation. It was not intended as a condemnation. UF leaders were simply unhappy that the UNC had gone against the wishes of the Confédération in deciding to march yet they recognised its right to protest. Pichot explained that at a meeting of eighty UF delegates on 8 February, a dozen or so had drafted the statement. It was then adopted unanimously. The UF president himself arrived at the meeting only after the decision had been taken.[84]

Likewise, in the UNC no single opinion dominated. The utility of citing examples of those sections who declared themselves 'for' and 'against' the GRP's action is questionable. In the absence of the opinion of every UNC section, which would facilitate a definitive tally, one is left with only a partial picture. The UNC did suffer a loss of membership in the months following February.[85] Lebecq claimed to have received letters of support and congratulations 'in their thousands', but he acknowledged that there had been losses too.[86] The Vaucluse group alone lost one-third of its members. Its president promised to remain at the head of the section but only if political action was henceforth ruled out.[87] Opposition arose in the sections of Villeneuve-sur-Lot, the Corrèze, Pompadour, the Ardennes, Touraine, the Haute-Garonne, the Dordogne, the Landes, the Oise and the Somme. Endorsements of the GRP's actions came from the

Nord, the Pas-de-Calais and Brittany.[88]

What were the reasons behind the opposition of some members? Some clue is provided by a group of former UNC members. In April 1934, they produced a poster that outlined their motives for resigning from the association in the aftermath of the riot. Police reported that the posters appeared across provincial France.[89] These veterans linked their decision to resign not only to the association's political action but also to the UNC's collaboration with the anti-republican extreme right. They denounced the CF as fascist and called on all true republicans within the association to follow their example and resign.[90] At the most this statement demonstrated that support for the parliamentary and democratic republic was still strong in sections of the UNC. At the least it showed distaste among some UNC veterans for political action and the extreme right.

New provincial sections were founded soon after the riot. In April 1934 veterans established a UNC section in Tarbes (Hautes-Pyrénées). They linked their decision to the association's role in the 'organisation and realisation' of the protest on 6 February.[91] The UNC's leadership alleged that new memberships had counterbalanced the losses suffered. Désiré Tritsch, vice-president of the Oise group, reported that the GRP had welcomed 3,000 new members in the fortnight since the riot.[92] The Pontivy group saw an increase of 230 members from January 1934 to February 1935.[93] The Montmartrois section of the UNC received 154 new members up to May 1934.[94] The UNC section in the second district of Lyon welcomed 1,000 new members between the riot and the end of the month.[95] From February to June 1934 the *landais* group gained 250 members and seven new sections.[96] While these new memberships came soon after the riot it is not possible to state that they were a response to the UNC's participation. Furthermore, one cannot say for sure that all resignations or new memberships were made in connection with the riot. Even when UNC sections made statements explicitly linked to the riot, these could be open to interpretation. In the end, the UNC certainly lost members yet veterans did not desert the association in droves.

The JUNC cited the veterans' participation on 6 February as the reason for an increase in its membership. Their parent organisation had shown a willingness to fight the 'gangrene' exposed by the Stavisky affair.[97] This had impressed new members. Raymond Schmitt, president of the *jeunes* in 1934, stated that if the UNC had not launched into political action on 6 February, the *jeunes* would not have followed the UNC. Now that the association had a 'doctrine', he could offer his members more than social engagements and sporting gatherings.[98] Franck d'Hennezel, president of the Saint-Quentin youth section, declared 6 February a watershed in the development of the youth movement. Inspired by the perceived cooperation of wartime and post-war generations in the CF, d'Hennezel claimed the time had come for the *jeunes* to join the *anciens* of the UNC and work towards national, social and moral renovation.[99]

The aftermath of the riot: the UNC's interpretation

The veterans' participation drew public attention to the movement as never before. In particular, focus fell on the UNC's national congress in Metz and the UF's meeting in Vichy. Police reports showed a variety of opinions among the public. Some feared that another attempt to replace the parliamentary republic would soon be made, this time in a bloody revolution.[100] Press opinion differed on the consequences of the night for the veterans' movement. *La Victoire* expressed a desire to see the veterans united behind a political programme and electoral action. *Le Figaro* warned against this action, desired by a minority of the veterans' movement.[101] The press furthered the myth that the events could be uniquely attributed to ex-servicemen. *Alliance démocratique* reported that 6 February was the 'veterans' work'.[102] Cartoons portrayed the veterans as victims of a government ambush, a premeditated massacre of France's bravest sons. One depiction showed a tribunal of dead veterans passing sentence, skeletons carrying tombstones engraved with the names of ministers: Pressard, Sarraut, Cot, Chautemps, Frot and Daladier.[103] Posters pictured dead veterans on the Concorde with the description: 'They escaped German bullets, the bullets of the Cartel did not spare them.'[104]

The UNC presented a contradictory picture of its role in the riot. On the one hand, the association emphasised the fact that it had turned away from the Chamber, did not have any political aims and was not involved in the rioting. Goy publicly denied Frot's charge that professional rioters had entered the ranks of the UNC column. He claimed that the police savagely charged the veterans with neither reason nor warning.[105] On the other hand, the UNC claimed to have been on the Place de la Concorde with the aim of chasing politicians from government and rescuing the republic. Goy and Lebecq boasted that it was the UNC that had forced Daladier to resign. If it had not been for the UNC's participation, the republic 'would have had its day'.[106] The *UNC de Normandie* condemned those in government, such as Daladier, who had effaced the role of the veterans in the riot.[107]

The UNC feted 6 February as a historic date when the people of France, embodied in the veterans, rose up against parliamentary corruption.[108] It was not alone in its claim to represent the popular will. With the fall of the government on 6 February, the street became an important territory in which the 'people', or rather the self-appointed representatives of the people, could air their views.[109] In parliament and press, discussion intensified on the location of popular sovereignty. Did it lie with the elected men of the Chamber or the man in the street? The UNC had not always been so sure of its popular character. Inherent to the veterans' claims to a privileged position in society was the difference between them and the mass of the population. The war had created in the veterans a certain mindset that non-combatants could not possess.[110] On 27 January 1934, days before the UNC would descend into the streets allegedly in the name of the people of France, Aubert wondered if the realm of the street would establish itself as 'the righter of wrongs'. However, following a month of leaguer agitation he described the streets as being in the grip of the party spirit and violence.[111]

Immediately after the riot Galland boasted that the UNC's Seine group's manifesto perfectly translated the wishes of all French citizens.[112] Lebecq stated '[w]e expressed the general sentiment of an opinion infuriated and sickened by the disconcerting spectacle of a parliament that for months had proved incapable of any discipline and useful work'.[113] Jean Ybarnégaray, a deputy and honorary president of the UNC's Saint-Jean-Pied-de-Port (Basses-Pyrénées) section, claimed that the protest was the 'cry of anger and indignation of a whole people'.[114] Goy condemned those who, disregardful of popular indignation, had manoeuvred behind the scenes to try and install Daladier as a dictator. He urged the French to support Doumergue's 'true antirevolutionary front'.[115] The UNC depicted the action as a popular uprising by the people of Paris on behalf of the whole nation.[116] The newspapers of provincial UNC sections concurred with the interpretation of the riot as a popular protest in the national interest.[117]

In their newfound role as the 'faithful interpreters of public opinion' the UNC now spoke of a divorce between parliament and the nation.[118] In a letter to the president of the republic in the days following the February violence the association claimed that a discrepancy existed between the political conduct of ministers and the wishes of the nation. It charged that the constitutional agreement between the two no longer existed.[119] The street now belonged to the veterans.[120] They were an invisible presence that guaranteed the stability and function of the regime. Still driven by the spirit of the demonstration, they continued to express the will of the free people and remained ready to intervene once again.[121] But to which veterans did the street belong? Unlike the UNC, Pichot claimed that it was not on 6 February 1934 that the people of France had defended the regime, but on 12 February, when the left mobilised its activists throughout the country.[122]

UNC veterans did not unanimously support the association's action yet their condemnation of it was no less unanimous. The UNC attempted to legitimise its role through the claim to represent the people of France against anti-national politicians. It was not the first time that the ex-*poilus* had represented the people of France. Veterans claimed that trench life had created a classless society where all social differences took second place to the wider conflict. The front had been a microcosm of the French nation. According to Roux-Desbreaux, such a levelling of social differences during the war meant that the veterans truly represented the people of France during the riot: 'We are, as in times past, all the people of France.'[123]

Saving the republic

The UNC continued to frame its action as republican against a government that was not.[124] When the association claimed it had saved the republic one must consider this declaration in relation to its claim that the Daladier government was *not* the republic. It did not mean that the association had embraced the democratic and parliamentary regime. According to the UNC, for fifty years an organised gang had lived off the republic, financed by secret funds. The association could not support a government that had come to represent the worst excesses of the *ancien* regime: the arbitrary use of power, a biased judiciary, favouritism, waste, the privilege of castes, injustice, fraud and the new feudalism of electoral fiefdoms.[125] *La Voix du combattant* railed against the deputies who claimed to be republican but were not.[126] The *cartelliste* Chamber had governed against the will of the country and had relied on armed force to remain in power. Though the UNC claimed that politicians should not be confused with the republic, it nevertheless identified the constitutional regime, and its inherent worth, with the political content of the government.[127]

Indeed, the UNC had not mentioned its loyalty to the regime before the riot. On the contrary, the association had claimed that the republic no longer existed. In a situation where the very life of the nation itself was deemed to be under threat, the regime no longer represented the country and had to take second place to that of the *patrie*.[128] When statements congratulated the association on saving the republic one must bear in mind what this implied. The departmental congress of the UNC at Ernée congratulated Lebecq and the GRP for the results they had achieved. These 'results' amounted to the fall of an elected government and the arrival in power of a conservative administration. The group did not express loyalty to the republic yet nor was it explicitly anti-republican.[129] It is possible to reconcile statements equating the fall of the government with the salvation of the republic if one accepts the subjective definition of the 'true' republic. Though the UNC did express loyalty to the republic this came *after* it had helped to force out an elected government, so reversing the mandate of 1932. At that time the association believed that a 'true' republic was but a few reforms away. The post-riot 'republic' was, for the time being at least, more acceptable than the 'republic' that had gone before it.

The UNC presented the Daladier government as an anti-national force. It did this through framing the riot as a premeditated massacre of French heroes. *Le Combattant d'Ille-et-Vilaine* published an elegy on the riot. The poet, Jean Douarre of the Courbevoie section, compared the march to the Place de la Concorde to a wartime advance into battle. Their torsos shining with medals hard-won in battle they marched, unarmed, only to be greeted by a salvo as they arrived at the square. Police had attacked without warning and so confirmed suspicions of a government ambush.[130] Goy supported the explanation that the attack had been an ambush to massacre veterans.[131] In Creil, the local executive committee also made reference to the government ambush, as did the Normandy group.[132]

Alleged crimes committed against French national symbols reinforced the argument that the Daladier government was anti-French. *Le Matin* reported a confrontation between veterans and police in which the tricolour flags of the UNC were forced down, broken and torn, and their bearers beaten.[133] UNC official Croizier saw blows rain down on one flagbearer. His flag thrown to the ground and his medals stamped upon, the veteran cried out as a police officer shouted, 'Here's what I do to your medals, bastard!'[134] In a symbolic affront to the war generation, a policeman was reported to have torn off Lebecq's medals with a contemptuous 'Old scrap!'[135] According to UNC section vice-president Georges Bonne, mounted police reacted most brutally to flag-bearers and those wearing their war medals, both sacred symbols of the war.[136]

War culture influenced the UNC's treatment of the victims of the riot in several ways. The UNC and nationalist leagues used commemorative devices usually reserved for the war dead to link the fallen of the Place de la Concorde to the soldiers of the Great War. Members of the GRP were awarded a diploma and a medal for their services on the night.[137] Alexander Werth, Paris correspondent for the *Manchester Guardian*, commented that young men showed off the scars they received on 6 February with no less pride than if they had won them at Verdun.[138] Victims, whether they were participants or innocent bystanders, were elevated to a similar level as the war dead. Although none of the association's members were killed, a UNC delegation attended the funerals of some of the deceased, whether they were veterans or not. Lucien-François Garniel, for example, was fifteen when he died from wounds received on the night. Approximately 5,000 veterans of the CF and UNC were reported to have attended his funeral. Referring to the victims as 'our dead', the UNC observed a minute's silence in memory of the fallen at memorial services.[139]

Nationalist groups acted similarly. Degirard, president of the CF section in Neuilly-sur-Seine, compared the victims to all those who had given their life for the defence and grandeur of France.[140] In May 1934 the Association Marius Plateau, the veterans' wing of the AF, laid a wreath at the Place de la Concorde for the victims of the riot. They were joined by delegations from the JP, the SF, and the Phalanges universitaires. As the latter passed the wreath, their leader read a roll call of those in the organisation who had fallen on 6 February, to which the response 'Killed in action' was given.[141] To preserve 'the still-living memory of [France's] children who had died for the ideal of justice, public morale and virtue', a group of municipal councillors, including Lebecq, proposed that the victims be honoured with a commemorative stone on the Place de la Concorde, where the 'blood of the martyrs' had flowed. The councillor Georges Prade suggested that a Parisian street bear the name rue du 6 Février to commemorate the night.[142]

The UNC portrayed the actions of the police as if they had been wartime atrocities. During the war, propaganda presented evidence of the enemy's inhumanity to society's most vulnerable members: women, children, and the infirm. UNC veterans emphasised their own nature as defenceless blind and disabled pacifists, savagely knocked unconscious by police.[143] A. Godon, president of the UNC's section in Montmartre, reported that mounted policed slashed women, the blind, and the elderly with their sabres, while officers on foot beat veterans with their bloodied truncheons.[144] A witness quoted in *Le Matin* compared the government's actions to the 1914 massacre of the Dinantais, which the German authorities had blamed on the provocation of 'imaginary snipers'.[145] The Daladier government was the heir to the barbarous adversary of the Great War. Veteran P. Croizier wrote in the UNC's *Le Combattant landais* that 'nothing in my memories of Lorette and Verdun distressed me as much as to hear [on 6 February] truncheons beat down like maces on the heads of these veterans and to see a great number of them fall down bleeding on the road'.[146] Photographs of injured veterans illustrated reports from the night. Lebecq was pictured with blood pouring down his face. *La Voix du combattant* showed a veteran lying prone on the pavement, allegedly having suffered three truncheon blows to the head, a kick in the face, and four kicks to his body.[147] The UNC issued a statement to the press, emphasising the brutality shown towards veterans with 'wooden legs' and 'empty sleeves'.[148] The press used attacks on women to further demonstrate the brutal behaviour of the police.[149] Mlle Ogé, beaten on the head with a truncheon, headed the list of victims published in *L'Echo Montmartrois de l'UNC*.[150] Aubert asked: 'is it the usual behaviour of police to club and cut down war invalids, the wives of unarmed veterans and flag bearers who could not defend themselves?'[151]

The UNC's interpretation of the riot sought to discredit the institutions of the pre-riot parliamentary republic. It located popular sovereignty in the streets and not in the Chamber. In claiming the right to speak for the people of France the veterans legitimised the actions of a people allegedly divorced from their representatives. Speaking at the Sorbonne in February 1934 Lebecq denied the charge that the UNC had taken up politics on the night of the riot. It had simply fulfilled its duty and served the country. He argued that during the war those who had committed crimes against French honour and the nation had been punished and 'certain men among us even belonged to execution platoons'.[152] Men who had neglected their national duty were executed. The UNC treated the Daladier government in the same way. Should politicians face the firing squad too? The Daladier government had not been a legitimate regime and direct action against it was therefore justified.

Conclusion

Throughout the inter-war period, the UNC did not advocate violent action against its adversaries or the regime. It was not a paramilitary organisation like some of the leagues. Consequently, the UNC neither called for a coup against the government nor was it the driving force behind the violence on the Place de la Concorde. Its members were not involved in the worst of the rioting when the police opened fire. Yet the UNC's violent discourse suggested a potentially violent course of action. This was not compatible with the electoral and parliamentary practices of the Third Republic. Its use of military language hinted at an extra-parliamentary route to power in which violence was framed as a viable option. This was especially true when the government acted contrary to the perceived national interest embodied in conservative veterans. The 'true' republic lay with the people in the streets of Paris and their representatives, the veterans. Significantly, UNC veterans received decorations for their role in the service of France *against* this government. Some members, therefore, were prepared to be violent when the situation called for a 'republican' action (as defined by the UNC) against a government that was not. Ultimately the UNC endorsed the overthrow of a democratically elected government by street violence when it considered this government's action detrimental to its own definition of the national interest.

During the riot, no single group remained separate and it is difficult to identify discrete elements in such a tumultuous and fluid situation. The UNC was not as aggressive in its actions as the leagues but as the night wore on some veterans did turn to violence. As individuals, UNC veterans took part in violent acts against the police. However, in the confusion and volatility of the riot one cannot be sure what members of each group did. Historians such as Berstein, Prost and Winock have drawn too sharp a distinction between the various groups present and have exaggerated the rigidity of their boundaries. Reaction from the veterans' provincial sections was mixed. Some members left the UNC but new sections were founded and new memberships arrived, some in response to the February action. The outcome of the riot was not an end in itself. The UNC considered the Doumergue administration as the first step in an authoritarian reform of the regime. The desired reform did not happen. A year after the riot Aubert lamented the fact that despite the passing of twelve months the same men remained in power. The criminals and corruption had not been punished.[153]

The UNC's actions on the night and the reaction to the events on a national and local level illustrate the ambiguous nature of this veterans' association. The February riot would leave some UNC sections with a taste for militant action. After all, the GRP had been successful in bringing about the downfall of a left-wing government and the installation of a more palatable conservative administration. UNC veterans frequented the meetings of and joined leagues such as the CF and the extreme right-wing coalition the National Front. These formations could not be described as integral to the survival of the French republic. The riot was part of a longer process of radicalisation that destabilised the regime, a process in which the veterans of the UNC were one of many actors.

Notes

1 Maurice Chavardès, *Une campagne de presse: La droite française et le 6 février 1934* (Paris: Flammarion, 1970), p. 23; William L. Shirer, *The Collapse of the Third Republic: An Inquiry into the Fall of France in 1940* (London : Pan Books, 1972), p. 181.

2 Chavardès, *Une campagne de presse*, p. 59; Marcel Le Clère, *Le 6 février* (Paris: Hachette, 1967), p. 115; Pierre Pellissier, *6 février 1934: La République en flammes* (Paris: Perrin, 2000), p. 84.

3 *Ibid.*, p. 320.

4 Berstein's *Le 6 février* has been hugely influential on the French historiography of the riot. The most important work of recent years is Dobry's, 'Février 1934'. French works include Chavardès, *Une campagne de presse* and *Le 6 février: La République en danger* (Paris: Calman-Lévy, 1966), Le Clère, *6 février*, Pellissier, *6 février* and Michel Winock, *La Fièvre hexagonale: Les grandes crises politiques, 1871–1968* (Paris: Seuil, 4th edn, 2009), pp. 193–239. The fullest treatment in English is Brian Jenkins, 'The Paris Riots of February 1934: The Crisis of the Third French Republic' (Ph.D. dissertation, London School of Economics, 1979) and 'The *six février* 1934 and the "survival" of the French Republic', *French History* 20 (2006), 333–51. Also worth consulting, if a little outdated, is Max Beloff, 'The sixth of February', in James Joll (ed.), *The Decline of the Third Republic* (London: Chatto & Windus, 1959), pp. 9–35. Specifically on the veterans' involvement in the riot see Shaw, 'The anciens combattants and the events of February 1934'. Works written at the time include Laurent Bonnevay, *Les Journées sanglantes de février 1934* (Paris: Flammarion, 1935) and Philippe Henriot, *Le 6 février* (Paris: Flammarion, 1934). The findings of the commission of inquiry set up to examine the events are available in *Commission parlementaire d'enquête chargée de rechercher les causes et les origines des événements du 6 février, 1934: Procès verbaux, rapports, annexes* (1935). The archives of the commission may be found at the AN in Paris, C/15092 to C/15103.

5 René Rémond, *La Droite en France de 1815 à nos jours* (Paris: Aubier, 1954), p. 210 (republished as *Les Droites en France* in 1982.)

6 Berstein, *Le 6 février*, pp. 247–51.

7 Winock, *La Fièvre hexagonale*, pp. 225–6.

8 Berstein, 'L'affrontement simulé des années 1930', *Vingtième Siècle* 5 (1985), 39–53.

9 See Introduction, note 66.

10 Jenkins, 'The *six février*', p. 339.

11 William A. Hoisington Jr., *The Assassination of Jacques Lemaigre Dubreuil: A Frenchman between France and North Africa* (London and New York: Routledge Curzon, 2005), p. 6.

12 Le Clère, *6 février*, p. 225; Beloff, 'The sixth of February', 16; 'Dans les grandes villes', *Le Matin* (7 February 1934); 'Une soirée d'émeute à Paris', *Le Figaro* (7 February 1934); 'De nouvelles manifestations se produisent en province', *Le Petit Journal* (9 February 1934); 'Manifestations de protestation', *Le Matin* (11 February 1934); Hoisington Jr., *The Assassination of Jacques Lemaigre Dubreuil*, p. 6.

13 Pellissier, *6 février*, p. 108; Philippet, *Le Temps des Ligues*, V, annex III-B-3, p. 276.

14 Edouard Daladier, *Prison Journal, 1940–1945* (Boulder, CO: Westview Press, 1995), p. 259; Pellissier, *6 février*, p. 135. Jacques Nobécourt mentions a meeting between Lebecq and Marshal Lyautey that suggested a nascent coalition of nationalist groups; *Le Colonel de La Rocque (1885–1946) ou, les pièges d'un nationalisme chrétien* (Paris: Fayard, 1996), p. 274.

15 Dobry, 'Février 1934', 511–33; Jenkins, 'The *six février*', 336–40.

16 Archives de la préfecture de police, Paris (hereafter APP), BA 1852/B1, anonymous, 'Le mouvement Croix de Feu', undated.

17 Paul Chopine, *Six ans chez les Croix de Feu* (Paris: Gallimard, 1935), p. 115.

18 Shaw, 'The anciens combattants', 304–5 ; 'La vérité: Paris la connaît mais la province qu'en sait-elle ?', *Le Jour* (26 February 1934).

19 Chavardès, *Une campagne de presse*, p. 63.

20 Prost, *Les Anciens Combattants*, I, p. 162 ; Berstein, *Le 6 février 1934*, p. 170.

21 *Ibid.*, p. 170; UNC/EC, 24 February 1934.

22 On violence in French politics during the inter-war years see Stéphane Audoin-Rouzeau, 'Le parti communiste et la violence, 1929–1931', *Revue historique*, CCLXIX/2 (1983), 365–83; Douglas, 'Violence and Fascism'; Passmore, 'Boy scouting for grown-ups?'; Daniella Tartakowsky, 'Stratégies de la rue. 1934–1936', *Le Mouvement social*, 135 (1986), 31–62; Andreas Wirsching, 'Political violence in France and Italy after 1918', *Journal of Modern European History*, 1 (2003), 60–79.

23 P. Delore, 'Pensées d'automne', *VC* (11 November 1933).

24 H. Rossignol, 'Parallèle de départ', *VC* (21 October 1933); P. Delore, 'Pensées d'automne', *VC* (11 November 1933).

25 A. Goudaert, 'Ayons confiance … en nous', *VC* (12 January 1935).

26 For example see 'Chéron contre la Génération du Feu', *VC* (21 January 1933); G. Heldet, 'L'infernel dilemme', *VC* (28 January 1933); 'L'heure des Anciens Combattants', *L'UNC de Paris* (22 February 1934).

27 H. Aubert, 'Toujours dans le bourbier', *VC* (22 December 1934) ; 'A la recherche des responsables', *VC* (6 January 1934); A. Goudaert, 'De quoi

s'agit-il?', *VC* (23 December 1933); G. Heldet, 'L'infernel dilemme', *VC* (28 January 1933); C. Vilain *Les Combattants exigent … Du manifeste de la salle Wagram au congrès de l'UNC à Metz* (Rouen: Imprimerie commerciale du Journal de Rouen, 1934), pp. 10–17.

28 M. Schmitt, 'L'orage gronde', *VC* (6 January 1934).

29 P. Galland, 'Ambassadeurs de la justice', *VC* (10 March 1934).

30 Soucy, *The First Wave*, p. 61; *The Second Wave*, pp. 77 and 86.

31 G. de Cromières, 'Vérité', *Le Combattant du centre* (March 1934).

32 Shirer, *The Collapse of the Third Republic*, p. 186.

33 H. Aubert, 'A la recherche des responsables', *VC* (6 January 1934); 'Toute la vérité?', *VC* (20 January 1934).

34 UNC/EC, 3 February 1934.

35 Centre des archives contemporaines, Fontainebleau (hereafter CAC), 19 9490459, anonymous, 'Georges Lebecq', undated; UNC/EC, 3 February 1934.

36 'Dimanche prochain, 4 février 1934', *VC* (3 February 1934).

37 UNC/EC, 3 February 1934.

38 APP, BA/1853, anonymous, untitled, 6 February 1934.

39 Chavardès, *6 février*, p. 163.

40 Pellissier, *6 février*, p. 316.

41 Le Clère, *6 février*, p. 121; 'Nous serons ce soir 50, 000 dans la rue déclare M. Jean Goy', *L'Ami du peuple* (6 February 1934).

42 'Lendemain d'émeute à Paris. A l'Hôtel de ville', *Le Journal* (8 February 1934).

43 F. Malval, 'Les projets financiers du gouvernment sont inadmissibles', *VC* (21 October 1933); H. Aubert, 'A la recherche des responsables', *VC* (6 January 1933).

44 Le Béguec, 'L'entrée au Palais Bourbon', p. 313.

45 Berstein, *Le 6 février*, p. 120; G. Pineau, 'L'Affaire Staviski', *VC* (13 January 1934); G. de Cromières, 'Vérité', *Le Combattant du centre* (March 1934).

46 H. Aubert, 'La racine du mal', *VC* (3 February 1934).

47 G. de Cromières, 'Vérité', *Le Combattant du centre* (March 1934); G. Berthau, 'Servir et non desservir: Lettre à Albert Sarraut, Ministre de l'Intérieur', *VC* (21 April 1934); 'MARIANNE: C'est l'Union des Anciens Combattants et des Jeunes qui réalisera la République de demain', *VC* (6 June 1936); 'Congrès départemental du groupe de la Sarthe', *VC* (6 December 1937).

48 H. Aubert, 'Testaments politiques', *VC* (29 February 1936).

49 H. Pichot, 'Ou l'on voit que le Président Doumergue, revenant de Tournefeuille, a passé près de Vichy', *CUF* (1 October 1934).

50 Passmore, 'Boy scouting for grown-ups?', 536.

51 J. Goy, 'La réforme électorale', in *XVe congrès national de l'UNC: Rapports, Discussions, Discours* (Paris: Editions Voix du Combattant, 1934), p. 485.

52 UNC/EC, 24 February 1934.

53 AN, F7/13024, 'Le Préfet des Côtes-du-Nord à Monsieur le Ministre de l'Intérieur', 4 June 1934.

54 'Garde à vous!', *Le Poilu*, March 1934.

55 P. Galland, 'Ambassadeurs de la justice', *VC* (10 March 1934); 'Raisons de la crise', *VC* (24 March 1934); 'La Révolution dans l'ordre', *VC* (21 April 1934); 'Refus d'obédience', *VC* (31 March 1934); 'D'étape en étape', *VC* (14 April 1934).

56 'Dimanche prochain, 4 février 1934', *VC*, 3 February 1934.

57 APP, BA/1853, anonymous, untitled, 6 February 1934.

58 AN, C/15092, '25 février 1934, Entendu, le gardien Gurney, Max, 42 ans, du 10e arrondissement, a déclaré', 25 February 1934.

59 AN, C/15092, '25 février 1934, M. Broissiat, Victor 51 ans, Inspecteur Principal du Xème Arrt, a déclaré', 25 February 1934.

60 AN, C/15094, 'Rapport de l'adjudant-chef Laurence, commandant le Peloton no. 135, 8 février 1935', 8 February 1934.

61 'L'histoire d'une émeute', *Le Matin* (1 March 1934).

62 Philippet, *Le Temps des Ligues*, III, p. 1468.

63 AN, F7/13320, 'Assemblée générale des sections de la Seine de l'Union nationale des Combattants, clôturent le congrès de la Région Parisienne', 8 April 1935.

64 Shirer, *The Collapse of the Third Republic*, p. 198.

65 'La manifestation de l'UNC', *VC* (10 February 1934).

66 'Les Associations d'anciens combattants et les événements du mardi 6 février', *JM* (14 February 1934).

67 J. Péricard, 'Après la nuit tragique: La manifestation de l'UNC', *L'Intransigeant* (8 February 1934).

68 AN, C/15092, 'Lettre à Monsieur le Président de la Commission de C. Roëland, Conseiller municipal de Paris, 2 mai 1934', 2 May 1934.

69 AN, C/15092, 'Rapport spécial, Préfecture de police, Compagnie de circulation, Paris, 15 février 1934, du commissaire spécial Tiha', 15 February 1934; AN, C/15094, 'Rapport du Capitaine Gilles, Commandant de la 9e Compagnie, 9 février 1934', 9 February 1934; Philippet, *Le Temps des Ligues*, III, p. 1519.

70 Le Clère, *6 février*, p. 151.

71 Pellissier, *6 février*, p. 167.

72 Le Clère, *6 février*, p. 151; Philippet, *Le Temps des Ligues*, III, p. 1519; V, annexe I-A, p. 54.

73 Report from the commission of inquiry into 6 February 1934 in *L'UNC de Normandie* (August 1934)

74 Chopine, *Six ans chez les Croix de Feu*, p. 115.

75 AN, C/15092, 'Paris 17 mars 1934, L'inspecteur général des Services de la Préfecture de Police à Monsieur le Préfet de Police', 17 March 1934.

76 APP, BA/1853, anonymous, untitled, 6 February 1934; APP, BA/1852 :B1, anonymous, untitled, 7 February 1934; 'L'histoire d'une émeute', *Le Matin* (27 February 1934); 'Après les fusillades: Nouveaux témoignages', *Action française* (25 February 1934).

77 Pellissier, *6 février*, p. 177; Shirer, *The Collapse of the Third Republic*, p. 199.

78 APP, BA/1853, anonymous, untitled, 6 February 1934.

79 Pellissier, *6 février*, p. 179.

80 APP, BA/1854, anonymous, untitled, 7 February 1934.

81 Pellissier, *6 février*, p. 183.

82 UNC/EC, 24 February 1934.

83 Ménard, 'L'Union fédérale devant la crise financière', *La Liaison* (April 1934); J. Pintout, 'La Politique', *Le Combattant creusois* (February 1934).

84 'L'Assemblée générale de l'UCL. 15 avril 1934', *Servir* (April 1934).

85 'Réunion du 11 mars 1934', *Le Trait d'union* (April 1934); E. Marchand, 'Groupe départemental de l'Eure: Communication du Président', *L'UNC de Normande* (March 1934).

86 Roux-Desbreaux, 'Après', *L'UNC de Paris* (22 February 1934).

87 AN, F7/13029, 'Le Préfet du Vaucluse à Monsieur le Ministre de l'Intérieur', 24 September 1934.

88 Prost, *Les Anciens Combattants*, I, pp. 161–2.

89 For example see AN, F7/13024, 'Le Préfet du Calvados à Monsieur le Ministre de l'Intérieur', 16 April 1934; F7/13025, 'Le Préfet de l'Hérault à Monsieur le Ministre de l'Intérieur', 6–16 April 1934; F7/13026, 'Le Préfet d'Indre-et-Loire à Monsieur le Ministre de l'Intérieur', 9 April 1934. AN, F7/13027, 'Le Préfet de la Manche à Monsieur le Ministre de l'Intérieur', 9 April 1934.

90 AN, F7/13028, copy of the poster 'La vérité sur l'Union nationale des combattants', in the weekly report from the Haute-Saône, 9 April 1934.

91 AN, F7/13027, 'Le Préfet des Hautes-Pyrénées à Monsieur le Ministre de l'Intérieur', 9 April 1934.

92 D. Tritsch, 'Réponse à des Histoires', *Le Trait d'union* (March 1934).

93 'Dans nos sections. Pontivy', *Le Cri du poilu* (March 1935).

94 Untitled, *L'Echo montmartrois* (May 1934).

95 'La vie des sections. Lyon: Sous-section du 2e arrondissement et 5e (Saint-Jean)', *Le Combattant du Sud-Est* (March 1934).

96 Compare the figures on membership in R. Dorlanne, 'La répercussion au Groupe landais des événements du 6 février' and 'Organisation et Propagande', *Le Combattant landais* (April 1934 and May–June 1934); P. Monredon, 'Le Rapport Moral', *Le Combattant landais* (June-July 1934).

97 'Groupement de Lagny', *VC* (31 March 1934).

98 R. Schmitt, 'Au travail de Suite!' *VC* (21 July 1934).

99 F. d'Hennezel, 'L'heure des Jeunes', *VC* (3 March 1934).

100 AN, F7/13033, 'Le Commissaire Spécial à M. le Directeur de la Sûreté Géné-

rale', Quimper, 7 February 1934; F7/13039, 'Le Commissaire Spécial à M. le Directeur de la Sûreté Générale', Boulogne-sur-Mer, 5 March 1934.

101 G. Hervé, 'L'heure des anciens combattants', *La Victoire* (23 March 1934); 'Les Anciens Combattants et l'action politique', *Le Figaro* (24 March 1934).

102 'Le beau Congrès des Combattants', *L'Alliance démocratique* (16 May 1934).

103 AN, F7/13320, 'Le Vernissage du Salon des Dessinateurs de Journaux', 7 April 1935.

104 AN, F7/13027, 'Le Préfet de la Manche à Monsieur le Ministre de l'Intérieur', 26 March 1934.

105 'M. Frot, vous ne dites pas la vérité', *Le Jour* (13 February 1934); 'Une lettre ouverte ...', *Le Journal* (13 February 1934); 'Une lettre ouverte à M. Frot', *Le Figaro* (14 February 1934).

106 UNC/EC, 24 February 1934; 'Dans nos sections: Vannes', *Le Cri du poilu*, March 1934; H. Aubert, 'Le Bilan d'un soir tragique', *VC* (17 February 1934).

107 'Le Trait', *L'UNC de Normandie* (March 1934).

108 J. De Rufz, 'Tribune des Militants: Préface à l'Action Combattante', *VC* (16 March 1935); G. Lebecq, 'Les anciens combattants dans la Nation', *VC* (20 April 1935).

109 Jessica Wardhaugh, *In Pursuit of the People: Political Culture in France, 1934–1939* (Basingstoke: Palgrave Macmillan, 2009), pp. 40–3.

110 'Henri Rossignol à Limoges', *Le Combattant du centre* (15 February 1930).

111 H. Aubert, 'L'ordre dans la maison', *VC* (27 January 1934).

112 P. Galland, 'Le vent d'orage', *VC* (10 February 1934).

113 Roux-Desbreaux, 'Après', *L'UNC de Paris* (22 February 1934).

114 AN, F7/12963, 'Conférence de M. Ybarnégaray, donnée le 23 février au Théâtre des Ambassadeurs', 24 February 1934.

115 AN, F7/12963, 'Transmission', 26 February 1934.

116 Roux-Desbreaux, 'Après', *L'UNC de Paris* (22 February 1934); P. Galland, 'Confusion', *VC* (17 February 1934).

117 D. Audollent, 'Réformes nécessaires', *Le Combattant du Cantal* (March 1935); L. Vandewalle, 'Le Sang a coulé', *Le Créneau* (February 1934); M.J. Victor, 'Troisième commission: Les Combattants dans la Nation', *L'UNC de Normandie* (June 1934).

118 'Lettre au Président de la République', *VC* (10 February 1934); Roux-Desbreaux, 'Il faut sauver la République et la France: deux entités qui ne font qu'un', *L'UNC de Paris* (March 1934); 'Entre le Parlement et le Pays le divorce s'accentue', *VC* (16 June 1934).

119 'Lettre au Président de la République', *VC* (10 February 1934).

120 Vilain, *Les Combattants exigent*, pp. 10–17.

121 J. De Rufz, 'Préface à l'Action Combattante', *VC* (16 March 1935); F. Gauthier, 'Les Fascistes du 6 Février! ...', *Le Combattant du Sud-Est* (March 1934).

122 H. Pichot, *Pour le rajeunissement français* (Vichy, 1934), p. 1.

123 Roux-Desbreaux, 'Après', *L'UNC de Paris* (22 February 1934).
124 G. Berthau, 'Servir et non desservir. Lettre à Albert Sarraut, Ministre de l'Intérieur', *VC* (21 April 1934).
125 H. Aubert, 'Le Bilan d'un soir tragique', *VC* (17 February 1934); P. Galland, 'Raisons de la crise', *VC* (24 March 1934).
126 H. Aubert, 'Le Bilan d'un soir tragique', *VC* (17 February 1934).
127 *Ibid.*
128 H. Aubert, 'Des volontés en caoutchouc', *VC* (10 February 1934); La Louve, 'Il faut en finir!', *VC* (6 April 1935).
129 AN, F7/13027, 'Le Préfet de la Mayenne à Monsieur le Ministre de l'Intérieur', 18 June 1934.
130 J. Douarre, '6 février 1934', *Le Combattant d'Ille-et-Vilaine* (April 1934).
131 Untitled, *Le Créneau* (May 1934).
132 'Vie des Sections', *Le Trait d'union* (June 1934).
133 'Les bagarres dans la rue', *Le Matin* (7 February 1934).
134 Pellissier, *6 février*, p. 169.
135 A. Soubiran, 'La vérité', *L'Ancien Combattant du Berry* (March 1934).
136 'L'histoire d'une émeute', *Le Matin* (4 March 1934).
137 AN, F7/13320, 'Assemblée générale des sections de la Seine de l'Union nationale des Combattants, clôturent le congrès de la Région Parisienne', 8 April 1935.
138 Alexander Werth, *The Twilight of France, 1933–1940* (New York: Howard Fertig, 1966), p. 19.
139 AN, F7/12963, 'A.S. des obsèques de M. Garniel, blessé mortellement le 6 février et décédé le 1er novembre', 2 November 1934; 'Réunion publique organisée par les 'Grandes Conférences Politiques, Salle Bullier, le 14 mars', 15 March 1934.
140 AN, F7/12963, untitled, 4 November 1934.
141 AN, F7/13306, 'Manifestation organisée à l'occasion de la Fête Nationale de Jeanne d'Arc (Paris)', 13 May 1934.
142 'Une dalle commémorative place de la Concorde', *L'Echo de Paris* (10 February 1934); 'Les collisions sanglantes du 6 février 1934: Une rue du 6 février 1934', *Le Matin* (10 February 1934).
143 H. Aubert, 'Le Bilan d'un soir tragique', *VC* (17 February 1934).
144 A. Godon, 'Menteur, Lâche, Assassin', *L'Echo montmartrois* (February 1934).
145 'L'histoire d'une émeute', *Le Matin* (February 1934).
146 Croizier, 'Le récit de la nuit tragique par un ancien combattant', *Le Combattant landais* (March 1934), also printed in 'La fusillade de mardi', *Le Figaro* (8 February 1934).
147 Photographs of the riot can be found in *VC* (17 February 1934).
148 Statement from the UNC's GRP in *Le Figaro* (10 February 1934)
149 'Une soirée d'émeute à Paris: Les manifestations sanglantes', *Le Journal* (7 February 1934).

150 List of section members injured in the riot, *L'Echo montmartrois* (March 1934).

151 H. Aubert, 'Le Bilan d'un soir tragique', *VC* (17 February 1934).

152 'La Commémoration de Verdun: La belle manifestation de la Sorbonne, 21 février 1934', *VC* (7 April 1934).

153 H. Aubert, 'Pour que ça aille bien', *VC* (2 February 1935).

3

Building a combatants' republic:
The campaign for state reform, 1934

In June 1934, police in Lille reported on the state of public opinion. Generally, the public was favourably disposed toward the new government but a nagging fear of further violence remained. Bloodshed in Paris in February had been followed by growing leaguer and left-wing agitation on the streets of France. The 'atmosphere of battle' had not yet dissipated. In particular, though, the *lillois* police commented on the public's fear that the veterans could again take violent if not revolutionary action.[1] In the months following 6 February 1934, a new assertiveness permeated the veterans' movement. The associations' belief in their self-appointed role as moral arbiter of the nation strengthened. Certainly, political allegiances still divided the two largest associations. The UNC's participation in the February riot continued to rankle the UF, which was suspicious of its rival's apparent political turn. Nevertheless, in spring 1934 both associations came together in a campaign for reform of the republic that involved groups across the veterans' movement. Consequently, the Confédération's own commission on state reform, the so-called 'commission of the nineteen', gained new impetus. At a meeting of the Confédération's national council during 23–25 March 1934, member associations adopted the commission's recommendations: a programme of electoral reform that included female suffrage and proportional representation to be followed by the dissolution of the legislature and new elections. The associations were confident that constitutional reform was but a matter of time.[2]

The veterans had long advocated reform of the state. Until 1934 they had been alone in doing so. Now state reform became a panacea for France's political and economic crisis. In domestic politics, the worsening financial predicament, parliamentary scandals and the recent violence drew attention to the perceived deficiencies of the regime. With the deaths of their comrades on the Place de la Concorde, the leagues howled about republican bankruptcy and illegitimacy. For the regime's more moderate critics, the elusiveness of ministerial stability was worrying, particularly in light of developments across the Rhine. Hitler's first year in power signalled that further challenges were to come to the Versailles treaty. Governmental stability would be essential to confronting a resurgent Germany and the menace to French security that this entailed. As the press took up the reformist campaign, the previously ignorant and those who had simply paid lip service to such projects became convinced that the republic, now covered as much in blood as in the 'mud' of corruption, was indeed in need of change. The Chamber and the hitherto reluctant Senate founded the Marchandeau commission to examine reform projects.[3]

Realignments took place in the veterans' movement too. While the UNC had supported institutional revision since the 1920s, the UF was traditionally reticent on matters of state reform. This did not mean that its rhetoric was no less anti-parliamentarian than other veterans' groups. Yet the UF considered discussion of reform too vulnerable to the corrupting influence of politic forces: constitutional revision aimed at correcting the failings of the regime could easily be derailed by politicians with more sinister intentions. Wary of the threat to the republican regime, the UF preferred the collaboration of the veterans' associations with the public powers to solve governmental problems. Reforms would be both 'modest' (leaving the constitution untouched) and 'objective' (because formulated by the veterans). Only ex-servicemen, untainted by political intrigue, possessed the required disinterested technical ability to propose viable reforms.[4] Subsequently the UF opposed discussion of reform at the Confédération's congress of March 1933. In June 1933, UF members reaffirmed their 'acute reluctance' to revise the constitution at the association's annual congress.[5] Similar opinions were expressed in the provinces. The *loiretaine* UF section agreed that the constitutional laws, although not perfect, should remain as they were. It was the politicians, not the regime, who were not fit for purpose.[6]

From March 1934, the UF's policy on reform began to change.[7] No longer would the association shun reformism. Street violence had deposed the radical government. The association could not accept the extra-parliamentary manner in which Doumergue and his 'government of old men' had come to power. If this was now the means by which governments were formed there was indeed something wrong with the functioning of the regime. Pichot outlined the choices that France now faced: either parliament would enact reform, of which the veterans would be the 'nucleus and the pivot', or France would fall into dictatorship. Pessimistic, he expressed small hope in parliament's ability to spare France such a fate. The task of reform therefore fell to the 'informed and organised forces': the veterans.[8] The UF section in the Loiret that had previously rejected institutional revision now recognised its necessity.[9]

Excitement spread through the veterans' movement as the rare opportunity for a unified reform campaign presented itself. Spurred on by the newfound consensus and enthusiasm that pervaded the Confédération, in April 1934 the veterans made their most audacious public demand. In an attempt to economise, prime minister Doumergue requested that the veterans accept a 3 per cent reduction in pensions. If the veterans refused, the premier would resign and the government would fall. On 12 April 1934, an extraordinary meeting of the Confédération's council met to discuss Doumergue's proposal. Split between those who wanted to reject the offer and those who did not wish to see the veterans blamed for the fall of the government, the Confédération accepted the reduction. However, it attached a condition to its acceptance: before 1 July the government should begin the process of 'national recovery' defined according to the Confédération's programme of March. When the Confédération next met on 8 July, it would judge whether or not the government had acted upon the good faith of the veterans. If the government's actions were deemed unsatisfactory, the associations would topple the government by forcing Rivollet, minister for pensions and head of the Confédération, to resign his portfolio. Speaking to the Confédération, Jean Goy sent out a warning to the government: 'Let's arrange an appointment with the government and may it apply its programme controlled by us. The regime is playing its next to last card. You, you are the last card. Let's keep ours in reserve, for we will not have the right not to succeed.'[10]

The Confédération's ultimatum did little to calm an anxious public. The day of the veterans' deadline promised to be tense. The socialist and communist Common Front, the CF and the UNC all announced street demonstrations for 8 July. With the forces of the left and the right taking to the streets, the July deadline preoccupied both press and public.[11] *La Croix* noted that the deadline had caused some amount of fear in 'high places'.[12] *Le Populaire* reported that 'everyone' was speaking about 8 July.[13] Police described the anguish of citizens who feared a veteran 'revolution' should the decision on 8 July not favour the government.[14] The left was concerned enough for communist Paul Vaillant-Couturier to offer the hand of the Communist Party to veterans lest their leaders dupe their former comrades-in-arms into dangerous adventures.[15] La

Rocque warned his followers to maintain their sang-froid, amid stories of 'mysterious meetings' and 'interchangeable and sensational alliances' that threatened bloodshed in the capital.[16] Some were more sceptical. Nationalist politician Gustave Hervé condemned scathingly the veterans' programme and reminded his readers that whatever happened, revolutions did not occur on fixed dates.[17]

Reforming the republic

Reformist thinking had a long tradition under the Third Republic.[18] In the decades before the Great War, social elites expressed concern for the perceived competence and quality of parliamentarians entering the Palais Bourbon. Various solutions were proposed, each one thought necessary to improve the calibre of men entering parliament. Some revisionists recommended a more frequent recruitment of ministers from outside parliament in order to raise levels of competence.[19] Anti-parliamentarianism was common but the strength of this differed among reformist elements.

Reform programmes often appeared to be similar but the difference between a genuine concern for the improvement of parliamentary mores and the desire for a more radical overhaul (or destruction) of the republic split conservatives. The centre right criticised the poor quality of parliamentarians and recommended reform within the system to correct the decline. In 1896, certain *progressistes*, including Raymond Poincaré, Louis Barthou and Paul Deschanel, while accepting to work within the republican system, envisaged a change in the spirit of the regime through the modification of parliamentary rules, conduct and suffrage in order to restore efficiency and authority.[20] The right and extreme right condemned parliamentarianism itself. Intellectuals such as Maurice Barrès, who described the 'rootedness' of all French in the land's 'blood and soil', and Charles Maurras, leader of the most energetic exponents of anti-republicanism, the AF, denounced the divorce between the people and the regime. However, as the parliamentary right entered the Republican fold soon after the turn of the century, extremists would have to wait for success in the crisis of the inter-war years.

After the elections of November 1919 numerous reformist groups and publications sprung up. They drew inspiration from the desire for post-war change called the 'spirit of 1919'. Most were concerned with a modification of the parliamentary regime. Members of the new veterans' associations were immersed in the reformist milieu. Ernest Pezet, president of the

UNC's Parisian section immediately after the war, contributed to the pages of reformist publication *Quatrième République*. UNC member Marc Sangnier revived the Jeune République group, of which Hubert Aubert was also a member.[21] Though in the decade to come, the major political parties would include state reform policies in their manifestoes, republicans continued to regard the notion of reform, in which they saw a potential departure from the republican model, as suspect. Reform without constitutional revision was possible, yet few projects, if put into practice, would have left the constitution completely untouched.[22]

By the mid-1920s, more drastic conceptions of reform gained favour. Left-wing agitation in the strikes of 1919–1920 and the electoral victory of the Cartel des gauches in 1924 spread the fear of communist revolution. With the subsequent appearance of the leagues in response to conservative fears, a growing number of groups came to express dissatisfaction with the regime. Doubly alarmed at the victory of the left and France's nascent economic difficulties, the right perceived the crisis as institutional; the republic itself was failing. This concern ran parallel to a crisis of political programmes among the parties, who, it was alleged, were unable to adapt to the problems of the time. Compared to the youthful and dynamic doctrines of fascism and communism, the French system seemed old and rusty as it clunked from one crisis to another.[23] Set against a background of the rising cost of living, the declining value of the franc and growing political confrontation, the government's recourse to decree laws did little to remedy the image of parliamentary incompetence.

The fading of the left after the 1928 elections effectively relegated the reform campaign to a secondary concern, though the veterans' movement and certain political figures such as Alexandre Millerand continued to espouse reformist doctrines. The onset of the worldwide economic depression in France and the return of a centre-left radical government in 1932 revived rightist dissatisfaction with parliament. Allegations of political corruption and the accompanying press hysteria amplified discontent to an unprecedented level.

On the initiative of the Semaine du combattant (SDC) an interassociational veterans' meeting took place in February 1932. Members reached a decision on four changes to the constitution: a strengthening of the executive, an independent and reorganised legislature, the representation of economic and social forces in the state and the creation of a supreme court. The motion ended with a call to form a constituent assembly. While the discussion of a constituent assembly worried orthodox republicans within the movement, the argument of the SDC's Maurice de Barral – that the most serious circumstances demanded exceptional remedies – persuaded attendees to back the idea.[24] The meeting created a permanent executive commission charged with making the French understand that, in the present situation, constitutional reform was the first condition of any recovery.[25]

In January 1933, SDC veteran Robert Monnier's report to the Confédération on constitutional change concluded that the present parliament was unable to reform itself. The report repeated the call for the formation of a constituent assembly composed of one hundred elected representatives and extra-parliamentary elements, specifically fifty 'great personalities' chosen by their peers. Reported in *La Voix du combattant*, the article concluded with a desperate call for reform, legal or otherwise: 'Whoever the man is who, tomorrow, takes up the reins of power legally or illegally, we submit to him the idea of forming a constituent assembly demanded by the veterans' Confédération. The national will must be freely expressed. A constituent assembly! [O]r the country is done for …'[26] The UNC agreed.[27] An extra-parliamentary method of reform was the solution. In itself, such recourse was not detrimental to the republic yet there was nevertheless scope for authoritarianism in the plan.

At the turn of the decade, few political parties had expressed serious interest in state reform. In the wake of the 1932 elections and the February 1934 riot, conditions were propitious for parties to take up the issue. The veterans, previously the vanguards of the reform agenda, now faced a field of competitors. Political parties each presented their reform programmes as unique yet there was common ground between groups. Characteristic of most were the desire to grant the prime minister the right to dissolution without the prior agreement of the Senate, the enforcement of limitations on parliament's financial freedom and the reorganisation of the premier's office. The majority of groups advocated the involvement of economic forces in the state, usually through the Conseil national économique (CNE).

Reform programmes were ostensibly similar yet the illusion of consensus hid conflict. Historically, both left and right had focused on the return of 'competence' to government. However, depending on the political colours of the incumbent regime, all groups laid claim to competence in government or alleged a lack thereof.[28] Parties across the political divide could therefore propose similar measures with different aims in mind. Concerning proportional representation, the centre-right Alliance démocratique (AD) hoped that electoral reform followed by new elections would break the Cartel's majority in the Chamber.[29] The FR's support for proportional representation stemmed too from a belief that this reform would increase the conservative share in the Chamber.[30] On the left, the socialist and communist parties saw proportional representations as a means to increase their share of seats in parliament.[31] Even extra-parliamentary groups showed the influence of the competence debate. The CF desired to see its own men (veterans and youth) in power. Whether precipitating a national crisis in which La Rocque would be called into government, or via electoral politics as the PSF attempted after 1936, the movement itself would rule. These men were the competent ones.[32]

Differences lay, too, in the method of reform and who would be called on to carry it out. At the centre, the AD and the centrist radical party sought to effect change within the confines of the existing regime. Reform would progressively improve the efficiency and competence of the system without straying from the republican model. To grant the prime minister the right to dissolve the Chamber was too great a threat to parliamentary sovereignty.[33] Proportional representation would give the public a fair means by which to express itself and simultaneously improve the quality of men entering parliamentary posts. For supporters of this idea, there would be no trip to Versailles to redraw the 1875 constitution.

Right-wing plans for state reform generally targeted the left. Denouncing the left-wing menace at the heart of parliament, André Tardieu claimed that socialism threatened the existence of the French state and undermined the nation through the spread of division and atheism. His programme aimed to erode socialist power. Tardieu took up a long-established argument of the right when he claimed that left-wing deputies needed spending powers more than their right-wing counterparts, in order to satisfy the demands of the interest groups that controlled them. The enfranchisement of women, believed to be conservative, would strengthen the right's share of the vote. Granting the government the right to dissolve the Chamber without the prior consent of the Senate would bypass this left-wing stronghold.[34]

In the atmosphere of crisis in spring 1934, the reformist fervour caused policy shifts, if only temporary, in the parties of the centre. The AD's manifesto of May 1934 adopted Tardieu's ideas on dissolution, the financial initiative and followed the FR in supporting proportional representation and the family vote. The radical party too harboured revisionists in its right wing including some who were prepared to call a constituent assembly to reform the republic.[35] This conversion to the reformist cause did not survive the cooling of passions as 1934 progressed.

The veterans' programme

The seriousness of thought now devoted to state reform ideas caused an expectant optimism to permeate the ranks of the veterans' movement. Was the era of the parties, selfish parliamentarianism and the *République des camarades* truly in its death throes? Prior to the riot the UNC had favoured constitutional revision by means of a constituent assembly of extra-parliamentary figures.[36] Yet with the arrival of the Doumergue government, the UNC acquired a renewed confidence in parliamentary reform. The association placed great hope in Doumergue: France had taken the first step on the road to French salvation.[37] With the right in power, reform could come from *within* the parliamentary system. The UNC hoped that Doumergue would swiftly introduce proportional representation, dissolve parliament and hold new elections. Electoral reform would banish forever the 'impotent spectacle', 'impasse' and 'paralysis' that the socialists and the radical party brought to the Chamber as they tried to transpose their electoral alliance into a functioning government.[38] The UNC's plan sought to reduce the number of deputies in parliament altogether, perhaps to as low as 200 deputies and 100 senators.[39]

Once more apparent consensus hid divisions. Certainly, the UF's discourse on state reform now came to resemble that of the UNC yet its motivations were different to those of its rival. The UF did not support Doumergue's government. If anything, the formation of the new government had discredited the parliamentary system.[40] Reform was needed and by extra-parliamentary means if necessary. The UF's conversion to reformism was sealed in the association's meeting of 11 March 1934. The association decried the divorce between an incompetent parliament and the French nation. Consequently, the UF specified a recreation of the 'political instrument of power' – the government. This did not mean a change in the ministerial team, but a fundamental change in the institution. Created by parliament or a National Assembly, the new government would rule for four years. Parliament would then be dissolved and elections would subsequently determine the next government's mandate. When one takes into account the UF's desire that veterans be at the centre of reform and Pichot's belief that a regime was incarnated in the men that governed it, it is likely that veterans would play a preponderant role.[41]

Having previously condemned all plans to amend the constitution, the UF now justified its own plans for constitutional reform by reference to the republic. Pichot claimed that the republic emanated from the revolution of 1789 and as such it could never be finished. Reform then was permissible within the context of perpetual progress toward the republican goal. Though Pichot wrote that the veterans of the UF were republican, the republicans of 1934 would appear very suspect to those of 1900.[42] In its motion of 7 July 1934, the UF specified that if parliament could not enact the necessary reforms then a constituent assembly should do so.[43] This National Assembly would appoint the new government for a fixed term.[44]

Provincial sections were divided over the UF's entry into the reformist camp. In the Loiret, the section in Tigy deplored the 'political' action of the federation. In Cravant and Coulmiers, veterans threatened to leave the UF for it no longer offered the political neutrality that they believed it once had. Conversely, the section in Bernon backed the UF's programme.[45] In the Deux-Sèvres, UF member Charbonenau feared that Pichot had allowed himself to be fooled by the UNC. Without a doubt, he continued, a constituent assembly would be 'bought' and used for ill ends.[46]

What form would the veterans' regime take? Some indication may be drawn from the UF and the UNC's writings on the matter throughout the 1930s. Divided in their motives, the UF and the UNC agreed on several points. Most importantly, the veterans would be at the centre of any reformist project.[47] They were uniquely qualified to claim this privileged position for their experience of the war had rendered them competent. Untainted by 'politics' and immune to the 'party spirit', the veterans' sole concern was the national interest.[48] How were the veterans to undertake this reform? The associations were not political parties; this idea was rejected in the 1920s. The veterans' programme therefore implied reform by extra-parliamentary means. True enough, deputies belonged to the UF and the UNC yet they were not bound to vote in line with the associations' demands. The associations' exclusion from political power meant that a populist appeal for veteran-led reform was their only means to pursue reform. The veterans' campaign used press and propaganda to establish direct contact with the people, in whom, the veterans believed, lay the power to reform the French regime. At a time when only two conceptions of action existed, that of reform through parliament, and reform from the people, the veterans' plan, based on the associations' claims to historical legitimacy, situated itself squarely in the anti-parliamentarian camp.[49]

Neither the leadership of the UF nor the UNC expressed the desire to lead France. To lead a government would require political action whether through election to office or a coup. The physical eviction of democratically elected representatives was not openly discussed in the UNC, much less the UF. It is unclear, therefore, what the associations meant when they spoke of 'sweeping' the politicians from power or 'cleansing' France of the party spirit. Whatever the associations' intentions, in the tense atmosphere of the time, their statements were ambiguous. To what extent did attacks on parliamentarians amount to an attack on the regime itself? At times, the boundaries between the two appeared blurred. Aubert claimed that parliamentarians were unlikely to reform the state because, in fact, they *were* the state.[50] The UF argued that a regime and the men who manage it were inextricably linked. These men incarnated the regime.[51] At the very least, to attack the content of an institution rendered the value of the institution itself uncertain.

Given the veterans' emphasis on military service as the ultimate qualification of competence, it is likely that a prominent figure from within the army, perhaps Marshal Pétain (whose name was raised occasionally in the veterans' plans), would have assumed the role of national leader. Deemed to be above partisan politics and therefore incorruptible, some believed that the Marshal would, unlike a politician, be a leader with French interests at heart. Goy supported this choice as Pétain's alleged distance from party politics heightened his prestige.[52] In March 1938, Pichot suggested to president Lebrun that Pétain be called to lead France.[53] The veterans were not alone in their admiration for Pétain. In 1935, the results of a poll in *Le Petit Journal* declared Pétain the most popular choice of dictator in France.[54] The team around the new head of government would contain veterans and it was these men who would restore order to France. Described as competent, sincere and honest, these qualities qualified the veterans for the task at hand and it was in them alone that salvation lay.[55] Around this national saviour and his veteran collaborators, ministers would almost certainly have been drawn from outside the parliamentary milieu, from men assumed to have proved their 'national' credentials.

Once the veterans had installed a worthy man in power, the mass of the veterans' movement would function as a support base for the new government. There would be a reduced number of parliamentarians and ministers. The associations hoped to fulfil the role of a supportive moral force upon which the government could rely. In some ways this role would be analogous to that of the single party in authoritarian regimes.[56] When their plans for the disbandment of political parties are taken into account with this envisaged role, concern for political pluralism in the associations seems slight. Goy made it clear in 1938 that the veterans' government, although 'national' in character, would not include representatives of every party.[57]

The government would function as an army's general staff. The successful outcome of the war for France proved that such a leadership was effective. Compared to the rapid turnover of republican cabinets – Doumergue's was the ninety-sixth – an army-style structure of government promised stability, order and discipline. Pichot was bemused at the number of men needed to form republican governments. Arguing that what democracy needed most was authority, the commanding and controlling will of a leader was essential to a government 'composed in the image of the army staff'.[58]

The hierarchical structure of government would be reflected in a similar organisation of society. The UNC in particular espoused this plan, describing the nation as an army. Ostensibly, the association celebrated the egalitarianism of the trench community yet the military values of duty and hierarchy, in which everyone 'knew their place', remained attractive. Galland saw no contradiction in remaining a free man who consented to his 'servitudes' and put his duty before his rights.[59] Aubert also concluded that the nation would function more efficiently if everyone was 'put in their place'.[60] The UNC's conception of a society dependent on a single national interest was incompatible with a regime based on equality, parliamentary debate and the vote.

The UF and the UNC's conceptions of the new regime were necessarily gendered. To some extent political context constrained the associations. Without the vote, women in France were excluded from elective office. The UNC supported female suffrage, citing the cause of democracy and fair representation, though it believed that when voting women would pay special attention to traditionally feminine issues such as public health, hygiene and social problems.[61] Regardless of this, the association did not envisage a role for women in the new French administration. In practical terms, the veterans' associations were founded by and for those Frenchmen who had served in the military during the war. Women were therefore ineligible for membership. Women were present in the associations in a different capacity. War widows were represented on the UF's executive committee. Young women and girls could join the UF's youth group. The UNC's youth group recruited women to its Action féminine groups too. Unlike the UF, women were not present at the upper levels of the UNC proper.

Taking into account the overwhelmingly masculine character of both French politics and the veterans' associations and the prevailing gender hierarchy it is unsurprising that the UF and UNC ceaselessly referred to the 'men' and the *chefs* who would assume power. References to women, at least in their capacity as potential leaders of France, were absent. Women had not fought in the war and thus were alien to the combatant spirit, the quality that made veterans fit for power. The inherent masculinity of the spirit did not solely disqualify women from power. The UF and the UNC used it to exclude politicians too. The associations specified that the men worthy of leading France possessed certain qualities: courage, competence, honour, selflessness, honesty, 'good sense', sincerity and a moral nature. It was these qualities that defined their masculinity. Such attributes were not self-evident. The veterans required proof and there had been no better place to prove one's manliness than in the crucible of the trenches.[62] Politicians were antithetical to the combatant spirit. Incompetent, dishonest, dishonourable, untrustworthy and selfish, politicians possessed none of the veterans' masculine qualities. They were governed by passions, a distinctly feminine affliction in the context of contemporary understandings of gender in which men alone were capable of mastering their emotions and thinking rationally.[63] The veterans' stipulation that men who had proved their manliness in the trenches alone could lead France challenged the perceived masculinity of elected politicians.

The JUNC's feminine sub-section, Action féminine, cast its attacks on politicians in gender terms. It blamed men for transforming politics into an 'abstract science' in which eloquence and fine words mattered more than action. Paulette Chailleux posed the 'natural' qualities of women as the remedy. A woman's sense of devotion, her intimate experience of suffering and her heartfelt spirit made her ability to 'observe and understand' superior to that of men.[64] Female suffrage was a particularly passionate issue for the women members of the JUNC. They demanded the right for fair representation in state affairs and they criticised the Senate for blocking the attempts of the Chamber to enfranchise women. Female members' claims sat uncomfortably next to the UNC's plans for an exclusively male government.[65] Claude Gauden warned that if women no longer wanted to have children it was because, without the vote, they had few weapons left with which to fight the 'ferocious selfishness of men'.[66] The implication was that women would refuse to bear children if the Senate continued to deny them enfranchisement.

In spite of the UNC's support for female suffrage, the association prioritised the family vote over that for women. To give the family due weighting in national life, the UNC proposed granting one extra vote to fathers of families with three or more children.[67] The family occupied a special place in the UNC's plans for state reform. It considered the family to be the basic cell of French society, termed the 'mother cell'. The future of the family was therefore intimately bound up with the future of France.[68] Parenthood was a national duty.[69] The UNC denounced the individualism and selfishness that it blamed for the decline of the family and the low rate of births.[70] These attacks could shade into denunciations of the regime. Action féminine specifically accused 'demagogic' republican politicians and France's 'stale democracy' for causing the decline of the family. The baseness of contemporary moral standards stemmed from parliamentarians who regularly waxed lyrical on the topics of duty, honour and probity, but who knew nothing of the meaning of these words.[71] Once again, the role of men came to the fore. The decadence of France had resulted from the diminishment of paternity, patriarchy and patrimony.[72] If the family was the key to the return of authority to France, it was a patriarchal conception of the family. Fathers, not mothers, would represent the family in state institutions. To some extent, the father was comparable to the veteran. Both had fulfilled their national duty, the veteran in the trenches of the war, the father in siring a child. In carrying out this service, they had demonstrated similar qualities necessary for the leadership of France: the veteran had shown selflessness and devotion to the nation, the father his 'assured probity' and 'hard toil'. Both stood in opposition to those who had neglected their national duty, the self-interested politician and the individualistic childless man.[73] The nation owed a debt to fathers and veterans.[74]

Corporatism informed the UNC's plans for the state representation of families. Inspired by the work of René de La Tour du Pin and Social Catholics at the turn of the century, corporatists had long supported the institutional representation of the family in the form of an assembly of fathers alongside which would be an assembly of professions, both considered 'natural' social groups. Corporatism went hand in hand with antiparliamentarianism and the well-worn debate over competence in government. While advocates of corporatism contested its content, with no single project agreed upon, all recognised that politicians did not possess the requisite competence for economic and social intervention.[75] Outside intervention alone could restore harmony to society and the economy.[76] Both assemblies would therefore collaborate in a council that would advise an authoritarian leader.[77] Corporatism implied a move toward authoritarianism. The assumption of a common interest among all members of a profession allowed corporatists to evade discussion of coercion.[78] The authoritarianism of the corporative system lay in the very claim to the existence of a single professional and national interest. Of course this national interest was subjective but it was always perceived as identical to the individual's self-interest.[79] Enemies of the professional interest such as communists, trade unions and foreign elements were thus deemed enemies of the *national* interest and to be eliminated.

The UNC's vision was for a society that rested upon the two fundaments of the profession and the family. It developed plans for what it termed the organised profession. Deputies and Senators simply did not possess the economic knowledge needed to run the economy.[80] The partiality of government in a democratic society meant that it could not fulfil its role as arbiter in industrial and social matters.[81] Corporations would put an end to industrial conflict, favour French nationals in the job market and remove the welfare burden from the state.[82] Parliament would not be replaced with an assembly of families or producers. Instead, the UNC prescribed a reinvigoration of the CNE. The UF also advocated a role for the council in national life. Accusing parliament of incompetence in economic matters, it recommended that the CNE advise the government in this domain.[83] Economic and political communities would thus collaborate for the good of France. Families and professions would be represented in the CNE. The government would consult the CNE on all matters relating to economic and social legislation, whether this was in the object of a law or its implications. In addition, amendments made in the Chamber would return to the CNE for further consultation.[84]

The organised profession did not require immediate reform of the constitution. Isaac, author of the plan, resisted calls for the establishment of corporative assemblies. Rather, the UNC would inculcate a 'corporative conscience' in society. Isaac recognised that this may take generations to achieve. He admitted that his plan did not go far enough for those veterans in the UNC who desired that a 'mixed assembly' of elected political and economic figures replace the Chamber. In answer to these concerns, Isaac saw 'nothing to prevent reflection' upon the CNE replacing the Senate in the future. The CNE would be better qualified to represent the social and economic forces of France than the upper Chamber. At this point the French regime would function like a business, with the government as management, parliament as the executive committee and members of the CNE as technical advisers.[85] Isaac's reluctance points to the co-existence of divergent tendencies in the UNC when it came to reform. Moderates, conservatives and authoritarians co-existed.

The UF and the UNC's plans for state reform were not democratic. Founded on the idea of their own historical legitimacy, both associations believed that sovereignty lay with the veterans. They opposed party competition and would likely seek to curtail political pluralism. The combatants' republic, led by competent men and a providential leader, would rely upon the natural elite of the veterans to form a government and as a reservoir of support. 'Natural' national communities (fathers and business) would also have a role in state institutions. Certainly the UF and UNC differed on several points, not least their motivations for reform. The UNC supported proportional representation specifically to exclude the radicals and socialists from power. The UF denied legitimacy to the Doumergue administration. Nonetheless, in 1934 both associations, while ostensibly concerned for the well-being of the republic, defined good government as a regime of military figures and veterans that would sweep elected representatives from power, limit political pluralism and reduce the role of parliament.

8 July 1934: The veterans' ultimatum

In spite of the proliferation of reform programmes in spring 1934, reformists would ultimately be disappointed. In May, the Doumergue government abstained from the vote on electoral reform, which was the first condition of reform in most parties' programmes. The partisans of proportional representation lost by eleven votes. If electoral reform enjoyed cross-party support, why did it fail to pass? Wary that reformists may try to force his hand, Doumergue allowed the post-February atmosphere of crisis to pass. He failed to profit from the high confidence he enjoyed from the public and parties, which may have forced the Senate to accept dissolution of the legislative house. For the left, Doumergue had come to power through the action of leaguers and fascists, a fact that always undermined the legitimacy of his government. Although hailed by some as a national saviour, he was still a man of the right. Socialist Léon Blum led a concerted campaign against Doumergue's plans, behind which he saw the threat of Tardieu. Denouncing the autocratic designs of the Doumergue-Tardieu partnership, Blum found support in the radical party. On the right, followers of the FR and the AD were not unanimous in their support for dissolution and revision. The question of constitutional revision was still the bane of the conservative camp. In the end, reformers could not escape the fact that their campaign began on the night of 6 February.[86]

For the veterans, Doumergue's failure to initiate a reform programme appeared to confirm parliament's inability to reform itself. Aubert remarked bitterly that this should come as no surprise. Politicians were not in the habit of committing political suicide. The men of the Chamber were concerned only with remaining in office until the end of their mandate, whether this was in accordance with the will of the nation or not. Deputies would not enact any serious reform of the state.[87] Yet despite the breakdown of the reformist project in parliament, attention remained fixed on the 8 July deadline. Meetings of the Confédération's commission of the nineteen became more frequent as the veterans planned for the failure of the government. The press devoted more attention than usual to the national veterans' congresses that year. In May 1934, the UNC held its annual congress at Metz. *Le Matin* recognised the significance of the UNC's meeting. Moving beyond the concerns of a single association, the veterans were meeting to decide once again whether to respond to the call of the country. The newspaper emphasised the strength of the association and described it as 'powerful' and a 'formidable army' similar to that which had entered Metz after the Great War.[88] The left-wing press saw more sinister motives behind the UNC's congress. *L'Humanité* warned that the 'fascists' in the UNC were using the congress to prepare another assault in the style of the February troubles.[89] Press reports focused on Goy's statements on electoral and state reform. Goy explained that 6 February was not intended to be the end of the UNC's political action.[90] The UNC had not prepared a team to take power by force and so, Goy claimed, the revolutionary period was still under way. The next step would be constitutional and state reform according to the UNC's long-established programme.[91]

The UF's congress at Vichy fell under the spotlight later that month. Pichot declared his conviction that reform was necessary to the survival of the republic. He condemned the Doumergue administration as a government of old men, which promised neither order nor security. Parliament was faulty. The veterans' revolution had begun.[92] The congress unanimously accepted Pichot's report and on the strength of it, installed him as president of the association. In his statement to the congress, the new president issued a warning to the government. On 8 July, if the government had neither stamped out fraud nor initiated reform the veterans would 'take the rudder'. Astounded, the audience applauded.[93]

As the July deadline approached and it became clear that the government had not satisfied the Confédération's demands, doubts began to surface about the consequences of toppling the government. Aubert was wary of government dupery but he knew too that the government enjoyed a majority in the Chamber and the Senate, as well as public sympathy. In bringing down Doumergue, the veterans would be committing a revolutionary act.[94] Others were less hesitant. The UF's Cher federation gave parliamentarians a stark choice: obey the veterans or abdicate.[95]

The UNC decided *not* to vote in favour of toppling the government. It announced this decision prior to the July meeting, which allayed some public fears. In the national press, Goy made it clear that the UNC did not want to cause another ministerial crisis. It did not believe that Doumergue had satisfied the veterans' demands but the association favoured the postponement of the deadline.[96] The UF did not share this view.[97] Subsequently, in spite of the apparent unity of the combatants' movement, at the July meeting the veterans could agree upon little else but the failure of the government. A motion intended to oblige Rivollet to resign was defeated by 292 votes to 290.[98] The Confédération split along established political lines. Groups on the right, such as the UNC and the AGMG supported Doumergue; the UF, FNCR and FOP on the left did not.

When the July deadline arrived, the UF's reaction indicated just how far it had moved into the reformist camp. It delivered a stinging criticism of the Confédération for failing to follow through with the veterans' threat to topple the government. Raymond Grasset, president of the federation in the Puy-de-Dôme, declared the inter-associational body dead.[99] Opinion among UF sections was divided. Members in the Creuse agreed that the government had indeed failed yet they were split evenly on whether to oblige Rivollet to resign. Nonetheless, the sections voted to follow the national UF's decisions.[100] However, following the July meeting, the president of the Creuse federation lamented the veterans' indecision and regretted that they had not taken power.[101]

As for the UNC, Aubert reassured members that in spite of the postponement the association would not be duped.[102] The conservative press congratulated the UNC for defeating the motion against the government.[103] *Le Figaro* expressed relief at the veterans' decision, as did *La Croix,* which claimed that the veterans had avoided being drawn into the revolutionary plans of the neo-socialists and trade unionists.[104] While affording the veterans the right to judge the acts of the national government, *Le Temps* nevertheless required that this judgement be moral and not political.[105] Some provincial UNC groups did not echo the press's congratulations. On 8 July, the Limousin group voted against granting the government an extension, in opposition to the vote of the national

UNC. Section president Gérard de Cromières criticised the Parisian leadership for its ignorance of provincial opinion and its vulnerability to government intrigue.[106] Even within the UNC's executive committee, members expressed reservations, considering the association's action as simply the postponement of difficult decisions. Gauthier argued that two options now remained: demand a constituent assembly, or descend into the street.[107]

The postponement of the deadline did not signal the UNC's support for parliamentary democracy. The value and legitimacy of the republic in the eyes of the UNC was dependent upon the political colours of the incumbent government. A right-wing administration, installed by street violence, was simply more acceptable than an elected left-leaning government. In any case, the association could not be sure that a new *cartelliste* government would not replace Doumergue. The UNC's opposition to the parliamentary regime still ran deeper than partisan politics. During Doumergue's reign, the association placed its confidence in the government but still expressed 'some anguish in this confidence'.[108] With Doumergue's government approaching two months in power, Aubert warned that 'gangsters' were still the masters of the Third Republic.[109] Lasting reform was all the more urgent.

Once reform failed to materialise, the UNC's confidence in Doumergue began to falter. In the final weeks of the administration, the UNC's disillusion seemed complete. On 29 September 1934, confronted with a regime as indolent as its predecessor, Aubert suggested a more radical treatment: 'The time when oratorical pills could have an effect is passed. Today, the sick country needs a severe treatment and we must have the courage to give some slices with a surgical knife here and there to avoid the wider spread of the gangrene.'[110] A week later, Etienne Bourrut-Lacouture wrote: 'If electoral reform … does not happen with parliament, then it will happen without it.'[111]

In October, Doumergue belatedly took up the revisionist cause once again in an attempt to shore up his failing popularity. Proposing measures that were accepted as necessary in spring 1934, Doumergue found that the fever of February 1934 had passed and cool heads had reasserted themselves. His plan chilled the hearts of deputies who once more feared constitutional revision and its implications for the parliamentary regime. The radicals, searching for allies on the right to oppose Doumergue, found support in Pierre-Etienne Flandin's AD and his centre-right allies. The AD renounced reformism and opted to effect improvement through a concerted bi-partisan effort. In November 1934, Flandin succeeded

Doumergue to the premiership and the following January expressed his opposition to constitutional revision. Reliant on the support of radicals, Flandin did not wish to jeopardise his position.[112]

The UNC once more confronted a regime it deemed incapable of change. Ten days after the Doumergue government fell, Lebecq spoke at a meeting of the UNC's Lyon section. Expressing the discontent of some within the association's ranks, he claimed that ultimately the state of France before and after 6 February remained unchanged.[113] The UF did not share its rival's pessimism. The association had always questioned the legitimacy of the Doumergue administration. It was now satisfied to see the radicals back in government. Pichot nevertheless warned Flandin that this was parliament's last chance for, if a country could not continue without a government, it could do so without a parliament.[114] The UF's support for extra-parliamentary reform now faded. Tellingly, on the occasion of the UF's national congress at Le Touquet in April 1935 the *Cahiers de l'UF* published no motion on state reform. There was no renewed call for a constituent. The UF now criticised parliament for placing too much power in the hands of the executive, the reverse of the UNC's argument.[115]

Conclusion

Analysis of the veterans' campaign reveals a complex story of political fluctuations that defies simple explanation. From March to November 1934, the UF and the UNC's programmes may have converged yet their motives diverged according to each association's political loyalties. The UNC, which had helped to remove the Daladier government, placed great hope in Doumergue. It believed that his right-wing ministry would reform the republic according to the association's own programme. For the UF, France had reached a nadir. Considering the Doumergue government illegitimate, Pichot's association moved closer to the UNC's position on reform, abandoning its neutrality when it feared that the functioning of the regime had finally broken down.

The UF and the UNC's programmes for state reform were ostensibly similar. United in the Confédération, an unelected body, the veterans formally threatened to bring down a government if their demands were not satisfied. They had long condemned the flaws of the parliamentary regime and presented themselves as the only men qualified to restore authority to France. Veterans were the sole holders of the relevant technical expertise and disinterested morality to remedy what they considered objective malfunctions in the regime. This belief was founded on the veterans' claim to an immanently authoritarian and undemocratic historical legitimacy that trumped the perceived authority of parliament. In this context, though the July 1934 ultimatum marked an escalation in veteran tactics, it should not give cause for surprise.

Parts of the UF and the UNC's plans *were* more moderate than those of other groups. They did not envisage taking power for themselves under a providential leader as fascist groups desired. However, to disprove the fascist attributes of a reform plan does not prove its democratic or republican nature. The UNC's preference for reform by means of a constituent assembly placed it closer to the right and extreme right than the republican centre. The same was true of the UF, though its demand for a constituent was short-lived. Nevertheless the UF's conversion to an authoritarian reformist project showed the willingness of 'moderates' to embrace extreme solutions in times of crisis.

The associations' plans for state reform were neither modest nor limited. They were not content to campaign solely for a change of government. The veterans' campaign demanded extra-parliamentary reform of the republican regime. A new government would then assume office for a predetermined period. Given the association's belief in the veterans' unique understanding of the national interest, it is likely that ex-servicemen would play a leading role in the administration. An administration of veterans and military figures would see deputies and ministers severely reduced in number. Following elections to validate the government's mandate, a team of national personalities and veterans would reform republican institutions.

The veterans' campaign demonstrates the complexities of opposition to the institutions of the Third Republic at this time. It is true that elements of the veterans' programme appear to have pre-empted some of the constitutional provisions of the Fourth and Fifth Republics. To interpret the veterans' plans in this way posits the Fifth Republic as the supreme goal toward which the French (as conscientious citizens) endeavoured. The deficiencies of the Third Republican regime are thus rendered objective and technical matters. There are two problems with such an interpretation. First, this teleological approach obscures the ignorance of historical actors of their role in the seemingly inevitable route to the present French regime. Second, state reform projects were not a 'neutral' and 'technical' matter, seeking to adapt the 'archaic' regime to the challenges of modernity.[116] Social and political agendas informed all reformist programmes. Consequently, the UF and the UNC's antiparliamentarian programmes were neither disinterested responses to objective systemic malfunctions nor objective and farsighted adjustments. In 1934, both associations reacted to a complicated and fluid political environment, which caused adaptations and reversals of policy. Rather than essentially supportive of the regime, the veterans' 'republicanism' and their ideas for reform were dependent on the ideological content of the government and how closely it conformed to each association's perception of the competent government.

Notes

1 AN, F7/13038, 'Le Commissaire Divisionnaire de Police Spéciale à Lille à Monsieur le Directeur de la Sûreté Nationale', June 1934 (specific date unreadable).

2 Prost, *Les Anciens Combattants*, I, p. 167.

3 Monnet's *Refaire la République* offers the best overall account of reform projects. Le Béguec provides an excellent study of parliamentary recruitment in 'L'entrée au Palais Bourbon'. See also Kevin Passmore, 'The construction of crisis in interwar France', in Brian Jenkins (ed.), *France in the Era of Fascism* (New York: Berghahn, 2005), pp. 151–99, especially pp. 177–86. A brief examination of state reform projects and the reasons for their defeat can be found in volume 5 of Edouard and Georges Bonnefous, *Histoire politique de la Troisième République*, 7 vols (Paris: Presses universitaires de France, 1962), p. 313 and volume 6 of Jacques Chastenet, *Histoire de la Troisième République*, 7 vols (Paris: Hachette, 1962), p. 105. William Irvine's *French Conservatism in Crisis: The Republican Federation in the 1930s* (Baton Rouge, LA: Louisiana State University Press, 1979) contains little on the subject within the FR – see pp. 100–2. Kalman's *The Extreme Right*, pp. 13–61, examines in detail the plans of the Faisceau and the CF/PSF. On La Rocque's movement see also Kéchichian, *Les Croix de Feu*, pp. 235–57; Kennedy, *Reconciling France*, pp. 112–19 and pp. 157–89; Passmore, *From Liberalism to Fascism*, pp. 117–23 and pp. 226–29. On individual politicans and state reform see, among others, Gilles Martinez, 'Joseph Barthélemy et la crise de la démocratie libérale', *Vingtième Siècle*, 59 (1998), 28–47 and Thibaut Tellier, 'Paul Reynaud et la réforme de l'Etat en 1933–1934', *Vingtième Siècle*, 78 (2004), 59–73.

4 G. Rogé, 'La réforme de la constitution ou le voyage inutile', *CUF* (15 July 1933).

5 'Notre XVIIe Congrès National, Limoges, 3–7 juin 1933', *CUF* (15 June–1 July 1933).

6 E. Bernon, 'Il faut revenir à de saines pratiques parlementaires', *Servir* (February 1934).

7   H. Pichot, 'Pour que vivent tous les Français dans une France vivante', *CUF* (15 March 1934); 'Le XVIII Congrès de l'Union Fédérale, Vichy, 20–22 mai 1934', *CUF* (1 June 1934).

8   H. Pichot, 'Pour une autorité républicaine: Que fera l'Union fédérale?', *CUF* (1 March 1934); AN, 43 AS/1, H. Pichot, 'L'Union fédérale au service du pays: Les délibérations du 11 mars 1934', undated.

9   'Un ordre du jour de l'Union fédérale du Loiret', *Servir* (March 1934).

10   'Les anciens combattants et les décrets-lois: Le Conseil national s'est réuni hier pour étudier la réponse à faire aux propositions gouvernementales', *L'Ouest-Eclair* (13 April 1934).

11   'A la veille du 8 juillet', *La Croix* (6 July 1934); C. Planche, 'Chez les anciens combattants: L'échéance du 8 juillet', *Le Populaire* (28 May 1934); 'Ce qu'est l'échéance du 8 juillet', *Le Matin* (29 May 1934).

12   'A la veille du 8 juillet', *La Croix*, 6 July 1934.

13   C. Planche, 'Chez les anciens combattants: L'échéance du 8 juillet', *Le Populaire*, 28 May 1934.

14   AN, F7/13033, 'Le Commissaire Spéciale [à Quimper] à Monsieur le Directeur de la Sûreté Générale', 7 February 1934; F7/13038, 'Le Commissaire Divisionnaire de Police Spécial à Lille à Monsieur le Directeur de la Sûreté Nationale', June 1934 (date unreadable); 'Le Commissaire Spécial de Lens à Monsieur le Directeur de la Sûreté Générale', 1 June 1934.

15   P. Vaillant-Couturier, 'Aujourd'hui: Anciens combattants nous vous tendons la main', *L'Humanité* (27 June 1934).

16   F. de la Rocque, 'Sang-froid', *Le Flambeau* (1 July 1934).

17   G. Hervé, 'L'échéance du 8 juillet ?', *La Victoire* (27 June 1934). See also an excerpt from *Le Temps* reproduced in H. Aubert, 'La voix des sirènes', *VC* (2 June 1934).

18   Specifically see Monnet, *Refaire la République*, p. 21 and pp. 179–90; Le Béguec, 'L'entrée au Palais Bourbon', pp. 156–276 examines reformism prior to the Great War.

19   *Ibid.*, pp. 158, 160–76, 206–14.

20   Monnet, *Refaire la République*, p. 186; Kalman, *The Extreme Right*, p. 14.

21   Monnet, *Refaire la République*, note 44, p. 556.

22   *Ibid.*, p. 317.

23   *Ibid.*, p. 199.

24   *Ibid.*, p. 223.

25   *Ibid.*, p. 224.

26   A. Colleau, 'L'Action civique des AC: De quoi demain sera-t-il fait?', *VC* (4 February 1933).

27   'A la Sorbonne: La réforme de la constitution', *VC* (28 January 1933); Monnet, *Refaire la République*, p. 247.

28   Le Béguec, 'L'entrée au Palais Bourbon', p. 313.

29   Monnet, *Refaire la République*, p. 339.

30 Irvine, *French Conservatism*, p. 101.
31 Monnet, *Refaire la République*, p. 320.
32 Passmore, 'The construction of crisis', p. 181.
33 *Ibid.*, p. 190.
34 Monnet, *Refaire la République*, pp. 300–1.
35 *Ibid.*, p. 319.
36 A. Colleau, 'L'Action civique des AC: De quoi demain sera-t-il fait?', *VC* (4 February 1933); 'A la Sorbonne: La réforme de la constitution', *VC* (28 January 1933); J. Goy, V. Beauregard and L. Berthier, 'La Réforme de l'Etat', *VC* (28 April 1934).
37 P. Galland, 'Ambassadeurs de la justice', *VC* (10 March 1934); 'Raisons de la crise', *VC* (24 March 1934).
38 Jean Goy, Victor Beauregard and Léon Berthier, *Le programme d'action civique des anciens combattants* (Paris: Edition de l'Action Combattante, 1935), pp. 35–6.
39 Prost, *Les Anciens Combattants*, III, p. 192.
40 G. Rogé 'La réforme de l'état: Une trouble tâche', *CUF* (15 September 1934).
41 H. Pichot, 'Pour que vivent tous les Français dans une France vivante', *CUF* (15 March 1934); Pichot, *Les Combattants avaient raison* ..., p. 72.
42 H. Pichot, 'Où l'on voit que le Président Doumergue, revenant de Tournefeuille, a passé près de Vichy', *CUF* (1 October 1934).
43 'Ordre du jour de l'UF, 7 juillet 1934', *CUF* (15 July 1934).
44 Pichot, *Les Combattants avaient raison* ..., p. 71.
45 'A l'UCL : Le Conseil communal du 4 novembre', *Servir* (December 1934).
46 'Conseil d'Administration,' *La Liaison* (July 1934).
47 P. Galland, 'La Révolution dans l'ordre', *VC* 21 April 1934; H. Pichot, 'Pour une autorité républicaine: Que fera l'Union fédérale?', *CUF* (1 March 1934); Hoffmann, 'Les Anciens Combattants et la politique', *VC* (2 March 1935).
48 Goy *et al.*, *Le programme d'action civique*, pp. 71–2; Hoffmann, 'Les Anciens Combattants et la politique', *VC* (2 March 1935).
49 Monnet, *Refaire la République*, p. 253.
50 H. Aubert, 'Celle sans laquelle on ne pourra rien faire', *VC* (9 June 1934).
51 Pichot, *Les Combattants avaient raison* ..., p. 66.
52 Prost, *Les Anciens Combattants et la confédération générale du travail* (Paris: Edition de l'Action combattante, 1934), p. 16.
53 Jean-Paul Cointet, *La Légion française des combattants: La tentation du fascisme* (Paris: Albin Michel, 1995), p. 22.
54 Jackson, *France: The Dark Years*, p. 124.
55 H. Aubert, 'Pour que ça aille bien', *VC* (2 February 1935).
56 Prost, *Les Anciens Combattants*, I, pp. 197–8.
57 'Réunis à la Salle Wagram les anciens combattants réclament un gouvernement de salut public', *Le Figaro* (27 March 1938).

58 'Un Nouveau et Magnifique Succès: Arcachon réserve aux participants du XX Congrès un inoubliable accueil', *VC* (20–27 May 1939).

59 P. Galland, 'Les bons ambassadeurs de la République', *VC* (20 July 1935); 'Les Droits et le Devoir', *VC* (23 January 1937); 'Etrennes 1938', *VC* (1 January 1938).

60 H. Aubert, 'Pour que ça aille bien', *VC* (2 February 1935).

61 A. Loez, 'A propos du vote des femmes', *VC* (30 March 1935).

62 Roberts, *Civilization without Sexes*, p. 138.

63 Vimal, 'Demain … ', *VC* (11 November 1933); M. Schmitt, 'L'orage gronde', *VC* (6 January 1934); H. Pichot, 'La vraie révolution', *CUF* (15 June 1934); C. Héline, 'L'UF entre courageusement dans la nouvelle année', *CUF* (10 January 1937); 'Oui, l'expérience est à faire', *CUF* (10 October 1937).

64 P. Chailleux, 'La Révolution féminine', *VC* (6 April 1935).

65 P. Chailleux, 'A un antiféministe', *VC* (3 November 1934); M.-A. Rocchesani, 'Action féminine: Les Jeunes filles et la crise', *VC* (2 February 1935); C. Gauden, 'Voterons-nous en mai 1935?', *VC* (16 February 1935).

66 *Ibid.*

67 See Humbert Isaac, *La Route de salut: Pensées, espoirs, volontés des anciens combattants et des jeunes* (Paris: Union nationale des combattants, 1935).

68 A. Debèvre, 'La décadence et la famille', *VC* (18 April 1936); M. Dupouey, 'Danger Social', *VC* (9 January 1937); A. Loez, 'Famille d'abord', *VC* (22 January 1938).

69 A. Loez, 'De l'Echo de Paris au … "Popu"', *VC* (12 December 1936).

70 *Ibid.*; 'Après le mal le remède', *VC* (10 April 1937).

71 'Action féminine: Sauvons l'enfance', *VC* (26 January 1935); P. Chailleux, 'Une conscience et des actes', *VC* (9 February 1935).

72 'Un impérieux problème', *VC* (9 June 1934).

73 A. Debèvre, 'La décadence et la famille', *VC* 18 April 1936.

74 P. Delore, 'La Famille dans la nation', *XVe congrès national de l'UNC*, p. 209.

75 Suzanne Berger, *Peasants against Politics: Rural Organization in Brittany, 1911–1967* (Cambridge, MA: Harvard University Press, 1972), p. 122–4.

76 Kevin Passmore, 'Business, corporatism and the crisis of the French Third Republic: The example of the silk industry in Lyon', *Historical Journal*, 38 (1995), 982.

77 Kalman, *The Extreme Right*, p. 27.

78 Berger, *Peasants*, p. 129; Passmore, *From Liberalism to Fascism*, p. 169; 'Business, corporatism', 961; Kéchichian, *Les Croix de Feu*, pp. 278 and pp. 318–33.

79 Passmore, 'Business, corporatism', 982.

80 Goy *et al.*, *Le programme d'action civique*, p. 88.

81 Joublin, 'La corporation, c'est l'union organique des classes', *VC* (24 September 1938).

82 'Rôle et fonctionnement de la Corporation', *VC* (17 September 1938);

Joublin, 'La corporation, c'est l'union organique des classes', *VC* (24 September 1938).

83 H. Pichot, *Les combattants avaient raison* ... p. 61 and 93.

84 H. Isaac, 'La Profession dans la Nation', *XVe congrès national de l'UNC*, p. 248.

85 *Ibid.*, p. 248.

86 Monnet, *Refaire la République*, p. 339–48.

87 H. Aubert, 'Celle sans laquelle on ne pourra rien faire', *VC* (9 June 1934).

88 'Le congrès de l'UNC à Metz: M. Lebecq parle du rôle des anciens combattants', *Le Matin* (12 May 1934); 'Le congrès de l'UNC a traité hier de la politique franco-allemande et de la réforme de l'Etat', *Le Matin* (13 May 1934); 'Le congrès de l'UNC à Metz', *Le Matin* (14 May 1934).

89 'Le Congrès des anciens combattants: A Metz, l'UNC élabore un programme nettement fasciste', *L'Humanité* (12 May 1934).

90 J. Goy, 'La réforme de l'Etat', *XVe congrès national de l'UNC.* p. 283.

91 J. Goy, V. Beauregard and L. Berthier, 'La Réforme de l'Etat', *VC* (28 April 1934); 'La réforme de l'Etat', p. 498.

92 H. Pichot, 'Union Fédérale. A Vichy: Le choc', *Le Poilu tarnais* (June 1934).

93 'Le Congrès à Vichy de l'Union fédérale des anciens combattants', *Le Matin* (22 May 1934).

94 H. Aubert, 'Examen de conscience', *VC* (7 July 1934).

95 'Congrès de la Fédération du Cher', *Le Retour au foyer* (2 trimester 1934).

96 C. de Rollepot, 'Que se passera-t-il le 8 juillet prochain ?', *Excelsior* (29 June 1934); '8 juillet?', *Le Peuple* (29 June 1934); H. de Kérillis, 'M. Déat n'aura pas sa "révolution" du 8 juillet', *L'Echo de Paris* (7 July 1934); 'A la veille du 8 juillet', *La Croix* (6 July 1934); G. Sanvoisin, 'Le congrès des anciens combattants commence cet après-midi', *Le Figaro* (7 July 1934).

97 'Ordre du jour de l'UF, 7 juillet 1934', *CUF* (15 July 1934); L. Viala, 'Après le 8 juillet', *CUF* (15 July 1934).

98 Prost puts the vote at 291 versus 291, suggesting that the figures were doctored, *Les Anciens Combattants*, I, p. 170.

99 R. Grasset, 'Au seuil de l'action', *Journal des combattants et mutilés du Puy-de-Dôme* (July–August 1934).

100 'Conseil d'administration', *Le Combattant creusois* (July 1934).

101 J. Pintout, 'Après le 8 Juillet', *Le Combattant creusois* (September 1934).

102 H. Aubert, 'La voix des sirènes', *VC* (7 July 1934).

103 H. de Kérillis, 'Par 294 voix contre 288 l'Assemblée écarte une motion qui signifiait, pratiquement, la défiance au gouvernement', *L'Echo de Paris* (9 July 1934).

104 *Ibid.*; G. Sanvoisin, 'L'action gouvernementale et le conseil national des anciens combattants', *Le Figaro* (9 July 1934); 'Le Conseil extraordinaire de la Confédération nationale des anciens combattants', *La Croix* (10 July 1934).

105 'L'Etat et les anciens combattants', *Le Temps* (9 July 1934).

106 'Assemblée générale du 21 octobre 1934', *Le Combattant du centre* (December 1934).

107 UNC/EC, 28 July 1934.

108 P. Galland, 'Raisons de la crise', *VC* (24 March 1934).

109 H. Aubert, 'Lettre ouverte au Président Doumergue', *VC* (7 April 1934).

110 H. Aubert, 'En écoutant le Président Doumergue', *VC* (29 September 1934).

111 E. Bourrut-Lacouture, 'Pour la salutaire réforme nous arracherons l'Etat à sa routine', *VC* (6 October 1934).

112 Chastenet, *Histoire de la Troisième République*, VI, p. 105; Monnet, *Refaire la République*, pp. 342–3; Bonnefous, *Histoire politique*, V, p. 313.

113 Archives départementales du Rhône, 4M, 33:1, 'Le Commissaire Divisionnaire de Police Spéciale [à Monsieur le Ministre de l'Intérieur]', 19 November 1934.

114 H. Pichot, 'Le gouvernment du 11 novembre 1934', *CUF* (15 November 1934).

115 L. Viala, 'Abdication', *CUF* (15 July 1935).

116 Passmore, 'The construction of crisis', p. 162.

~ 4 ~

'We are not fascists': The veterans and the extreme right

'We are not fascists', wrote Roux-Desbreaux, an activist in the UNC's Parisian section. His denial came in the wake of the section's involvement in the violence of February 1934.[1] The UNC had come under attack from the left for its role in the resignation of the Daladier government and thus the association found itself drawn into the unprecedented political mobilisation that followed the riot. The highways of France became a staging ground for extra-parliamentary politics as groups across the political divide rallied their activists. On 12 February 1934, in response to the leagues' 'fascist' coup, socialists and communists demonstrated in French cities. In Paris, though the processions of each group planned to remain separate, they came together in the streets. Collaboration between the groups was formalised on 27 July 1934 when both agreed a unity pact and formed the Common Front alliance. As left-wing cooperation continued through the local elections of October 1934, the socialists and communists sought to include the radicals in the alliance. Radicals were initially reluctant to participate in the Common Front. But the persistence of the right in power under Pierre Laval frustrated the party and grass roots activists impressed by the left's anti-fascist initiative. The radical party officially joined the Common Front, now renamed the Popular Front, at a vast demonstration on 14 July 1935. Demonstrators from the three parties swore an oath to the coalition. The combined forces of the left seemed stronger than ever. In May 1936, the coalition won the legislative elections. For the first time the socialist party participated in government and Léon Blum became the first socialist to lead France.

The extreme right founded its own alliance. Buoyed by its victory over parliamentary politics in February 1934, yet alarmed at the left's 'revolutionary' alliance, the JP and the SF created the National Front in May 1934. Through *L'Ami du peuple*, its official organ, the National

Front appealed to diverse nationalist movements in the name of counter-revolution.[2] Marches on days of national commemoration were often a cover for violent activity. On 13 May 1934, for example, the national day for Joan of Arc saw the JP and *camelots du roi* attack an ARAC protest against the decree laws. Later that month, *L'Ami du peuple* called for battle in the street against the left.[3] Yet the right-wing alliance was weakened by the CF's stubborn unwillingness to join its rival leagues. Fiercely jealous of his organisation's independence, La Rocque did not wish to see the CF subsumed into a nationalist alliance especially at a time when the league was rapidly becoming the largest formation on the right. Although the CF did not play a central role in the riot of February 1934, its astounding growth may be attributed to the colonel's appropriation of the plaudits for bringing down the Daladier government. While declarations of the size of the membership are not wholly reliable, it is safe to assume that the CF had fewer than 100,000 members on the eve of the riot. Only two years later, membership stood at approximately 500,000.[4] In November 1935, the Mouvement Social Français des Croix de Feu (MSF) was established as an umbrella group for various CF organisations and auxiliaries. Aimed at addressing the concerns of the economically and socially disadvantaged, the MSF sought broad support among women, the young, shopkeepers and peasants.[5] After the Popular Front's victory in the elections of May 1936, Blum's government dissolved the leagues and with them the CF. La Rocque established the PSF and ostensibly embraced electoral politics. This transformation did little to harm the popularity of the colonel's organisation. The PSF became the largest political party in France with over one million members in 1938.

Controversy surrounds the history of the French extreme right and France's alleged 'immunity' to fascism. In the debate the CF has garnered much attention from scholars. Due to its sheer size, historians on both sides of the argument agree that the league is key to the issue. At the risk of simplifying the debate, historians have largely concerned themselves with one question: was the CF fascist? If the CF was fascist, it would no longer be possible to dismiss the significance of fascism in inter-war France. Consequently, since René Rémond concluded that the CF prefigured mass democratic conservative politics in France rather than representing an authentically indigenous fascism, the thesis that France remained 'immune' to fascism between the wars has proved remarkably influential. Sustained attack on this 'immunity thesis' since the 1980s has considerably undermined the orthodox interpretation of the CF yet the Rémondian school still has its vigorous defenders.[6] Fundamental to the disagreement over the fascist credentials of the CF is the problem of defining the concept itself.[7] The irreconcilable difference of definition regarding fascism has left the debate sterile with historians on either side unable to agree.[8]

The veterans' movement is largely understood to have been an obstacle to the development of a French fascism.[9] Scholarship on the inter-war extreme right makes little mention of the veterans' associations. It is not the purpose of this book to prove or disprove the 'fascism' of French veterans. It is a mistake for scholars in the field (and this is true of the immunity thesis' defenders as much as their opponents) to focus on aspects of a group that 'reveal' its true 'nature', while they dismiss evidence to the contrary of this definition as unserious or anomalous because it does not conform to a definition of fascism that they find suitable. Instead of classifying a group as fascist or not (a categorisation that is then deemed to govern the group's behaviour) one should focus on how these groups operated in a society in which their actions, ideology and discourse were subject to interaction, collaboration and competition with rivals and allies in response to new and diverse situations.[10]

One such response from the UNC marked a deeper involvement in politics for this association. Following February 1934, the UNC launched a short-lived league-style organisation called Action combattante de l'UNC. The new group spoke to the desires of those veterans impressed by the contemporary political mobilisation. Action combattante served several purposes. It was intended to recruit veterans and non-veterans into a grass-roots movement sympathetic to the association's policies on state reform. The UNC hoped that the new group would halt the defection of UNC veterans to the leagues. It also used Action combattante to support the candidature of its members in the municipal elections of 1935.[11] This electoral involvement, the UNC planned, would prepare local activists for the upcoming national elections the following year. The creation of a veterans' party was not possible yet the UNC's executive committee agreed that because the veterans alone could initiate national renovation, it was necessary to increase the number of veterans in the Chamber.[12]

Disappointingly for activists in the UNC, by May 1936 Action combattante was effectively defunct. To explain the failure of Action combattante, one may point to the veterans' inherent rejection of 'politics'. This was certainly true of some moderate members but provides only a partial explanation. For those UNC veterans who desired to engage in political action, better established alternatives existed: the leagues.

On the right, analogous ideas were common to many groups and their boundaries were permeable. Members could share or switch allegiances at will, in spite of each organisation's jealously guarded independence.[13] UNC veterans were not different in this respect. The case of Yves Nicolaï is emblematic of the cross-membership of extreme right-wing groups in France. An activist in the Gironde UNC, as well as the Camarades de combat and the Légionnaires décorés au péril de leur vie, Nicolaï joined the Faisceau in 1926. He was responsible for the recruitment of veterans. The same year, Nicolaï founded a section of the JP. During the 1930s, he became secretary general of the Ligue des contribuables, an influential member of the Bordeaux CF and subsequently departmental president of the PSF in 1936.[14]

UNC president Georges Lebecq, too, was a familiar figure in extreme right-wing circles. A member of the JP and backed by the FR, Lebecq won a seat on the Parisian municipal council in 1929. His connection to the JP paid dividends after the loss of his seat to a Popular Front candidate in May 1935. Lebecq quickly found a post as a councillor of the Seine in Neuilly, where nationalist deputy Henri de Kérillis forced the local JP leader in the town to withdraw his own candidature.[15] Within the UNC's leadership, Lebecq was not alone in his patronage of the leagues. Among those members affiliated or sympathetic to the JP were vice-president of the UNC Nord group André Auguste, president of the UNC in the Aisne, Parmentier, Henri Rillart de Verneuil and national executive committee member and deputy for the Deux-Sèvres, Emile Taudière. Members and section leaders of the JP were present in the leadership of the JUNC.[16] UNC vice president (later president) Jean Goy was a member of the CF at least as early as April 1930. While he was reported to have only attended one meeting, as mayor of Perreux he always invited the local section to patriotic ceremonies. Its members sponsored his candidacy in the elections of 1932.[17]

Did membership of the leagues and the CF in particular make these veterans essentially 'fascist' or 'anti-republican'? No, they cannot solely be understood as such. A variety of reasons governed their decision to collaborate with the extreme right and their decisions could change over time, dependent on a multitude of circumstances. While it is always difficult to determine the motives of political activists, the context of the period during which veterans joined the leagues may give some clue to their motivation. Between 1934 and 1936, it was apparent that the CF was more than a veterans' association. It was a paramilitary organisation that portrayed itself as a force for order that would step into the breach once the republic collapsed. Meanwhile, other leagues such as the JP and the SF did not hide their contempt for the parliamentary regime. Whether through double memberships, attendance at meetings, combined street demonstrations or the open endorsement of political programmes, some UNC veterans consorted with and sought allies in the avowed enemies of the Third Republic.

Action Combattante de l'UNC

Founded in December 1933, Action combattante did not gain any real momentum until after February 1934. An undated document, produced by UNC vice-president Goy, marked the second phase of Action combattante's development. The document was perhaps produced between February and April 1934, during which time *La Voix du combattant* made several appeals for the intensification of propaganda efforts and subscriptions under the title 'L'Action combattante'. Goy believed that the UNC had reached a critical point in its history. His prognosis was pessimistic. He wrote that despite the UNC's membership of 900,000 veterans and propaganda activities, the association had not attracted the French to its programme on state, moral and economic reform. The stagnation of the UNC's membership amplified the urgency of the situation.

Goy was particularly worried by the success of the CF. La Rocque's league was in the ascendancy and Goy acknowledged that a section of the UNC membership participated in its activities.[18] His analysis reveals how closely Action combattante's development was linked to the perceived success of the CF. He located the key to the CF's growth in its populism, which reached beyond the veteran community, and its style of propaganda: 'Where does their [the CF's] success come from? From their propaganda in youthful and non-veteran milieus! From their mysterious gatherings! From their large and imposingly executed meetings! From their discipline! From their leadership mystique!' If the UNC did not undergo a 'rapid and brutal' reform, it would continue to lose its members and see its moral authority threatened. From now on, wrote Goy, *La Voix du combattant* should inculcate a faith in its readership. It should use simpler language to rouse the enthusiasm of members and create a 'mystique' for the association. The president of the UNC should act like a 'true leader' and take a greater role in the association's direction, propaganda and action. Finally, the dissemination of propaganda should be intensified, particularly through meetings. Four teams of orators comprising three speakers each would be able to hold four meetings a day in large

French towns.[19] Action combattante responded to these recommendations.

In spite of the importance that members such as Goy placed on Action combattante, others on the executive committee were ignorant of its workings. On several occasions, executive members debated the origins and purpose of Action combattante. Alfred Charron, president of the *poitevin* group, Paul Galland and national president Lebecq, who were in favour of the new group, were forced to defend themselves against those who feared that Action combattante would subvert the apolitical neutrality of the UNC. Originally, the leadership had agreed to undertake 'civic' action within the existing structures of the UNC, rather than establish a separate group for veterans and non-veteran sympathisers. To found a new group, Léon Berthier argued, would attract 'political black balls' who wished to improve their reputation through membership of the UNC.[20] Action combattante's ambiguous relationship with the UNC did not go unnoticed. Dr Patay of the Ille-et-Vilaine, Francisque Gauthier, vice-president of the Lyon section, and Daniel Desroches, UNC president in the Finistère, feared losing control of a group that acted with apparent independence yet was funded largely by the UNC.[21] Gauthier complained that the committee had not been informed from the start that the UNC was responsible for Action combattante.[22] Other executive members objected to the rumoured provenance of the group's funding, namely from industrialist Ernest Mercier. During the 1920s, Mercier developed close ties to the Parisian UNC and to Goy in particular through the Front Républicain.[23] In response to these concerns, Charron explained that given the success of the CF, it was necessary to found a separate group as quickly as possible. The anger of moderates was understandable given that a degree of secrecy surrounded the founding and operations of Action combattante. The new group had been founded without the express permission or the knowledge even of the committee.[24] Acting in effective secrecy, the activists in the UNC's leadership had successfully circumvented the executive committee and out-manoeuvred their colleagues.

Action combattante was open to veterans but it also recruited non-veteran sympathisers and sought collaboration with non-veteran organisations. The unrestricted recruitment policy did not please all members of the committee. For one thing, Nérisson, president of the UNC's fifteenth section, was disgruntled that the advertising campaign for the group used the work of Italian artist Leonetto Cappiello, doubly unsuitable for being both a foreigner and a non-combatant.[25] More seriously, vice-president of the Marne group Rasse looked for reassurance that Action combattante officials were veterans.[26] In fact the leadership of Action combattante included veterans from the UNC specifically treasurer Alfred de Pontalba, and vice-presidents Charron (who was the group's director), Goy and Paul Galland.[27] Nevertheless, the new group explicitly targeted those French who wanted to collaborate in the UNC's project for state reform, yet who could not ordinarily join the association itself. The only stipulation was that non-combatants be 'sincere men'. This did not exclude women from the association. Patay emphasised that women and 'all honest people' should be encouraged to attend Action combattante meetings.[28] The UNC was especially desirous that French youths become involved. Attendees at the Metz congress in May 1934 decided that all young people, not just the sons and daughters of veterans, would be allowed to join Action combattante.[29]

The foundation of Action combattante prompted the UNC to restructure its propaganda activities. At the Metz congress, Charron presented a report on the restructuring of the UNC's propaganda activities. He suggested that France be divided into zones of four or five departments each, presided over by a leader and a small administrative staff. Regional heads would be responsible for moulding public opinion through informing local newspapers of group actions and producing posters and tracts. When the time was right, the regional head's staff would organise meetings through a 'Comité d'Action combattante'.[30] Veterans were still required in order to ensure the establishment of Action combattante groups in their area. They gave access to established UNC networks and personnel and in some cases they provided office space and financial resources. Furthermore, each UNC departmental section was required to train orators and conference organisers. The national organisation did not possess the funds to run a nationwide training programme. Lacking the means to train activists, it is possible that the national UNC would have found it hard to resist the recruitment of ready-made propagandists from the leagues. Indeed, the Parisian leadership sent men, probably from the CF, under the auspices of Action combattante, to preside over departmental UNC meetings.[31]

Despite these efforts, the response of UNC veterans to Action combattante disappointed the leadership. In August 1934, *La Voix du combattant* announced the beginning of a national subscription campaign for Action combattante. Powerful financial resources were needed, it claimed, to launch a vast action on a civic, moral, financial and economic front.[32] From 25 August until 17 November 1934, six lists of subscriptions were published in *La Voix du combattant*. Though one must be cautious about self-publicised figures, the response was not encouraging. After an initial flurry of donations, including one of 10,000 francs from an anonymous donor (Mercier?), the generosity of UNC members was found wanting. In just under three months, the UNC raised 73,127 francs. The poor response to the campaign was noted. In May 1935, an article addressed to all UNC section chiefs demanded their efforts in support of Action combattante.[33] The same article appeared four months later. The meagre results of the campaign contrasted sharply with the amount received to fund a monument to king Albert I of Belgium, which had raised 802,452 francs by February 1935.[34]

Did this lack of enthusiasm result from a rejection of politics among the membership? Certainly, regional editions of the UNC's press neither published all the appeals for Action combattante nor did they dedicate a whole page to the movement as *La Voix du combattant* did from December 1934.[35] The organisation was aware of concerns among provincial members. Patay acknowledged the 'surprise' and 'worry' of some UNC veterans at the UNC's action. He assured readers that this political action was the 'good' politics of the veterans and not the 'bad' politics of corrupt politicians.[36] Nonetheless, a proportion of UNC veterans rejected league-style politics.

Action combattante found favour among some provincial sections. Evidence of this support is incomplete and one must rely on a few police reports and anecdotal sources in the UNC's own press to assess the extent of support. There was a limited implantation outside Paris. During 1934, police reported that a poster campaign took place in the Aisne, the Alpes-Maritimes, the Drôme, the Oise, the Morbihan, the Vaucluse, the Vienne, the Ille-et-Vilaine and the Pas-de-Calais.[37] At a meeting held in Rodez, in the Aveyron, Action combattante activist de Chalain presented the group's programme to local residents. New members soon joined up 'to prepare the ground in the Aveyron'.[38] One function of Action combattante was to found new UNC sections and groups affiliated to the UNC that could then be absorbed into the organisation proper. It was successful to this end in the Drôme, the Var, the Alpes-Maritimes, the Hautes-Pyrénées, the Basses-Alpes and the Gard.[39] Each of these departments had previously had a minor UNC presence, if a section existed there at all.[40]

Some existing UNC provincial groups showed support for Action combattante. The UNC's Berry group donated 100 francs to the association.[41] In May 1934, the departmental congress of the Basque and Béarnais group voted in favour of Action combattante's state reform project.[42] An Action combattante group existed in the Pyrénées-Orientales.[43] In the Seine-et-Marne, the Action combattante section counted twenty-two members in January 1935. By March, the group had forty members. During the months of April, May, June and August 1935, the section spread Action combattante propaganda, mainly through meetings, conferences and the sale of an Action combattante monthly newspaper. Commandant Thibaut of Action combattante spoke about the group's programme for civic action and national renovation at the general assembly of the Fontainebleau section of the UNC.[44]

UNC speakers held meetings to unveil the role and aims of the new group. The largest of these meetings took place at Rennes on 14 October 1934. Action combattante already had a presence in the area at least since June 1934, when a meeting of forty men took place under the auspices of local UNC president Patay.[45] At the October congress of Action combattante, Goy and Roger d'Avigneau, founder of the UNC's Loire-Inférieure group and secretary of FIDAC, addressed a reported 8,000-strong audience. Local police stated that the meeting demonstrated the discipline of the group and its willingness to 'enter into the struggle' if its 'demands were not satisfied'.[46] Later in October, a similar meeting took place in Caen at which 8,000 people attended.[47]

The same month, the Eure group accepted the task of founding an Action combattante section in the department. Non-UNC members were to pay ten francs for admission while UNC members could join free. At the meeting of the Eure departmental commission on civic action, Victor, founder of Action combattante in the department, reported that the organisation was doing well. It had already recruited regional and cantonal security officers. The local Action combattante shared the UNC's headquarters in Evreux. In addition, the commission agreed that as both groups had identical programmes, meetings of the departmental Action combattante group and the departmental civic action group would be combined.[48]

Provincial sections interpreted the new group in different ways and this affected its use. In some departments, such as the Eure, the group simply held meetings to promote and discuss the UNC's programme on state reform and civic action. In other cases, Action combattante groups mobilised for physical confrontation with perceived enemies. In the Ille-et-Vilaine, the local UNC designated district and cantonal Action combattante delegates. Each delegate possessed a telephone and a car. It was thanks to this organisational structure, wrote Patay, that the group had

been able to mobilise an entire district against potential political demonstrations, probably of the left.[49] This tactic was not dissimilar to contemporary CF strategy. At Tours on 27 June 1935, La Rocque declared,
'From now on we are able to affirm that thirty-six hours would suffice to
muzzle the red suburbs and to take power if necessary.'[50] In the Ille-et-
Vilaine, Action combattante used technology to assemble members in a
short space of time when perceived enemy action threatened.

On one occasion Action combattante members in the Drôme dis-
rupted a political meeting. In April 1935, at a gathering of the Ligue
des Droits de l'Homme, held in protest against the extension of military
service, an altercation occurred between members of the Ligue and UNC
activists. The speaker's declaration that he would rather die from French
bullets than fight an invading enemy sparked the clash. Taking exception
to this pacifism, the UNC veterans in attendance prevented the adoption
of an agenda. *La Voix du combattant* did not state whether this involved
violence or the simple shouting down of the opposition. In any case, as a
result of the disruption the organisers abandoned the meeting. Pleased
with this outcome, the UNC congratulated its loyal comrades. A new
style of political confrontation had proved successful and readers were
urged to do the same.[51]

Nonetheless, Action combattante was not a paramilitary arm of the
UNC. Though Isaac described the group as an auxiliary force in which
a taste for action, even combat, motivated its devoted activists, the use
of Action combattante as an apostolate for the UNC's broader campaign
for state reform trumped its use as a combat group.[52] Though the CF inspired the development of Action combattante, the UNC's auxiliary did
not simply ape La Rocque's league. Indeed, it was most vigorous during
the municipal elections of May 1935 when it supported the campaigns of
local UNC members and put up its own candidates for election. At this
time La Rocque rejected electoral politics (though provincial activists
could be less disinclined). The UNC hoped that engagement with wider
political issues through electoral action would prevent communist revolution and attract the peasant classes away from extremist groups.[53] Goy
summed up this new political direction: 'What it is necessary to establish
are ententes with sympathetic town councils ... the constitution of [elec-
toral] lists with youths and under the title Action combattante ... [to act]
purely on veterans' issues would result in failure.'[54] Participation in the
municipal elections would serve as preparation for the legislative elections
in 1936. By May 1935, the work of twenty-three departmental delegates
and seven hundred communal activists had allowed Action combattante

to discern the 'electoral mentality' of each area.[55] In Normandy, each section was charged with establishing a list of combatants 'in the UNC sense of the word'. The aim was to win all seats on the municipal council and install a UNC mayor in each area. Candidates would be listed as a 'UNC delegate'.[56]

It is difficult to gauge the influence of Action combattante on voters. Results were varied. In the Gers, a mayor won office as an Action combattante candidate yet in Clermont (Nord) a member stood unsuccessfully as an independent republican and a delegate of Action combattante.[57] In the Ardèche municipal elections, 812 UNC and 569 'youths and sympathisers' succeeded out of a possible 2,096 seats available.[58] It is possible that a proportion of these 'sympathisers' were Action combattante yet the UNC did not explain how it defined the word. Furthermore, support for a large conservative veterans' association was potentially large and so 'sympathy' cannot be limited to the membership of the UNC's small auxiliary. In the Ille-et-Vilaine, where Action combattante was relatively well-established, UNC veterans fared well. In total, UNC members or candidates won 53 per cent of council seats (701/1,317), with a majority share on 68 per cent (63 out of 93) of councils. The organisation boasted a UNC mayor in 54 per cent of councils (50 out of 93).[59] These results, in an area where Action combattante was well established, perhaps attest to a political militancy that extended beyond the leadership cadres of local UNC sections but given the variety of reasons for which candidates may have stood it is impossible to ascertain a definitive answer. Some veterans were in little doubt about where to attribute the UNC's success. In the month following the election, Jacques Toutain, president of the Seine-Inférieure section, hailed the victories of UNC delegates in the elections. He chastised some section presidents for not communicating the previous month's instructions on Action combattante to their members. In these areas, candidates had failed.[60] Presumably then Action combattante had contributed to candidates' success in other areas.

After May 1935, mention of Action combattante in the UNC's press became rare, though the group claimed to have 127,000 members.[61] In June 1936, the UNC accepted the failure of Action combattante. Galland blamed the broken promises of members, while executive member Grasseau accused unnamed rivals of stealing the UNC's programme. Does Action combattante's failure prove a general distaste for political action among UNC veterans? In some areas this was the case. In the absence of membership lists one cannot specify the proportion of veterans that was favourable to Action combattante. The veterans' rejection of militant political action was not unanimous but it was not insignificant. The desire for politically motivated action existed but it did not pervade the association. However, it was greater than historians have allowed. The group set a precedent and provided a framework for future civic action. Local UNC initiatives, under the title Action combattante and operating within the group's former structures, continued in some regions.[62]

Despite its short existence Action combattante embodied the desire of some UNC veterans to go further in their political activism than their association previously had. This very desire was a site of conflict between factions in the UNC. Members with an activist tendency, who favoured entry into politics and relations with political groups, clashed with those of a more moderate inclination who shunned political involvement. The latter for whom political activism was abhorrent fought to maintain the association's ostensible neutrality in the face of the UNC's evident political turn under presidents Lebecq and Goy. Yet even the founders of Action combattante could not control its operation in the provinces. The group's function varied, dependent on the (variable) enthusiasm of local activists. One further factor worth noting is the competition that Action combattante faced. It emerged onto the political landscape at a time when the CF was experiencing unprecedented membership growth. It faced competition from the Volontaires nationaux (VN), which came into being at largely the same time as Action combattante.[63] Even within the UNC framework itself, Action combattante competed for youth members with the JUNC. For UNC veterans who wished to pursue political action Action combattante did not present the best option. With the CF having appropriated the mystique of the veteran and 6 February, some UNC veterans may have preferred to join a group with a perceived record of success.

The UNC and the extreme right

The forces of the extreme right had long confronted the Third Republic. In the late 1880s, the emergence of Paul Déroulède's Ligue des Patriotes and the success of General Georges Boulanger's opposition to the republic saw the right combine authoritarian nationalism and populism. In 1898, the AF was founded in response to the Dreyfus Affair and the subsequent revitalisation of the left. For the next forty years, under Maurras's leadership the group relentlessly attacked the republic, while it championed monarchism and integral nationalism. After the Great War, the extreme right once again took up the anti-republican cause in the wake of left-wing electoral victory in 1924. Valois' Faisceau and the JP under Taittinger often engaged in violence in their campaigns for an end to the parliamentary republic. In the early 1930s, as the economic crisis worsened and dissatisfaction with the regime grew, François Coty and Jean Renaud's SF and Marcel Bucard's Francisme swelled the ranks of the republic's enemies. In rural areas, Henry Dorgères exploited economic hardship to attract peasants to his anti-republican Greenshirts movement.

The exemplar of the extreme right's growth was the CF. From its foundation in 1927 to the creation of the Fils et Filles des CF (FFCF) youth section in 1932, the CF's membership was restricted to veterans decorated for their bravery under fire and those who had served at least six months on the front line, known as *briscards*. Like many other combatants' associations the CF condemned politicians and laid claim to the heritage of the trenches yet it sought to situate itself as a new force within the veterans' movement. La Rocque, who assumed leadership of the movement in 1931, emphasised the CF's uniqueness in the combatant world. He condemned combatant leaders whom he blamed for the inertia of the veterans' associations and their failure to capitalise on the prestige they enjoyed after the war.[64] The colonel further separated the CF from the rest of the veterans' movement in describing his followers as 'true' veterans.[65] Ideologically, the league presented itself as sole representative of the national interest, above political disputes and class struggle.[66]

How did veterans perceive the CF? True enough, the CF's elitism and admiration for the military set it apart from the mainstream veterans' associations such as the UF and the UNC. Yet in spite of La Rocque's effort to differentiate his movement from the mainstream veterans' associations, in several respects the CF resembled a veterans' association. It took part in the commemorative events of the veteran calendar throughout France. It spoke of a future action, referred to as 'H hour', in which the veterans would take centre stage. For the CF, the UNC, and countless other combatants' associations, the veterans were a moral force, above political factions and parliamentary infighting. They alone were capable of returning order to France and effecting a national revival.[67] Like the veterans, the CF made it clear that the emphasis was on action instead of the 'chitchat' of politicians and the 'noise' of parliament. La Rocque condemned the parliamentary system and its preference for words over action, the deputies 'trembling before the magic of words', and playing the 'miserable game' of electoral politics.[68] The UNC expressed a similar contempt for the vain words of politicians. Though the CF's paramilitary and elitist complexion did not conform to the mainstream of veterans' associations, differences between it and veterans' groups have been exaggerated.[69] One should not therefore exclude the CF from the veterans' movement for veterans themselves did not.

UNC veterans were amenable to the CF. After all, both groups targeted the same clientele: right-wing veterans. However, when examining the extent of cooperation and cross-membership between the UNC and the CF, the picture is unavoidably partial. One must rely upon police reports, anecdotal evidence and the information printed in partisan newspapers. One can be sure neither of the number of veterans who took this course of action nor the motivation of veterans who did so. Local circumstance and idiosyncrasies were undoubtedly important but are often unclear. A comparison of departmental CF membership figures with those of the UNC for the year 1933–34 draws mixed results. A strong UNC presence within a department did not guarantee the CF success in that area. The league did not rely solely on UNC veterans for its recruits.[70] Moreover, motivations could change dependent on the individual and the circumstance. Goy claimed to know of several cases in which veterans had left the UNC to join the CF, only to return to their original association.[71] It is safe to assume that defections from the UNC to the CF did not occur *en masse*.

In order to discern a veteran's motives for joining the CF, one may look to the evolution of the league during 1927–36, from an association exclusively for decorated veterans into a 'fascist' paramilitary league. Until the CF opened its ranks to non-veterans in 1932, it was a veterans' association and UNC members perceived it as such. In this period of its development, the league was not so alien to the veterans as to dissuade UNC members from joining. Certainly the CF was more militant than the average veterans' group but it was not yet the radical paramilitary movement that it would become. Though some of its members may have sympathised with the extreme right, others joined for reasons of solidarity with veteran comrades and there were moderate republicans in the movement too.[72]

In April 1928, Jacques Péricard, a member of the executive and policy-making committees of the UNC, wrote a short article on a new veterans' group: the CF. Péricard's attention to the CF was not disinterested. He was a founding member of the league and would remain a president of honour.[73] He described an apolitical, interclass organisation for 'true' combatants who wished to give 'a bit of splendour to their ribbons'. Reprinted in the national *La Voix du combattant* the following month, the article provided details on how to join the CF.[74] Didier Leschi is correct to conclude that the combatant world was the 'compost' in which La Rocque's league grew. No other league enjoyed the same illustriousness that the veteran mystique brought to the CF.[75] New CF sections relied in part on the membership and in some cases the leadership of UNC members in the locality. In February 1931, the Rhône section of the CF admitted in its press, *La Relève*, 'Many of its members [the CF's] belong to other associations (UNC, UMAC (Union des Mutilés et Anciens Combattants), *Gueules Cassées*, etc) and even hold important posts in them.'[76]

Relations between the UNC and the CF during this period were not always harmonious.[77] In May 1932, *La Voix du combattant* responded acerbically to La Rocque's accusation that the large veterans' associations were replete with 'false combatants'. The UNC denied the charge and invited La Rocque to come and inspect the quality of its members. Despite the colonel's attempt to clear up the matter, the UNC was piqued.[78] In some cases though, UNC veterans were willing to collaborate. The UNC's 9th section went as far as to open the pages of its bulletin to other groups, including the AGMG, the Médaillés militaires, the Ligue des chefs de section and the CF. It claimed that the arrangement would allow the groups to 'better exchange their ideas'.[79]

In 1933, the CF radicalised. A new, more vociferous manifesto in October 1933 denounced the failings of French leaders. If politicians proved incapable of restoring order to the nation, the league promised to use physical force to do so. At the same time, the CF's membership criteria became less stringent. Anyone with a subscription to *Le Flambeau* could join the new Regroupement national autour des CF. Younger men who had not fought in the war were eligible for membership in the VN. The VN went onto absorb the *briscards* and the FFCF in mid-1934. It became the most dynamic of all the CF's affiliates.[80]

The CF's new programme did not deter veterans from joining the league. Some UNC members, while still considering the CF a veterans' association, now perceived something different in the league. Toutain was invited to the first official meeting of the CF section in Rouen in November 1933. He was impressed by what he saw. While the large combatants' associations were formed around the basis of material demands, Toutain reported, the CF based itself on cordial and intellectual affinities in the work of national renovation. For Toutain, a 'particularly evocative sight' was that of the CF marching 'in rhythmic step ... crossing the great streets of the large town, sharply regimented'. This demonstration of discipline revealed that the CF was a group of the highest calibre, and perhaps the 'something' that France had been waiting for since the victory. It was one of the finest *combattant* groups one was ever likely to meet.[81]

Before the February 1934 riots, *Le Flambeau* reported warm relations between sections of both organisations. On 4 February 1934, the 65th CF section held a meeting at Choisy-le-Roi at which CF speakers described the struggle against communism. CF members, *dispos* and veterans of the Choisy UNC attended. All were noted to have 'acclaimed [the orators] with the same unanimous spirit'.[82] As has been argued, on the night of the 6 February riot, CF members joined the UNC's march to the Place de la Concorde. They fought alongside UNC veterans in clashes with police on the Rue du Faubourg Saint-Honoré.[83] The following month, *Le Flambeau* expressed admiration for its 'UNC comrades' who had, like the CF, confronted head-on the 'regime of mud and blood'.[84]

After February 1934, La Rocque presented the league as the only alternative to governmental impotence and the revolutionary threat from the left. This period did not witness a move towards moderation within the CF. Sean Kennedy, citing a survey of former CF activists in 1967, argues that it is unlikely that many members joined at this time with the defence of democratic institutions in mind.[85] Only after 6 February 1934 did the CF arrange its first paramilitary mobilisations.[86] Throughout this period of radicalisation, the league's sections continued to recruit members from the veterans' movement and especially the UNC.[87] Although the number of CF veteran members declined numerically, with the deaths of ex-servicemen, and proportionally, as the group expanded to admit non-veterans, by July 1935 perhaps one in three members was a veteran.[88] Certainly, a veteran may have still joined the CF for the relatively benign reason of showing solidarity with his former comrades-in-arms. After all, even up to 1936 the league used the image of the heroic and selfless veteran in its rhetoric. Yet the CF's increasing paramilitary activity after October 1933 renders this explanation less plausible. The league had moved beyond solely preserving wartime camaraderie to demand the wholesale renovation of France along authoritarian lines. Within the context of the CF's development, it is plausible that a proportion of UNC veterans were willing to join the movement because its political programme promised authoritarian, national and moral renovation. Some UNC activists abandoned their association altogether to defect to the CF. In Brittany, commandant Leclerc resigned from the UNC and founded the first section of the CF in the Finistère.[89] La Rocque's movement provided an image of action and success that proved attractive.

Cooperation between local groups of each organisation persisted. In April 1934, the CF section in the Vaucluse thanked and congratulated the Avignon UNC and especially its president for his 'attitude' to the CF.[90] Two months later, the same UNC section invited CF members to its departmental congress and banquet. The CF accepted and asked that members attend in as great a number as possible.[91] Yet other provincial UNC veterans feared that an alliance with La Rocque would ultimately see the UNC absorbed into the colonel's league. This was an obstacle to collaboration with the CF in the Somme. In the same month that links between the CF and the UNC were strengthening in the Vaucluse, a new CF section in Amiens met with little enthusiasm from UNC veterans. The veterans of the local UNC felt that to join the new group would be detrimental to the internal cohesion of their own association.[92] The size of the UNC's membership precluded political homogeneity and cooperation was not to the taste of everyone.

Nevertheless, La Rocque sought to maximise recruitment among veterans. In May 1934, after a conference held by La Rocque in Bordeaux, the local CF section welcomed five hundred new members, the majority of which came from the UNC. Police reported that UNC members preferred the CF as this association only admitted 'real' veterans, suggesting that some still perceived the league as an ex-serviceman's group.[93] Nevertheless, for a UNC veteran to join the CF suggests that some veterans gained something from the league that they found lacking in the UNC and other combatants' associations. Founded almost ten years after the majority of other veterans' associations, the group appealed to veterans who did not consider existing organisations up to the task.[94] This fact was recognised within the wider veterans' movement. André Gervais wrote:

> The veteran of the FOP who joins the Common Front does not leave the FOP; the veteran of the UNC who joins the Croix de Feu does not leave the UNC; but from then on they count on their former associations only for the defence of their material rights, because they have found elsewhere, outside the old groups, at least the momentary calming of their worries, the apparent satisfaction of their desire for action, the illusion of a profitably and efficiently directed fervour.[95]

Although UNC members could belong to both associations at once, the colonel's plan was to entice veterans away from the UNC. He ordered that new recruits 'must not come to us as UNC but as Croix de Feu'.[96]

In some instances CF activists worked to 'seduce' UNC members. CF section chiefs advised members to portray their action as 'strictly republican' in an attempt to belay fears among provincial UNC members that the association was fascist.[97] What did the veterans of the UNC understand by the term 'fascism'? During the 1930s, few French extreme right-wing groups claimed to be fascist. At the very least this rejection stemmed from fascism's association with foreign political movements and the desire of right-wing groups to be perceived as thoroughly French. After the riot of February 1934, the left used the term against the leagues and particularly the CF. The UNC, too, fended off the accusation that it was fascist. It recognised both the ambiguity and the power of the word.[98] Galland described it as a 'werewolf' that had frightened people into voting socialist in the municipal elections of May 1935.[99] The UNC publicly rejected both fascism and communism, which it termed 'red fascism'. It considered both doctrines largely the same in their violent pursuit of power and penchant for dictatorship.[100] It is therefore unlikely that the UNC considered the CF to be fascist. But some UNC members *were* suspicious of the CF. The group of veterans that resigned from the UNC in the aftermath of the February 1934 riot accused the CF of being fascist in its plans to install a dictatorship under La Rocque.

The CF was not the only league to target UNC veterans for recruitment during 1934. In May that year, the leaders of the National Front, Taittinger, Renaud and Jacques Fromentin, courted the UNC in an effort to secure the veterans' membership of the anti-revolutionary alliance.[101] The JP and the UNC were not strangers to collaboration. During the government of the first Cartel, they had both been members of the nationalist alliance of leagues. In 1934, the JP depicted UNC veterans and its own followers as the avant-garde of 'national ideas'. It proclaimed the similitude of the groups' programmes.[102] The SF recognised, too, the UNC's civic action programme as compatible with that of the National Front. Fromentin urged the UNC to enter into the Front and show the way to all other veterans. *L'Ami du peuple* named the affiliation of those men who attended National Front meetings yet it reported only 'anciens combattants' as having attended, suggesting either that UNC veterans did not attend or they did not do so in any official capacity.[103] The counter-revolutionary coalition would not have been unattractive to certain members of the UNC. The association had come under increasing attack from the Communist Party for its role in the February riots. Communists organised counter-demonstrations against UNC parades. In turn, the UNC threatened to disrupt communist meetings if such action continued. In the Vaucluse, in response to a loss of membership since February 1934, the president of the local UNC section promised to end political action *except* for the struggle against the left-wing front.[104]

Ultimately, the UNC did not join the National Front. Lebecq was wary of signing a pact with the coalition, which might provoke further attacks from the left and perhaps prompt the resignation of some UNC members. Instead, he decided to encourage UNC members to work with the anti-revolutionary alliance and attend its meetings informally. This tactic would obtain the desired collaboration without officially compromising the UNC.[105] Writing in October 1934, Fromentin could not hide his frustration at the UNC's apparent lethargy: 'The UNC … has missed a good chance! … The UNC *must* take its place in the National Front, not tomorrow but immediately, before it's too late.'[106] Collaboration with the National Front displeased some UNC veterans. In July 1934, president of the Nord group Aimé Goudaert advised his colleagues on the executive committee to avoid involvement in both the Popular Front and the National Front. In the Nord, he explained, the UNC had remained neutral. This stance meant that the association could hold meetings even in 'the most socialist regions' without the threat of disruption. He recognised that the UNC was hostile to the left but warned that if it declared this publicly the association could expect to lose one-third of its members. Eugène Félix of the Eastern group, Goy and Isaac agreed.[107]

Though the National Front was frustrated with the UNC's apparent reluctance, local veterans did indeed pursue informal collaboration with the coalition.[108] Tellingly, entry to National Front meetings was granted upon production of either a National Front or a UNC membership card.[109] UNC members and section presidents attended National Front meetings, alongside JP, AF and SF activists. At Metz in October 1935, Magny, head of a sub-group of the UNC, presided over a meeting of 600 people, with the presidents of the local JP and AF. He called for the fusion of all 'national' groups to 'clean up the country'.[110] On 23 June 1934, *Le National*, the JP's newspaper, advertised a meeting of the National Front in the sixteenth district of Paris at which Pierre Plument of the UNC would speak. In October 1934, at a meeting of 2,000 UNC veterans in Caen, police noted the presence of numerous CF and the AF's street fighters, the *camelots du roi*.[111] The veterans of the Association Marius Plateau, affiliated to the AF, and the JP's Association Raymond Rossignol joined UNC veterans in their collaboration with the National Front.[112]

Throughout 1934, the UNC's cooperation with the CF continued. Lebecq did not hide his personal endorsement of La Rocque's league. On 10 November 1934, Lebecq and La Rocque attended a joint ceremony in honour of King Alexander of Yugoslavia under the Arc de Triomphe. When the UNC's executive committee met later that month, several members questioned Lebecq about this meeting. He was reticent about the precise nature of relations. Lebecq denied cooperating with the league and refuted the claim that he was in contact with La Rocque. He added that he had forbidden members of the GRP's executive committee from being members of other groups.[113] Yet one week later, *Le Flambeau* published a communication from Lebecq that contradicted the president's explanation. In reply to a telegram from La Rocque, which expressed the colonel's 'cordial feelings' for the UNC, Lebecq wrote, 'I was particularly pleased about our meeting at the tomb of the Unknown Soldier: this gesture will be understood by our comrades and by the country.'[114] What was to be 'understood' from this 'gesture'? At the very least, Lebecq appeared to endorse the cooperation of CF and UNC members. Shortly after this incident, in January 1935, links between the CF and the UNC became closer. In one night, La Rocque spoke to approximately 17,000 CF across four venues in Paris. The colonel lauded cooperation with the UNC and affirmed the 'common thought' of both associations. La Rocque announced that he and Lebecq were 'working towards the close and united collaboration of [their] two great associations'.[115] On this subject, a press communiqué was published in the following days that bore the signatures of both the UNC and the CF presidents. Short of agreeing a formal pact, Lebecq and La Rocque tacitly endorsed collaboration.

In July 1935, the UNC's relationship with the CF once again came under scrutiny. Lebecq and Charron's presence at a CF march on 14 July caused confusion and consternation in the ranks of the UNC. In a meeting of the association's executive committee the week before, members had unanimously decided not to take part.[116] Lebecq protested that he had attended, 'in a personal capacity … wanting to associate [himself] with a patriotic demonstration'.[117] He stated that if the UNC and the CF had taken similar action in the past it was coincidental as both groups acted 'in a purely national mind (*pensée*)'.[118] Lebecq stated categorically that the UNC had never colluded with the CF and offered to resign if the committee believed him to have sullied the good name of the organisation. His offer was rejected. Goy and Rossignol profited from Lebecq's uncomfortable situation. Police reported that they had stirred up opposition among provincial members. If the right wing of the UNC, behind Lebecq, split from the left wing, police expected the former would join the CF.[119]

Lebecq's lack of forethought concerning the consequences of his attendance at the July ceremony is unlikely to have simply been a matter of political naivety. A public association with the CF would have pleased a man who had led street action on 6 February 1934 and desired political activism from his organisation. The president supported Action combattante from the start and was part of the select few on the executive committee who were fully aware of its existence and actions. This episode was not the end of Lebecq's collusion with La Rocque. In February 1936, La Rocque advised CF voters in the 8th arrondissement of Paris to vote for his 'kind friend, Georges Lebecq' in the upcoming municipal elections.[120]

Publicly, the CF took great profit from the ostensible entente. UNC executive member Maillard complained that CF propaganda in the Manche had focused on Lebecq's attendance at the July ceremony.[121] Certain UNC sections interpreted Lebecq's attendance as evidence that the associations were 'united in the same spirit' as the CF.[122] In October 1935, UNC section chief Desroches informed the executive committee that a CF member in his department had stated, 'We are the moving flank, the UNC is the main body of the group.'[123] The situation was doubly concerning because this very CF activist was also a member of the committee of the local UNC section. It was not unusual for UNC section leaders to be CF members. This was the case in the Loiret where a local UNC president was a 'very active' member of the league.[124]

Veterans in the wider movement were concerned about the relationship between the CF and the UNC. In December 1935, the UF expressed anxiety that the CF was attempting to infiltrate the veterans' movement via the UNC. It alleged that La Rocque's plan was to recruit the 'best elements' in an association while instructing them to remain in place and 'maintain their influence'. UF president Pichot claimed that CF scouts had already found a UNC section president who was responsible for 150 members. If the CF was successful in recruiting local veteran leaders it would gain a foothold in their associations without the knowledge of members. Ultimately, Pichot warned, the veterans of a village or a district could wake up one day and find they were CF members.[125] Pichot ordered all members of the CF in his Loiret section to resign from the league or face expulsion from the UF.[126]

Within the UNC, Isaac was the most prominent critique of La Rocque's league. Admitting that the UNC and CF programmes were similar, he nevertheless warned that to follow the league would lead to violence and civil war. As a moderate, Isaac was concerned for the defence of republican legality. He asserted that if an ostensible alliance had existed between the two organisations in the past, it was now time to clarify matters: this had never been the case. While he recognised that some UNC members held sympathies for La Rocque's league, Isaac warned that to leave the UNC and succumb to the colonel's siren call would be to betray the front generation and the country itself.[127] He was concerned too, therefore, that the UNC would lose members to the CF. Isaac had experience of cross-association membership in the Rhône department. He refused patronage to the CF in the Ardèche, founded by a UNC Rhône member.[128] Yet Isaac did not forbid UNC members from joining the CF.[129] Put simply, it would be disastrous for the UNC if its activists spent their energies on CF action, rather than on the important tasks for which they were needed in the UNC. Isaac's opposition demonstrates that republican voices were still strong in the UNC.

Conclusion

On 18 June 1936, Léon Blum's newly elected Popular Front government announced the dissolution of the paramilitary leagues. The UNC was angered that the leagues should be dissolved while more threatening leftist formations continued to exist. It pilloried minister of the interior Roger Salengro for being a 'frightened weakling' in his refusal to stand up to the communists and 'cholera-spreading Bolshevik *métèques*'.[130] Goy, who had assumed the presidency of the UNC in December 1935, warned that communists were preparing to replace the republic with a soviet regime. With the leagues dissolved, he argued, it now fell to the UNC to 'prevent the triumph of Asian barbarism' and rally all those who wanted 'France to remain for the French'.[131] Fears of violent resistance to the leagues' dissolution were unfounded. La Rocque accepted the decision and founded the PSF. Police reported that Lebecq and Goy attended the general constitutive assembly of La Rocque's new party. Both were elected to its executive commission. They hoped that local PSF anti-soviet committees would aid in the fight against the enemies of France.[132] Like its predecessor, the PSF continued to recruit veterans.[133]

Action combattante entered a competitive political arena at precisely the moment when the CF experienced huge growth. To some UNC veterans, the CF appeared to be a more dynamic wing of their association, the very image that Action combattante hoped to cultivate. Though it established a presence in some departments, the group failed to arouse the enthusiasm of UNC members. Without doubt, there were UNC veterans who rejected political action outright. These members refused to support Action combattante. However, one should not attribute the group's failure exclusively to this reason. An alleged wholesale rejection of politics among veterans does not, therefore, explain Action combattante's failure. Rather, some veterans preferred to pursue political action through one of the many more successful alternatives. In competition for members with leagues that appeared effective in combating the left and energetic in their plans for national renovation, Action combattante found little room for development.

In a similar way, the tendency to reject the leagues co-existed with a desire for collaboration. Provincial veterans' cooperation and membership of extreme right-wing groups demonstrates that some were sympathetic to their advances. The UNC's official relationship with the CF bordered on an alliance. Undoubtedly an admirer of La Rocque's league, Lebecq wanted to take the UNC in a political direction. This view found echoes among members throughout France, not just the more reactionary section presidents and vice-presidents and La Rocque's movement was successful in recruiting UNC veterans. While it pursued cooperation with the association the CF also attempted to encourage veterans to leave the UNC. Yet the opposition of moderate UNC members to the leagues prevented the agreement of a pact. Cooperation between members was therefore more an expression of shared aims than a commitment to assiduous collaboration.

It is thus incorrect to exclude out of hand the CF from the veterans' world. Given the collective wartime experience that their members shared, it is unsurprising that the UNC and the CF referred and laid claim to similar ideals, activities and styles. The CF presented itself as a veterans' association. Steeped in the veteran mystique and using similar language and rhetoric, both the CF and veterans' groups targeted similar clientele in the veterans' world. The league was not so foreign as to dissuade high- and low-level UNC veterans from joining it.

Some veterans of the UNC saw no contradiction in belonging to their association and the CF, while others abandoned their association to join the leagues. Certainly, some UNC veterans rejected the leagues altogether. Others joined a league but then returned to the UNC. A variety of reasons governed these decisions. Discerning the motivations of veterans who joined the leagues is problematic. The immediate context of the time gives some clue. Concerning the CF, between 1927 and 1932, it is likely that veterans joined the league because they perceived it to be a veterans' association, even if it was a little unlike all other groups. From 1934 to 1936, the league's expanding popular base and increasing paramilitary activity meant it was now discernibly different to a veterans' association. It was not concerned with defending the material rights of ex-servicemen. Its mission was to restore discipline to the nation through authoritarian methods and the decimation of the left. When one takes into account the CF's doctrine, its paramilitary tactics and the polarised political climate not a few veterans may have joined for political purposes. The violence and perceived fascism of the league repelled some. Others were concerned for the integrity of their associations and the veterans' movement in general.

Unlike the CF, the component groups of the National Front made no claim to be veterans' associations. Though they may have posed the moral authority of the veterans against the corruption of the political class, the JP and the SF were evidently political groups that violently opposed the parliamentary republic. This fact neither discouraged UNC leaders nor certain members from collaborating with these leagues.

An examination of the veterans' links to the extreme right serves to remind us that groups in inter-war France did not operate in a vacuum. They interacted with their allies and adversaries within a political, social and cultural context. The UNC adapted its tactics and attitude to immediate circumstances, as did its members. It saw no problem in cooperating with the extreme right, which it considered an ally, when the 'national interest' of France appeared under threat from the combined forces of the left. One cannot therefore reduce the veterans to a single definition whether this be democratic, authoritarian or otherwise.

Notes

1 Roux-Desbreaux, 'Avant', *L'UNC de Paris* (22 February 1934).
2 Tartakowsky, 'Stratégies de la rue', p. 39.
3 *Ibid.*, p. 40.
4 Kennedy, *Reconciling France*, pp. 37–52.
5 *Ibid.*, p. 74.
6 Zeev Sternhell presented the most controversial challenge to the immunity thesis in *La Droite révolutionnaire, 1885–1914: Les origines françaises du fascisme* (Paris: Editions du Seuil, 1978) and *Ni droite ni gauche: L'idéologie fasciste en France* (Paris: Editions du Seuil, 1983). The following works appeared largely in response to Sternhell's challenge: Serge Berstein, 'La France des années trente allergique au fascisme: à propos d'un livre de Zeev Sternhell', *Vingtième Siècle*, 2 (1984), 83–94; Philippe Burrin, 'La France dans le champ magnétique des fascismes', *Le Débat*, 32 (1984), 52–72; Michel Winock, 'Fascisme à la française ou fascisme introuvable?', *Le Débat*, 25 (1983), 35–44; Pierre Milza, *Fascisme français* (Paris: Flammarion,

1987). Since the early 1990s numerous works have challenged the French orthodoxy on Fascism. They include: Dobry, 'La thèse immunitaire'; Irvine, 'Fascism in France'; Passmore, *From Liberalism to Fascism*; Soucy, *Second Wave*. The publication of the French translation of Soucy's *The Second Wave* (with a rather notable change of title) as *Fascismes français? 1933–1939. Mouvements antidémocratiques* (Paris: Autrement, 2004) has reignited the debate to some extent yet consensus is still elusive. Winock's response to Soucy, and Soucy's reply, largely rehash old arguments: Michel Winock, 'Retour sur le fascisme français: La Rocque et les Croix de Feu', *Vingtième Siècle*, 90 (2006), 3–27; Robert Soucy, 'Enjeux: La Rocque et le fascisme français. Réponse à Michel Winock', *Vingtième Siècle*, 95 (2007), 219–36; Michel Winock, 'En lisant Robert Soucy', *Vingtième Siècle*, 95 (2007), 237–42; Serge Berstein's conclusion, 'Pour en finir avec un dialogue des sourds. A propos du fascisme français', *Vingtième Siècle*, 95 (2007), 243–6, sums up the immunity thesis historians' standpoint. See also Roger Griffin, 'Consensus? Quel Consensus? Perspectives pour une meilleure Entente entre spécialistes francophones et anglophones du fascisme. *Vingtième Siècle* 4 (2010), 53–69.

7 For a lengthy discussion of fascism and its definition see Roger Griffin, 'Fascism's new faces (and new facelessness) in the 'post-fascist' epoch', *Erwägen, Wissen, Ethik*, 15 (2004), 287–301 and the responses of historians in the field in *Critique 1*, pp. 301–61, and *Critique 2*, pp. 378–424. There are many works on fascism and it is impossible to cite them all here. The following works demonstrate some of the different approaches to the problem: Roger Griffin, *The Nature of Fascism* (London: Routledge, 1991); Kevin Passmore, *Fascism: A Very Short Introduction* (Oxford: Oxford University Press, 2002); Robert O. Paxton, 'The five stages of fascism', *Journal of Modern History*, 70 (1998), 1–23.

8 Jenkins, 'The *six février*', 337.

9 Prost, *Les Anciens Combattants*, III, p. 119.

10 Dobry, 'February 1934', p. 131; Jenkins, 'Introduction', pp. 16–18.

11 UNC/EC, 9 December 1933. In this meeting the UNC's leaders discussed the association's future political action. Though they did not mention Action combattante by name it seems that the group arose out of this discussion.

12 UNC/EC, 28 July 1934.

13 Jenkins, 'Introduction', p. 17.

14 Sylvain Trussardi, 'Faisceau, Croix de Feu, PSF. Trois mouvements girondins, du milieu des années 1920 à la fin des années 1930', *Parlement[s]*, 3 Hors-série (2005), 59.

15 Philippet, *Le Temps des Ligues*, IV, p. 2020; V, annex III-B-3, p. 276.

16 *Ibid.*, pp. 189, 201 and 210; E. Veysset, 'La propagande: Nous unissons, nous fédérons, nous ne démolissons pas', *VC* (7 September 1935).

17 Kéchichian, *Les Croix de Feu*, p. 70; p. 147.

18 UNC, Rossignol dossier, J. Goy, 'Quelques constatations', undated; 'Appel', *VC* (10 March 1934).

19 UNC, Rossignol dossier, J. Goy, 'Quelques constatations', undated.

20 UNC/EC, 9 December 1933.

21 UNC/EC, 30 June 1934.

22 UNC/EC, 28 July 1934.

23 Kuisel, *Ernest Mercier*, p. 106–8.

24 UNC/EC, 10 May 1934; 30 June 1934; 28 July 1934.

25 UNC/EC, 20 June 1934.

26 UNC/EC, 28 July 1934.

27 UNC/EC, 30 June 1934.

28 'Entre le Parlement et le Pays le divorce s'accentue', *VC* (16 June 1934); Patay, 'A tous les AC', *Le Combattant d'Ille-et-Vilaine*, September 1934; Prost, *Les Anciens Combattants*, I, note p. 156

29 'Assemblée Générale Statutaire, Vendredi 11 Mai: Les Jeunes', *VC* (19 May 1934).

30 A. Charron, 'Organisation, propagande et presse', *XVe congrès national de l'UNC*, pp. 346–8.

31 Prost, *Les Anciens Combattants*, I, p. 166.

32 'Pour l'Action combattante: Appel à tous nos camarades', *VC* (11 August 1934).

33 'Action combattante', *VC* (25 May 1935).

34 Results of the campaign were published in *VC* (9 February 1935).

35 The articles that appeared on the first 'L'action combattante' page provide a clue to its diversity of subject: 'L'Etat écartelé'; 'Planistes et révolutionnaires'; 'M. Benes optimiste'; 'Le système soviétique'; 'La filibuste'; 'Vers le suffrage familial'; 'Réponse à un neutre'.

36 Patay, 'L'Action Combattante', *VC* (20 October 1934).

37 AN, F7/13024, 'Le Préfet de l'Aisne à Monsieur le Ministre de l'Intérieur', 23 July 1934 and 19 November 1934; F7/13025, 'Le Préfet de la Drôme à Monsieur le Ministre de l'Intérieur', 17 September 1934; F7/13026, 'Le Préfet de la Loire-Inférieure', 11 June 1934; 'Le Préfet de l'Ille-et-Vilaine à Monsieur le Ministre de l'Intérieur', 18 June 1934; F7/13027, 'Le Préfet de l'Oise à Monsieur le Ministre de l'Intérieur', 4 June 1934; 'Le Préfet du Morbihan à Monsieur le Ministre de l'Intérieur', 13 August; F7/13029, 'Le Préfet du Vaucluse à Monsieur le Ministre de l'Intérieur', 11 June 1934; 'Le Préfet de la Vienne à Monsieur le Ministre de l'Intérieur', 16 July 1934; F7/13039, 'Le Commissaire Spécial, Chef de Service, [Boulogne-sur-Mer] à Monsieur le Directeur Général de la Sûreté Nationale', 5 August 1934.

38 'Chronique d'action: Aveyron', *VC* (5 January 1935).

39 UNC/EC, 28 July 1934; 'L'Action combattante', *VC* (31 May 1935).

40 Prost, *Les Anciens Combattants*, II, p. 63.

41 'Groupe de Berry', *L'Ancien Combattant du Berry* (September–October 1934).

42 Report from the departmental congress of the Basque and Béarnais groups, *Le Poilu basque* (June 1934).

43 Hoffmann, 'Tribune des militants: Les Anciens Combattants et la politique', *VC* (2 March 1935).

44 'Chronique régionale', *VC: Seine-et-Marne* (January 1935); 'Chronique régionale' *VC: Seine-et-Marne* (May 1935).

45 AN, F7/13026, 'Le Préfet de l'Ille-et-Vilaine à Monsieur le Ministre de l'Intérieur', 2 July 1934.

46 AN, F7/13026, 'Le Préfet de l'Ille-et-Vilaine à Monsieur le Ministre de l'Intérieur', 28 October 1934.

47 'L'Action Combattante: Le meeting régional de Basse-Normandie à Caen, 28 octobre', *VC* (17 November 1934).

48 'Commission départementale d'Action civique de l'Eure', *L'UNC de Normandie* (November 1934).

49 Patay, 'L'organisation de l'action combattante en Ille-et-Vilaine', *VC* (22 June 1935).

50 Passmore, 'Boy scouting for grown ups', p. 549.

51 'L'Action combattante', *VC* (13 April 1935).

52 H. Isaac, 'Propos de Rentrée', *VC* (22 September 1934).

53 UNC/EC, 28 July 1934.

54 UNC/EC, 24 November 1934.

55 'L'Action combattante', *VC* (31 May 1935).

56 J. Toutain, 'Rapport succinct sur la Question de l'UNC et des Elections Municipales du 5 mai 1935 envoyé à tous les Présidents de Section du Groupe le 22 février 1935', *L'UNC de Normandie* (March 1935).

57 'Chronique d'action: Gers, Puy-de-Dôme', *VC* (29 December 1934).

58 'Chronique d'action: Ardèche', *VC* (22 June 1935).

59 'L'UNC aux élections municipales', *Le Combattant d'Ille-et-Vilaine* (July and August 1935).

60 J. Toutain, 'Après les élections des 5 et 12 mai 1935', *L'UNC de Normandie* (June 1935).

61 Georges Lebecq, 'Rapport moral'. *VC* (31 May 1935).

62 Report from the general assembly of the Seine-Inférieure group, *L'UNC de Normandie* (June 1936); J. Toutain, 'Mise au point', *L'UNC de Normandie* (January 1937); 'L'Action Combattante Cantonale', *L'UNC de Normandie* (April 1939); UNC/EC, 18 February 1939.

63 Passmore, *From Liberalism to Fascism*, p. 220.

64 F. de la Rocque, 'Triptyque', *Le Flambeau* (1 December 1933).

65 F. de la Rocque, 'Réalisations', *Le Flambeau* (1 October 1933).

66 Passmore, *From Liberalism to Fascism*, p. 223.

67 AN, 451AP/83:24, F. de la Rocque, 'Comment les hommes de la victoire

sauveront la paix', undated.

68 F. de la Rocque, 'Méthodes d'action', *Le Flambeau* (1 November 1933); 'Controverses militaires', *Le Flambeau* (1 January 1934).

69 For a discussion of similarities between the CF and the veterans' associations see Chapter 1 of Rymell, 'Militants and militancy'.

70 Compare the departmental membership statistics of the UNC in Prost, *Les Anciens Combattants*, II, pp. 63–4 with those for the CF in Kennedy, *Reconciling France*, p. 189 and Kéchichian, *Les Croix de Feu*, p. 201.

71 UNC/EC, November 24, 1934.

72 Kennedy, *Reconciling France*, p. 39.

73 Cointet, *La Légion française des combattants,* see note, p. 429.

74 'Les "CF"', *L'UNC de Normandie* (April 1928); 'Sociétés diverses: Les "CF"', *VC* (6 April 1928).

75 Leschi, 'L'étrange cas La Rocque', p. 167.

76 AN, 451AP/83:31, *La Relève*, February 1931.

77 AN, 451AP/81:6, letters from colonel Chevassu to La Rocque, 2 August, 16 August and 22 August 1930.

78 'Echos: Quel dommage!', *VC* (7 May 1932); 'Echos: Précisions', *VC* (21 May 1932).

79 'La vie des groupements: UNC Par la Concorde vers la maîtrise', *Le Combattant du IX* (December 1932–January 1933).

80 Kennedy, *Reconciling France*, p. 41; Soucy, *The Second Wave*, pp. 109–10; Passmore, *From Liberalism to Fascism*, p. 220.

81 J. Toutain, 'Chez les Croix de Feu et Briscards', *L'UNC de Normandie* (December 1933).

82 'A travers les sections: 65e section', *Le Flambeau* (1 March 1934).

83 APP, BA/1853:B1, anonymous, 'Le mouvement Croix de Feu', undated; 'Les graves troubles de cette nuit', *Le Petit Journal* (7 February 1934); Chopine, *Six ans chez les Croix de Feu*, p. 115.

84 F. de La Rocque, 'Croix-de-Feu, Briscards, Volontaires Nationaux', *Le Flambeau*, 1 March 1934

85 Kennedy, *Reconciling France,* p. 94.

86 Passmore, 'Boy scouting for grown ups', p. 533.

87 Nobécourt, *Le Colonel de La Rocque*, p. 286.

88 Rymell, 'Militants and militancy', p. 20.

89 David Bensoussan, *Combats pour une Bretagne catholique et rurale. Les droites bretonnes dans l'entre-deux-guerres* (Paris: Fayard, 2006), notes 9 and 10, p. 608. Evidence of defections can be found also in Kennedy, *Reconciling France*, p. 94; Nobécourt, *Le Colonel de La Rocque*, p. 286; Rymell, 'Militants and militancy', pp. 12–13.

90 'A travers les sections: Section de Vaucluse', *Le Flambeau* (1 April 1934).

91 *Ibid.*

92 AN, F7/13029, 'Le Préfet de la Somme à Monsieur le Ministre de l'Intérieur',

16 April 1934.

93   CAC, 19 940500/237, 'Le Commissaire Divisionnaire de Police Spéciale [à Bordeaux] à Monsieur le Directeur de la Sureté Générale', 24 May 1934.

94   Rymell, 'Militants and militancy', p. 8.

95   A. Gervais, 'Les Anciens Combattants pensent-ils prendre le pouvoir?', *VC* (10 August 1935).

96   APP, BA/1901, 'Réunion des chefs de section des Croix de Feu et des Volontaires Nationaux, Salle de la Société d'Horticulture, le 30 octobre', 31 October 1935.

97   AN, F7/12990, 'Le Commissaire Central [à Bordeaux] à Monsieur le Ministre de l'Intérieur', 7 April 1934.

98   G. Vanderwalle, 'Sur la Sellette', *Le Créneau* (3 March 1934).

99   P. Galland, 'En plein désordre', *VC* (18 May 1935).

100   H. Isaac, 'Ni communisme, ni fascisme', *VC* (10 October 1936); 'Le Rassemblement Français', *VC* (21 November 1936).

101   CAC, 19 940500/237, 'Activité du Front National', 23 May 1934.

102   'Les JP à Sousse', *Le National* (24 March 1934); 'La vie et l'activité des JP: 13e arrondissement', *Le National* (19 May 1934).

103   J. Fromentin, 'Les AC et la réforme de l'Etat', *L'Ami du peuple* (14 November 1934); 'Les anciens combattants et les Jeunes générations: Ce qu'il reste à faire', *L'Ami du peuple* (12 May 1934).

104   AN, F7/13029, 'Le Préfet du Vaucluse à Monsieur le Ministre de l'Intérieur', 7 May 1934 and 24 September 1934.

105   CAC, 19 940500/237, anonymous, untitled, 30 May 1934.

106   J. Fromentin, 'Devant les menaces du Front commun: Tous unis comme là Haut', *L'Ami du peuple* (9 October 1934).

107   UNC/EC, 28 July 1934.

108   Writing in October 1934, Fromentin could not hide his frustration at the UNC's apparent lethargy: 'The UNC … has missed a good chance! … The UNC *must* take its place in the National Front, not tomorrow but immediately, before it's too late" (italics in original), J. Fromentin, 'Devant les menaces du Front commun: Tous unis comme là Haut', *L'Ami du peuple* (9 October 1934).

109   'La vie et l'activité des JP: 16e arrondissement', *Le National* (23 June 1934); 'La vie et l'activité des JP: 16e arrondissement', *Le National* (30 June 1934). See also the section on the National Front in *L'Ami du peuple* on 5 June 1934.

110   CAC, 19 940500/237, 'Le Préfet de la Moselle [à Moselle] à Monsieur le Ministre de l'Intérieur', 29 October 1935.

111   AN, F7/13032, 'Le Commissaire Spécial [à Caen] à Monsieur le Contrôleur Général des Services de Police Administrative', 5 November 1934.

112   CAC, 19 940500/237, 'Une lettre de M. Charles Trochu au président de l'UNC', 29 July 1936.

113 UNC/EC, 24 November 1934.

114 'Manifestations et propagande: A Paris, 10 novembre', *Le Flambeau* (December 1934).

115 AN, F7/13320, 'Maison de la Mutualité'; 'Salle Bullier'; 'Salle Magic-City'; 'Salle Wagram', 25 January 1935.

116 UNC/EC, 5 October 1935.

117 UNC, Lebecq dossier, letter from G. Lebecq to the executive committee, undated.

118 UNC/EC, 5 October 1935.

119 AN, F7/12960, 'La situation chez les Anciens Combattants', 22 July 1935.

120 Centre d'histoire de Sciences Po, Fonds La Rocque, LR 56II B4, letter from La Rocque to Mssrs Risacher and Brunhes, 11 February 1936.

121 UNC/EC, 5 October 1935.

122 AN, F7/13040, 'Le Commissaire Spécial [à Saint-Louis] à Monsieur le Sous-préfet', 18 July 1935.

123 UNC/EC, 5 October 1935.

124 Prost, *Les Anciens Combattants*, I, p. 188.

125 H. Pichot, 'Halte au noyautage!', *CUF* (20 December 1935).

126 H. Pichot, 'M. le Colonel de la Rocque se trompe lourdement,' *NF (Loiret-Pas-de-Calais)* (November 1935).

127 H. Isaac, 'Camps hostiles', *VC* (26 October 1935).

128 Prost, *Les Anciens Combattants*, I, p. 165.

129 H. Isaac, 'A propos de "camps hostiles"', *VC* (14 December 1935).

130 H. Aubert, 'Le bâton pour faire se battre', *VC* (27 June 1936); P. Galland, 'L'épuration nécessaire', *VC* (4 July 1936). Galland expressed similar views a year previous in 'Les ligues, les fronts de l'Etat', *VC* (13 July 1935).

131 A. Albaret, 'L'Espagne ruinée: Ruines matérielles et ruines spirituelles', *VC* (6 February 1937); J. Goy, 'Sommes-nous encore en république?', *VC* (11 July 1936).

132 CAC, 19 940500/238, 'Création du 'Parti Social Français' et les 'Comités de Rassemblement National', 26 June 1936.

133 Kennedy, *Reconciling France,* p. 133.

5

Rejuvenating France: The Jeunes de l'UF and the Jeunes de l'UNC

Inter-war France saw an extraordinary mobilisation of young men and women in associations designed to protect young people's interests and give voice to their concerns. Certainly, youth organisations had existed before the Great War. The Association catholique de la jeunesse (ACJF) aimed to provide members with wholesome values, lifestyle advice and a sense of collective identity while the AF's *camelots du roi* brought youthful anti-republicanism to the street.[1] Yet only after the war did young French men and women patronise youth groups in their thousands. Social and political youth associations represented a section of society that was only just becoming aware of its distinctiveness and which desired an action autonomous of the 'adult' world.[2] By 1935, half a million French youths belonged to a group.[3]

'Youth' was not confined to the groups who represented the younger generations. Youth and youthfulness was more than simply a stage of life. They became concepts laden with unprecedented political, social and cultural value.[4] Of course, youth and age were not completely detached from corporeality. Youthfulness still meant health, energy and strength while 'age' and 'old-age' brought impotence, degeneration, senility and, eventually, death. Yet both youth and age also implied a gamut of non-corporeal attributes. The young were intellectually dynamic, imaginative and open to 'modern' ideas. Conversely, 'aged' minds were stuck in the past, unable to confront 'modern' challenges and intellectually decrepit. For this reason, youth became a valuable political attribute. The 'young' or, rather, whoever claimed to be so, championed themselves as the solution to the French economic and political crises. They coupled the concepts of youth and age, life and death, to their political projects. If France ignored the young (and with them the chance to 'live') in favour of the outdated practices of the republic's 'old' parliamentarians, the result would be fatal.

In political discourse, the opposition between youth and age was embodied in a perceived generational split between the men of the pre-war era and those of the front generation. The notion of a generation gap was not new. Already in 1912 Agathon's narrow survey of bourgeois Parisian youths claimed to have discovered a generation gap. Compared to the bookish, intellectual and liberal youth of the 1880s, Agathon found that contemporary young men were men of action who loved sport and technology. They rejected the corruption and lethargy of the Third Republic.[5] Two years later, the Great War seemed to cut all ties with the pre-war world. The conflict exacerbated the apparent break between generations. But this break depended little on age. The war was a generation-defining event for a trench community that included millions of men from late adolescence to middle age. The claim to have survived humankind's greatest ordeal strengthened the veterans' belief in the uniqueness of their generation. This shared generational identity (recognised by the veterans only in the late 1920s) combined with the enormity of the war caused some returning soldiers to believe that one epoch was coming to an end and another, 'their' epoch, was about to begin.[6] Though the myth of the trench fraternity was largely constructed after 1918, the idea of the 'front generation' loomed large throughout Europe.[7]

Post-war hopes for a new era were soon dashed. The parliament elected in 1919 failed to live up to the expectations of those who desired renewal and traditional party politics reasserted itself.[8] Frustrated elements were left to search for alternatives. Some turned to the mythologised potential of French youth. From the communist left to the extreme right, groups employed a language of youth, hoping to capture the energy and dynamism of young recruits but also to stake their claim to these very qualities. Despite differing in ideological terms the movements all believed that their organisation would unleash the new forces needed to change the country. Susan B. Whitney has demonstrated the importance of the communist party not only to the founding of communist youth sections but also to the prominence of youth as an issue in the inter-war years. During the 1920s the Jeunesses communistes (JC) sought to employ youths in the revolutionary struggle of its parent party. After 6 February 1934, the JC embraced the antifascist struggle and pursued a Popular Front strategy. It abandoned its uniquely revolutionary approach and expanded its activities to include sport and leisure while adopting a more conservative view on women, marriage and the family.[9]

On the right, Catholics looked to attract young male and female workers to the Jeunesse ouvrière chrétienne (JOC). Alarmed at the advance of communism in the late 1920s, the Church hoped that the JOC would prise the young working class away from the left by redefining the Church's relationship with the proletariat. The JOC intended its working-class activists to spread Catholic doctrine in the workplace, depicting Christ as a worker and emphasising the spiritual, rather than economic, causes of proletarian distress in their campaign to push back communism.[10]

Meanwhile, radical young intellectuals, independent of political parties, defined far-reaching solutions to the French crisis in revues such as *Esprit*, *Jeune Droite* and *Ordre nouveau*. These men perceived a sharp conflict of generations. In a critique that went further than a denunciation of political corruption, young French thinkers scorned the established order, or 'disorder' as they termed it. The proposed solution not only entailed a wholesale rejection of conventional politics and contemporary values but also a redefinition of human civilisation.[11]

The war generation was an important constituency for groups looking to harness the power of youth. For men who believed the conflict was a regenerative experience, the vigour of youthful veterans contrasted sharply with the weary decadence of politicians. During the 1920s, Valois' Faisceau depicted the veterans as a youthful force for change. After all, many veterans were still young men. Consequently, the Faisceau directed little propaganda at the post-war generation. Veterans' age and war service therefore doubly qualified them for the task of national renovation.[12] By the 1930s, the situation had changed. Outside the veterans' associations at least, the belief in the youthful power of the veterans was waning. Though reformers continued to exploit the youthful mystique of the veteran, the advancing age and failing health of many ex-servicemen meant that they were no longer the vanguards of rejuvenation. The inability of the veterans' associations themselves to renovate France had compounded this 'failure'. Instead, political organisations targeted the post-war generation in their projects. The CF/PSF demonstrates this shift in attitude. La Rocque's movement regarded the younger generation as vital not only to toppling the republican system but also to the construction of a new order.[13] PSF youth doctrine in particular provided for the participation of young Frenchmen in the construction and leadership of the new state apparatus.[14] However, French youth, decadent from years spent living under the republic, required comprehensive physical and moral reform. For this reason, La Rocque and his collaborators developed wide-ranging plans on the reform of education, physical activity and youth initiatives for all ages such as the successful *colonies de vacances*. La Rocque's movement founded several organisations to educate and train thousands of young French boys and girls in his movement's values. The FFCF alone counted approximately 30,000 members by 1938.[15] Not all right-wing youth groups were as successful. The autonomy of the FR's youth group, the Jeunesse de la Fédération Républicaine, suffered from the presence of party personalities in its executive. The FR did not intend the group to attract mass support but to regenerate the cadres of the party. As a result, it became an imitation of the FR.[16]

Despite this loss of faith in the youthful force of ex-servicemen, the language of youth and generational conflict remained intrinsic to the veterans' political discourse. A desire to break with pre-war ways saw veterans' associations pit the dynamism and action associated with 'youth' against the allegedly ineffective policies of 'aged' career politicians. Though veterans depicted themselves as possessing the youth needed to solve the crisis, they nevertheless sought an alliance with the post-war generation. To this end, in the late 1920s the UF and UNC founded youth movements. The youth groups had their own programmes and some measure of independence but they were nevertheless intended to support the politics of their parent association.

The JUF, founded in 1927, believed that the entry of veterans into government would rejuvenate governing elites. The group was first formally represented at the UF's national congress in 1930 in Algeria. At Dijon in 1932, UF veterans agreed an official statute for the youth movement. Yet it was only in 1934 that the UF's congress at Vichy devoted a unique day to the discussion of 'youth'. By June of that year, the JUF counted 28,000 members and was represented in the UF's executive committee.[17] At first, membership was limited to those who had 'contact' with the combatant spirit. 'True' *jeunes* were the sons and daughters of the war dead, veterans or widowed mothers.[18] Recruitment was later widened to include all French youth. Based on evidence in the UF's press, the JUF was not as successful as its counterpart in the UNC. Certainly it continued to present reports at the UF's annual national congress but it was not granted a permanent page in the *Cahiers de l'UF* and the youth page in *Notre France* was short-lived.

The UNC laid the foundations for its own youth movement at the national Saint-Malo congress in 1928. At this gathering, the leadership recommended that its members participate in sporting societies. If no such societies existed in the local area members were asked to create a youth group for this purpose.[19] In July 1929, the UNC announced the creation of the Union Nationale générale des fils de combattants. Its motto was 'United like our fathers', an adaptation of the UNC's slogan 'United like at the front'.[20] The earliest youth section was the Gauchy group, Saint-Quentin, founded in 1930.[21] Only after youth members first presented reports at the 1932 Lille congress did the movement gather some momentum, though in January 1933 the JUNC admitted that membership was still small.[22] Membership increased throughout 1934 and in May that year the UNC's annual congress at Metz ratified the decision to allow the sons of non-veterans to join. At this congress for the first time the *jeunes* had their own commission.[23] By April 1939, the JUNC claimed to have at least 100,000 members across 1,100 sections.[24]

The year 1934 was important for both the JUF and the JUNC. The groups' recruitment efforts began to reap rewards. Simultaneously, youth members took part in the annual meetings of the UF and the UNC and thus finally gained recognition as serious sub-groups within their parent associations. It is doubtful that the veterans' renewed interest in young French men and women at this time was a coincidence. That year saw the beginning of the polarisation of French politics. The CF in particular widened its net to capture the allegiance of the young. Likewise, the Paris sections of the JC and the Jeunesses socialistes came to an agreement based on mutual pacifism and antifascist struggle. Never had political groups invested so much in the recruitment of the young. The JUF and the JUNC drew new momentum from the need to capture young hearts and minds from these political forces.

The JUNC and the JUF shared some common ground. In their function, both groups provided a variety of activities for their members, from sport to speech-making. Politics was a concern of both groups. Their political discourse was couched in the subjectively defined concepts of youth and age. The JUF and JUNC attacked the age of politicians and lauded the 'youth' of the veterans. Both groups supported their founding organisations' programme on state reform, though the JUNC went further than the UNC in its suggestion that republican institutions would be destroyed in the coming 'revolution'. This was consonant with its overall spirit for – more so than the JUF – the JUNC had explicitly political goals, which it developed in the UNC's press. It endorsed the programmes of and encouraged collaboration with the leagues. It was anti-communist, supported corporatism and the organised profession, eulogised the virtuous French peasant, family life and pursued a conservative policy on women. The JUNC became a virtual political wing of the UNC and was in some ways more radical than its veterans' association and the JUF.

The JUF and the JUNC were doubtless important to the UF and the UNC's wider projects for the renovation of France. Nonetheless the veterans' associations did not seek to prepare young members as future leaders. They required only the collaboration of the young. The veterans believed themselves to be the most youthful and healthy elements in French society. The *jeunes*, too, described the veterans as the 'most healthy, most stable, most secure elite' in France.[25] How could middle-aged men who for the most part had suffered some degree of psychological or physical impairment during the war live up to such claims? Precisely because age was no longer a physical attribute. It was a state of mind, a quality that one could possess, a political trait even, used to fortify the veterans' claims to competence and power and, likewise, to undermine the identical claims of parliamentarians. The veterans' discourse on youth and age was therefore an important component of their authoritarianism.

'Being' young

However much one claimed to be young at heart, the veterans' youth groups did qualify members by age. To be a member of the JUNC one had to have been born after 1 January 1899, unless foreign occupation had prevented one from fighting in the war.[26] Yet in veteran discourse 'youthfulness' neither depended on, nor was it defined by, one's age. It was an abstract principle and a quasi-spiritual value, equated with one's openness to new ideas and the energy needed to overcome the ordeals of the political and economic crisis.[27] Veterans across the combatants' movement held this view. De Barral of the SDC spoke of youth as a 'laboratory' of ideas that the government should immediately put into action, as if its very youthfulness was qualification enough.[28]

Youth was a state of mind even in those of advancing years. Upon Goy's accession to the presidency of the UNC he was forty-three years old. *La Voix du combattant* referred to him as a young man because he had maintained the 'soul' of an activist.[29] The JUNC recognised the youthful nature of its veteran collaborators. Raymond Schmitt, president of the JUNC until November 1936, praised the elders of the UNC for their 'youthful mystique', which allowed them to understand the aspirations of young French men and women.[30] The JUNC group in the Ille-et-Vilaine attributed its rapid growth to the veteran Loiseleux, whom it described as 'always on the go, still younger than the youngest of the young'.[31] As for the UF, Pichot argued that as long as their heart remained young and the fire of faith still burned in their souls, the greying hair and the deepening wrinkles of the war generation mattered not at all.[32] In the Puy-de-Dôme,

Grasset dismissed the wounded bodies of the veterans. What mattered for him was the age of their soul.[33]

How should one remain young? Youthfulness was explicitly linked to political and civic action. UNC executive member Delore, for example, arrived in the trenches of Verdun aged twenty and subsequently came to believe that he had not experienced youth. Upon leaving the army three years later, he claimed to have already lived a lifetime. Nonetheless, 'civic' action gave him a new lease of life.[34] The JUNC advised that although the movement was young, as were its members, the only means by which to preserve this youth was to be an activist, to fight, and to struggle. This was the *modus vivendi* of the youthful generation.[35] Similarly the UF linked youthfulness to activity. The young needed to 'move' and make themselves seen and heard.[36] Physicality was linked to moral and intellectual capacities. The JUNC warned against the 'intellectual scepticism' and 'physical cowardice' of the indifferent and indecisive, which led to premature ageing and sterility of both body and mind. Inactivity was not the only way that young men became virtual geriatrics. Politics undermined the spirit and could turn 25-year-olds into old men.[37] According to the JUF, the politician's preference for 'words' over 'action' led one to become an impotent old man.[38] 'Civic' action rendered a person youthful, while inaction led to mental and physical infirmity, even in those who were young of age.

The veterans used their conception of age as a discursive tool for the reinforcement of their claims to the leadership of France. According to the UNC, the quality of youth, like the quality of being a combatant, was qualification enough to supersede the democratic process and accede to power, in place of politicians who were 'too old and too corrupt to govern effectively'. These old men would soon abdicate the seats of power before the generation of young men who had fought so hard to defend their country. Such discourse could shade into anti-republicanism. Not only did the UNC level the charge of senility at politicians and parties, it did so at the regime too. Similar to the men of its institutions, the state was anarchic, aged, ill-equipped and had simply run out of steam.[39]

The UF condemned politicians in similar terms. Pichot attacked parliamentarians' aged policies and formulas, exhausted ideas, quaint and old-fashioned habits and the worn-out expedient measures that dominated political assemblies. It was time for younger men to replace the generation of old men who had clung onto power for forty years.[40] The UF's Léon Viala admitted that contemporary French youth was just as dissatisfied with the democratic regime as the veterans. He blamed the 'old men' and the 'degenerate descendants' of the republic's founders who had barred the route to government of younger men.[41] Yet the UF was slower to condemn the regime than the UNC. It believed still that republican institutions were essential to the resurrection of France. Nonetheless, such a resurrection required the eviction from government and parliament of politicians and the investiture of 'new men'. The republic needed to bathe in this fountain of youth.[42]

Intrinsic to the associations' conception of youth was a discourse of life and death. To be young was to be alive. JUNC members brimmed with vitality and its activists incarnated life itself. Activist Guyot wrote, '[W]e [are] the Young! We are life! And a life that is not at all stilted or in decline, but bold, "living".[43] The JUNC had its own 'living spirit', founded on the young's immersion in 'the real and in life'.[44] Pichot agreed. Youth lived neither for the past, the present nor the future; it was living and eternal.[45] Camille Héline, president of the UF in the Deux-Sèvres and a vigorous proponent of his association's youth group, wrote that the young men and women of the JUF 'needed' to live, and so spread the 'healthy and fertile' doctrine of the association.[46] The young no longer wanted to be a 'dead mass'.[47]

Parties, politicians and their politics were the antithesis to youthful action. The JUNC accused 'criminal' politicians of leading France to its death. Its opposition to this seemingly inevitable 'death-by-politics' formed the basis of the JUNC's challenge to what it termed the 'established disorder'. The very rejection of 'that which leads to death' lay at the heart of the JUNC's claim to be revolutionary.[48] The UF, too, associated politicians with death. Héline expressed exasperation at the 'old men' and 'old transgressions' of parliamentarians. They had led France to the edge of the abyss, when the nation wanted to live.[49] According to Pichot, moribund parties had sterilised French democracy. The answer lay with French youth and the 'non-continuation' of the present. Only then would France be resurrected.[50]

The condemnation of politicians for their alleged age was an important component of the veterans' challenge to the perceived legitimacy of deputies and the regime. Discourse of youth and age was inherently linked to modernity and the perceived challenges it brought. When the veterans demanded that young men enter government, they were arguing for 'modern' solutions for 'modern' problems.

In these discursive offensives, the notion of age and senility condemned those in power as outmoded and anachronistic. Politicians would lead France only to its demise. These men were denied membership of their own generation and exiled to the generation of an earlier period. Exactly what qualified as youthful or modern depended on the political agenda of each group. The detachment of youth from the fact of physical age meant that to call for youthful ideas and leaders was thus not an objective or technical matter. It was wholly political and contained the potential for authoritarianism in its prioritisation of an abstract principle over the electoral process. Aged parliamentarians populated the institutions of the republic, a fact that could render these very institutions archaic and exhausted.

The JUF

From the outset, the JUF encountered a measure of reluctance from some UF veterans. The UF initially rejected recruiting youths beyond the descendants of veterans. It argued that the children of veterans and war widows were the 'true young' for they had been raised and educated in contact with the combatant spirit.[51] To admit non-combatant youth may bring division to the association. Others were wary of losing control of the youth sections.[52] The intransigence of its parent association on this issue frustrated the JUF. It argued that certainly the sons and daughters of veterans were important but they were already members of the 'combatant family'.[53] The group desired to bring all youths into the combatant fold in support of its campaign for 'peace and democracy'. Local variations were important. In the Creuse, though recruitment was limited to veterans' descendants, 'sympathisers' could be honorary members.[54]

Though the UF acknowledged that French youth would play a vital role in ensuring the veterans' moral and political legacy and consequently in guaranteeing the future of the nation, it determined that young men and women were not ready for the task ahead of them. The veterans' task was to imbue the youth of France with the combatant spirit through a relationship akin to that between teacher and pupil. Until 1934, Pichot, though conscious of the need to engage French youth in the combatants' plans, remained optimistic that in spite of their advancing years the veterans themselves would ultimately fulfil their much vaunted programme for national recovery.[55] Others in the UF did not share Pichot's optimism. Héline foresaw the disappearance of the generation of fire before its project could come to fruition. He predicted the eventual replacement of the veterans of the UF with younger men as the front generation passed away. Ultimately, the UF would become a 'parliament of youth'.[56]

Developments during 1934 and 1935 influenced the UF's policy on youth. In spite of the optimism of the reformist campaign of spring and summer 1934, the veterans had failed to implement their programme. With the Confédération paralysed following the 8 July meeting, the leagues in the ascendancy and the Common Front taking shape, the veterans' accession to power seemed as distant as it had ever been. Pichot came to accept that the front generation had turned out to be a transitional cohort, bridging the gap between the outdated politics of 1914 and the generations to come. It would not be the veterans who constructed the new France. This task fell to the youth of France. When the time came for the young to 'seize the reins of the state', Pichot would submit to them.[57] The pessimism of the UF president was echoed throughout the UF. The veterans were 'disappointed, exhausted, revolted and resigned'. The 'generation of fire' had amounted to little more than the 'first instruments' of a revolution that would be completed by the young.[58]

However, even if the veterans' revolution was to be accomplished by the young, the UF faced a difficult task. Young people were not perfect. On the one hand, JUF activist Albanie Costes bemoaned the indifference of young men who lived out their lives like leisurely old bourgeois.[59] On the other hand, Héline warned of the political influences on young French men and women who, embittered before their time, joined leagues and revolutionary movements.[60] Some in the UF worried that inexperienced, impulsive and rash French youth was not up to the task asked of it.[61] It appeared that a gulf separated the young from the veterans. But, with the right teachers, this gulf was bridgeable.[62] While the veterans still lived, it was up to them to guide the young and instruct them in the ways of the combatant spirit. Such an alliance would perpetuate the work of the association while facilitating the unity needed for national recovery. For the young to ignore the veterans would be perilous indeed. Héline warned youngsters not to reject their country and the republic, as this would be tantamount to a betrayal of their fathers' generation.[63]

For the most part, members of the UF and the JUF were receptive to each other's programmes. Collaboration was the norm. The JUF edited a short-lived youth page in the UF's *Notre France* national publication and veterans usually sat on JUF executive committees. Much of the JUF's programme was therefore similar to that of its parent association. Likewise, the UF included the youth group in its most prominent campaigns. The plan of 11 March 1934, which specified that the UF would now enter into the state reform debate, called for the mobilisation of youth interested in the campaign. In return, youth members promised to work in collaboration with the veterans towards the associations' plan for a combatants' republic.[64]

As the JUF grew it became more confident in making policy decisions of its own. In June 1934, youth leaders decided that to campaign solely on veterans' issues would divide them from the children of non-combatants. The group announced that youth had 'awoken' and it was time for action. Its principal preoccupation was now the veterans' civic action programme. Likewise, UF veterans sometimes appeared uninterested in the preoccupations of younger members. Costes warned the *anciens* against undermining the JUF in this way. If youth members could not rely on the veterans, they would look elsewhere for support. In doing so, it was quite possible that the JUF would oppose its founding association.[65] Deference to the war generation was no longer guaranteed. By 1936, the JUF depicted itself as the stimulus of the UF; the two groups marched in tandem.[66]

The activities of JUF sections were diverse. Jean Mouraille, the UF's commissioner general to the JUF, recommended four modes of youth action.[67] As a protest group, JUF sections could champion young people's rights. The JUF was particularly concerned for the material condition of French youth and especially youth unemployment.[68] If a protest group was not to members' tastes then youth activists could found an artistic and sporting club or a scout group. Indeed, the JUF's programme emphasised moral and physical probity. Sport would improve the race and create virile young men while combating the nefarious effects of alcohol and poverty. Héline praised the Eclaireurs youth movement for their moral and physical education that kept the young off the streets and away from cafés. As for other leisure pursuits, JUF groups were encouraged to nurture internationalist values in members. Sections were asked to found a pacifist library in their local area and classes in Esperanto should be made available.[69] Finally, JUF sections could be civic action groups. Whether this meant involvement in politics depended on local circumstances. In the Nord, discussion of politics, religion or foreign policy was punishable by expulsion.[70] In the Creuse, the JUF rejected political action as an association yet encouraged its members to join political movements and parties as individuals, to spread within them the combatant spirit.[71] Collaboration with political leagues was forbidden. Though it drew inspiration from the youth policies of neighbouring countries, expressing a particular admiration for Mussolini's efforts to unify Italian youth, the JUF aimed to do the same in France through human and republican values rather than uniformed regimentation.[72] Certainly, the

JUF declared itself to be revolutionary, as many youth groups did, but this meant political, social and economic reform in line with the UF's programme.[73]

The JUF reflected the comparative temperance of the UF. Concerned with the moral and material well-being of French youth, it rejected collaboration with the leagues. The JUF expressed loyalty to the republic. It backed the UF's state reform programme and its inherent ambiguities. The group believed in the veterans' inherently authoritarian claim to power in France. Equally, it subscribed to the association's discourse on youth and age, which buttressed the veterans' apparent legitimacy. Nevertheless, the JUF, with its emphasis on moral and physical health, internationalism and leisure pursuits, was less political than its counterpart, the JUNC.

The JUNC

If one is to believe the JUNC's self-publicised membership figures, the group was remarkably successful. One should be cautious regarding the reliability of such information, which is open to exaggeration. Nonetheless, regular appeals for information about groups, reprimands for sections that had not replied to these appeals and the fact that the JUNC admitted the sons and daughters of non-veterans too suggest that the information is of some use. In May 1935, François Aubert (son of UNC executive Hubert) for the first time gave an approximate figure for overall membership: 30,000 *jeunes*.[74] Though the JUNC's claim to have 100,000 members by April 1939 is likely an exaggeration, nevertheless the JUNC proved more successful than Action combattante.[75] The rapid expansion of the JUNC is reflected in reports from local groups.[76] The JUNC retained ever-expanding national and local youth pages in the association's press. Throughout the 1930s, there was a high level of cooperation between the JUNC and the UNC proper, with youth members sitting on the veterans' executive committee.[77] Ultimately, the UNC's executive committee did not concede the failure of the JUNC as it did in the case of Action combattante.

Despite this apparent faith in the JUNC, the UNC shared the UF's pessimism on the state of French youth. The association did not believe young French men and women alone were up to the task of saving France. Morally and physically out of shape, French youth could not compete with the images of the disciplined, enthusiastic and dynamic youth of Nazi Germany, Fascist Italy and Soviet Russia. Preferring detective novels and bad cinema, young Frenchmen were sceptical and prematurely old, 'clapped out' by useless sporting competitions.[78] Youth, the UNC alleged, had fallen into disarray, a symptom of existing within a decadent society that was heading for oblivion.[79] The young were therefore unprepared to lead France. For this reason, when the time came, the veterans would enter government with youth at their sides. Only then would it be the turn of French youth to learn the methods of administration. The UNC did not state how long this would take.[80] Until then, its veterans would guide and instruct the youth of France, who would swell the ranks of the veterans' moral elite and work toward recovery.[81] In return the *jeunes* would defend the rights and interests of the veterans and fight for the aims of their programme.[82]

The JUNC disagreed. From its point of view, youth members were already qualified to join the veterans' moral elite. In believing this, the JUNC co-appropriated the role of national saviour.[83] As men of order and high morality like the veterans, JUNC members were willing to take up the torch of the combatant spirit and were better qualified to lead the country than those 'blinded by the party spirit'.[84] Some members of the UNC spoke of the veterans' relationship to youth in grander tones than the simple replacement of politicians. For Isaac, youth members would become better than the generation that went before them, better than the generation of fire.[85] Delore linked a youthful national renovation to the future of the French race. An infusion of youthful blood would allow France to face up to modern problems. Subsequently, Western culture would be reborn through institutions that befitted its grandeur.[86] Delore's millenarian vision contrasted with the rather more apocalyptic pronouncements of de Cromières. He regularly used his editorial in *Le Combattant du centre* to launch diatribes against Jewish influences in France. De Cromières implicated French youth in the wider struggle for French civilisation against bolshevism and international Jewry. De Cromières believed it was essential that the veterans pass on to the young the notions of 'good' and 'justice' for, without this tutelage, France would not break free from the shadowy hold of the Jewish banker in the City of London and the torturer of 'bloody and revolting' Russia. The solidarity between the UNC and its youth wing would thus defeat both the excesses of capitalism and the barbarity of communism.[87]

The relationship between the UNC and its youth movement was not always harmonious. On occasion, youth members questioned the right of the veterans to speak on their behalf.[88] They described the veterans as broken men, despondent and paralysed, whose rejection of politics was their ultimate mistake. In spite of its promise to be at the side of the veterans, the JUNC warned that it would not act as the 'walking stick' of UNC veterans.[89] Youth sections would not wait indefinitely for the call to action and may launch action independently. Second JUNC president Jacques Raudot condemned the veterans for liking the security of speeches and discussion, which sometimes resembled the worst squabbles of the Palais Bourbon, while youth members took action. He pressed the UNC's executive committee for more support and warned that if the youth members were not with the veterans, they would be against them.[90]

Like the JUF, the JUNC initially accepted that it was up to the veterans, and not their sons, to make the necessary reforms and to take into their hands the direction of the country. This changed as the movement grew during 1935. The JUNC's commitment to fight for the material rights of veterans was no longer a worthy raison d'être. According to Emile Veysset, the JUNC's propaganda chief, youth members were not interested in the revision of pensions. He stated somewhat bitterly that the 'sacred rights' of the veterans, which the JUNC nevertheless recognised and defended, only concerned young men to the extent that they financed state payments as taxpayers.[91] After the elections of 1936, JUNC vice president Roger Pinoteau judged that the *jeunes* now occupied a place in society as important as that of the veterans, who were on the verge of disappearing. The tables had turned. The young now held the power and, in order to remain relevant, it was the veterans who needed *their* collaboration.[92] The UNC remained unconvinced. Unlike the UF, as late as 1939 the UNC was optimistic about the veterans' ability to complete their own mission.[93]

JUNC sections engaged in a diverse range of activities. Certainly some youth groups existed merely as social associations to provide young people with a means to pursue leisure activities and to take holidays. The basic activities of a youth section included participation in national commemorations, the organisation of *fêtes*, regular meetings and marriage and death notices. Groups provided intellectual, sporting and recreational pursuits for their members and these opportunities attracted new recruits. Activist Dauguet of the Caudéran group cited social activities as the reason for the group's growth from 25 to 105 members over three years.[94]

Political action was the goal of some sections. Writing in July 1934, Schmitt congratulated the UNC on its actions on 6 February 1934 as, before 1933, he could only offer sporting activities to his group. The UNC's new political turn had provided a doctrine for JUNC members and the promise of action.[95] Youth sections were encouraged to collaborate with political parties and leagues. Franck D'Hennezel urged readers not to forget their comrades in the CF, the SF or the JP, who, like the JUNC, desired ordered, non-revolutionary action.[96] The JUNC admitted to the presence of its members and leaders in groups such as the JP and La Rocque's VN.[97] Yet the JUNC was careful about its relations with political groups. In order to preserve its autonomy, the JUNC as an organisation did not conclude ententes or official alliances with other groups. Rather, on an individual level members had a duty to engage in political action with the political 'parties of order' and leagues as soon as possible.[98]

The JUNC was vigorous in its propaganda activities. In January 1934, it founded the Permanent Youth Action Centre to coordinate these efforts. From August that year, the Centre met each month and founded technical committees concerned with press, propaganda, general activities and 'feminine action'.[99] Two years later the JUNC initiated training courses for prospective orators and conference organisers.[100] It sought to make its youth page in *La Voix du combattant* one of 'combat' and 'action'.[101] The JUNC valued street demonstrations as large, vital and disciplined displays that would cow rivals and impress public opinion.[102] Youth groups embraced innovative ways of spreading their propaganda such as the radio and cinema. The Haut-Rhin section produced its own films on the JUNC. In November 1935, the general assembly of the JUNC asked the head of the Suresnes section Robert Gautron to take charge of cinematographic propaganda and establish relations with Pathé.[103]

The leadership of the JUNC considered political intervention the ultimate goal for all youth sections. Once members had founded a section and nurtured a strong local implantation, there would come the time for political action. The *jeunes* would infiltrate existing organisations in an effort to spread the spirit of duty and discipline. Veysset claimed that this 'politics of infiltration' had worked well for the JUNC's adversaries and so the movement must take up this action itself. He admitted that few groups were currently at this stage.[104] Whether any JUNC groups reached this stage before the UNC suspended its activity in 1940 is difficult to say. Even so, sections that did not reach this level of autonomy could act as a reserve force for parties, movements and leagues until the time for intervention came. This intervention would then 'happen as our elders' interventions have happened'. It is unclear what this meant. It could be a reference to the direct action undertaken by the UNC in February 1934 or the rather more sedate public pressure campaigns familiar to the veterans' associations. Veysset's ultimate vision for the movement was to overtake the success of the UNC. He predicted a future time when the *jeunes* would found UNC sections to complement and aid youth members in areas where JUNC sections were isolated.[105]

Like the JUF, the JUNC declared itself a revolutionary movement. To some extent this quality was inherent to youth members: to be young was to be, in essence, revolutionary.[106] Yet while the JUF defined its 'revolution' in accordance with the UF's reform programme, the JUNC conceived of its revolutionary nature in accordance with the ideas of contemporary young intellectuals. Revues such as *Esprit, Ordre Nouveau* and *Jeune Droite* defined a 'spiritual' revolution in contrast to the 'established' revolutions of fascism, Nazism and Marxism. They expressed some sympathy for the established revolutions, recognising in them the attempts of young men to transform society. Yet the results of these new political projects were disappointing. Capitalist society had undergone little change. Conversely, the young intellectuals' revolution necessitated a complete overhaul of human practices and values. A new order could not be built on the basis of contemporary principles. Institutional reform was therefore useless unless accompanied by the overthrow of modern values and a reformulation of the relationship between men and between man and himself. Extremist action was not discounted, though its proponents – men such as Thierry Maulnier and Robert Francis of the *Revue française* – were small in number.[107]

The JUNC's proposed spiritual and institutional revolution drew on similar themes, reflecting the intellectuals' mix of reactionary and revolutionary ideas. The JUNC purported to have inherited its 'national spirit', its rejection of internationalism and its desire for national defence, empire and the autarkic organisation of the country from the leagues, rightwing parties, 'radical patriots' and neo-socialists. It attacked liberalism as the root of the class struggle during the past century. The complete freedom that reigned had led to a freedom of pleasure, a reference to the decadence of French society. From the left, the movement drew an anticapitalism directed against high finance, trusts, cartels and 'irresponsible anonymous societies'. As the rate of salaries declined and quality diminished, money had become the master. The JUNC reviled the excesses of the capitalist system, epitomised in monopolies, the abuse of credit, the market and, above all, speculation with other people's money. This anticapitalism nevertheless respected private property whether from savings or inheritance.[108]

The JUNC would neither wait for the structure of the state to collapse nor attempt to shore up its weaknesses. The JUNC would begin reconstruction immediately through a necessary but controlled revolution.[109] There would not be a violent seizure of power even if, on occasion, violent language entered JUNC discourse. In April 1936, activist Georges Merchiez expressed the belief that if the JUNC was to breathe new life into the 'old trunk' of government, it would first need to kill the 'worms' inside.[110]

What would follow the revolution? In the first instance, the state required reform. French youth organisations had shown their interest in state reform at the Etats généraux de la jeunesse in June 1934. Hopeful of an accord based upon a perceived shared generational identification, the youth groups unanimously condemned the capitalist regime and affirmed the revolutionary nature of French youth. The '9 July Plan' represented another attempt by youth groups of various affiliations to demonstrate their will to unite across political cleavages.[111] For the JUNC, the modification of republican institutions would not be sufficient. New institutions should be created only after the destruction of the old.[112] Whether this destruction would come after a 'managed revolution' or with the 'sweep of a broom by vigorous fists' was unclear.[113]

The JUNC's plans for reform were often vague. The content of the future regime, though not democratic, mattered less than the fact that it would be new. In any case, according to the JUNC, the form of the French state was variable. The best one was that which adapted most easily to the needs of the nation. This was hardly an endorsement of the French republic. The democratic system dealt in the 'empty' and 'intangible' notions of liberty, equality and fraternity. Parliamentary democracy degraded man into an abstract being, detached from 'natural' moral, familial and professional communities.[114] When the JUNC did publish the specifics of its vision, elements of it were close to the right. In August 1935, Veysset expressed his association's support for the reformist programmes of the leagues and politician André Tardieu.[115]

The new state would be based on the maxim 'Family, Profession, Nation', a slogan strikingly similar to Vichy's 'Work, Family, Fatherland'.[116] Close to the doctrine of its parent organisation, the JUNC's faith in the family and the profession was expressed in corporatism. Corporations would run the economy, free from state intervention and the influence of international capitalism. In industry, class struggle would fade away as corporative institutions settled disputes, revived a sense of community and made property owners of the proletariat. Under a strong executive and a legislature that would not 'surpass its mandate', corporations would make social laws without recourse to parliament.[117] In rural France, each rural commune would possess a *maison* for the JUNC in which local youngsters would receive a practical education in farming and education in the doctrine of the UNC. Social work in the countryside would combat rural depopulation and encourage the urban unemployed to return to the land.[118] In its family policy, the JUNC conceived of the nation as an organic whole, in which the family unit was the basic cell. Like the UNC, the association proposed the return of French mothers to their homes. Recognising the importance of fathers to the nation, the youth group proposed that election to parliament be restricted to fathers with at least two children.[119]

Given the close relationship between the UNC and the JUNC, it is unsurprising that the youth group's programme complemented that of its parent association. The JUNC approved of both the Wagram manifesto of October 1933 and the UNC's participation in the riots of February 1934.[120] However, there were several differences between UNC and JUNC policies. Firstly, youth sections were not afraid to declare their political intent. The UNC always claimed to be apolitical, in spite of its right-wing preference. The veterans believed that this self-imposed exclusion from politics added further credibility to their claims to lead France. Conversely, the *jeunes* considered political intervention essential and endorsed the initiatives of other groups.[121] Secondly, the *jeunes* based their claim to national salvation on youth. In veteran discourse, though youth was an important component of the veterans' claim to power, their perceived legitimacy rested primarily on the fact of their war service. The JUNC's prioritisation of youth was another means by which to attack the politicians for their incompetence. Young Frenchmen were better qualified to save France than old and outdated politicians. Finally, the *jeunes'* ostensible amalgamation of left- and right-wing politics and their desire for spiritual revolution were similar to the ideas of contemporary young intellectuals. Unlike the UNC, the JUNC prescribed the destruction rather than the revision of the old institutions as the precondition for national recovery.

Youth and gender

The connection between youth and gender in communist and catholic youth groups has recently been explored.[122] The veterans' associations and their youth groups present an interesting case study for they were dominated by men and their conception of masculinity depended so much on service during the war. Conversely, their youth associations admitted women as well as men too young to have fought. In a physical sense, the veterans' movement was masculine, made up of those men who had fought as soldiers at the front, a service from which women were excluded. Gender division ran deeper than the simple fact that only men could fight. War was a male undertaking and the *poilu* became a warrior, 'a new masculine type', based on military valour and youth. 'Male' qualities such as courage, honour, sacrifice, bravery and heroism defined the veteran himself.[123] The UNC reflected this masculine domination. Women were not present in the upper levels of the UNC. The UF, which was an association for all victims of the war including war widows, counted Jeanne Callerac and Elisabeth Cassou as national vice president and secretary general respectively. The UF nevertheless characterised itself as the 'male defender' of veterans' rights.[124]

The UF and UNC's definition of youth encompassed men and women. The admission of young girls and women to the JUF and the JUNC is therefore an important difference between the youth groups and their parent associations. Both planned to transform young men and women into beings worthy of joining the veterans' elite. Contemporary cultural understandings of the 'natural' attributes of men and women informed their plans. The JUNC's conservative policy aimed to return women to the home as wives and mothers though, as will be seen, this was not an uncomplicated stance. Concerning young men, the JUF and the JUNC sought to strengthen the health of French males and consequently the fortitude of the race. The JUNC spoke of 'remaking' French men in discourse that was similar to the extreme right.

The existence of women's sections attached to larger associations was not uncommon. The JC admitted women, though their concerns were subordinated to the demands of the androgynous revolutionary struggle. In 1936, it founded the Union of Young Girls of France which adopted a gender-specific approach to youthful organisation.[125] On the catholic right, the Jeunesse ouvrière chrétienne féminine targeted young working women and hoped to encourage them back into the family home.[126] The leagues also showed concern for the fate of young French women though some were more enthusiastic than others. Founded in January 1926, the Faisceau féminin was powerless to affect decision-making and policy within the larger movement.[127] Far more successful were the women's sections of the CF and the PSF. Mainly concerned with social work, recruitment and propaganda, they numbered approximately 300,000 at their peak. The CF's Section Féminine played a key role in promoting the movement's burgeoning network of social services, which was a crucial component of the movement's strategy for taking power. Despite the priority given to women's activism though, female members were restricted from political meetings and important associational activities such as parades and ceremonies commemorating veterans.[128]

Though the UF was eager to attract girls and young women to its youth groups, it was the JUNC that came closest to establishing a sub-group for women. Women members played an important role in the leadership of the JUNC both nationally and locally. Of the thirty-one members of the JUNC's national youth council elected in November 1934, three were women: Yvonne Luzier (Les Lilas), M.A. Rocchesani (Courbevoie) and Liégeois (Sedan).[129] A year later, the council admitted five new members, one of which was Yvonne Boulet. Boulet became women's propaganda delegate in the JUNC and a member of the Action féminine commission for the Seine group.[130] Luzier was elected a vice-president of the JUNC at the general assembly in November 1935. Perhaps an indication of the regard in which she was held, Luzier received 241 votes, equal to the number received by François Aubert and more than those received by Pinoteau and Veysset.[131] In the provinces, women were involved in the youth groups as JUNC vice-presidents, secretaries and council members, though never as president. In April 1934, the Arcachon group voted in a new executive committee of which seven out of fifteen members were women.[132] The JUNC directed the beauty queens elected by UNC sections to act as local propaganda activists. It hoped that they would help found JUNC sections in new territory.[133]

At the JUNC's third general assembly in November 1936, the leadership announced that the Action féminine commission was to become a semi-autonomous group.[134] This measure was intended to maximise recruitment as some parents did not want their daughters to join mixed-sex groups. JUNC president Raudot ordered all groups to provide a delegate to the autonomous Action féminine sections.[135] But this greater independence of action did not last long. At the general assembly in 1938, Action féminine renounced all claim to administrative and financial autonomy. Young women had encountered hostility from regional groups who refused to admit them or attempted to obstruct their action. Contrarily, the group had achieved great success in the Somme and the Loire-Inférieure where local UNC presidents had encouraged its action.[136]

While women could act as vice-presidents and treasurers of local sections, they were usually responsible for leisure and charitable activities such as soup kitchens, second-hand clothes collections and the running of holiday camps, of which the UNC possessed several.[137] In some cases social work subsumed a political motive. Luzier, president of Action féminine, reminded male members of the UNC that social work made for the best propaganda.[138] In March 1935, sixty-three children attended a monthly meal organised by the Lilas JUNC group. The accompanying report on the youth page revealed the desired consequence: 'these children will say to themselves when they are old enough to understand: 'It was not the communist who offered that, even with Moscow's money'.[139] While politics did not inform all of the JUNC's social work, it cannot be discounted as a motive in some cases.

The JUNC's youth page reported the involvement of women at local meetings. Women spoke on their role in politics and society, which was explored in Chapter 2. In these meetings, women's ability as controlled and competent speakers was reiterated and their speeches were noted as having been warmly applauded and appreciated.[140] Rocchesani's report at the JUNC general assembly in November 1934 was cited as testament to 'the measure, level-headedness [and] perceptiveness that women can bring to intellectual work'.[141] In late Third Republican France, rational thought and control over one's emotions were perceived to be distinctly masculine characteristics. Consequently, while the JUNC appeared to offer women a visibly political role at meetings, which was unusual by the standards of the time, it understood its female members' involvement within a defeminising and masculine framework. The JUF attributed similar qualities to female orators at its meetings. Viala reported that women speakers had proved themselves capable of 'intelligence' and 'good sense'. Yet this judgement rested on Viala's understanding of what constituted the appropriate behaviour of women. JUF women had rejected the pastimes of many young girls, which he summarised as dancing, the cinema and flirting with young men. In a similar manner, Viala praised male speakers for their 'strong' and 'vigorous' monologues.[142] Both were suitably masculine attributes.

The JUNC did not confine its praise solely to women as orators. Women were held as an example to follow. François Aubert portrayed female members as more efficient and better organised than their male counterparts.[143] Boulet wrote of a section whose very existence depended on the incessant action of its female element, despite the presence of male members. She encouraged women members to found their own JUNC sections if the enthusiasm of male members was lacking.[144] In March 1936, Mme Schmitt, wife of the JUNC national president at the time, recommended that if a woman could not find a man to become president of her local group, she should act as a vice-president and name Raymond

Schmitt as president. In this case, the female vice-president would effectively run the new section.[145] Nonetheless, some women members did not want their role to expand beyond social work and the planning of festivities. In the Lot-et-Garonne, Mlle Magné, vice-president of the local JUNC, asked that female members not be encumbered with the collating of reports. It would be more logical, not to mention gallant, for the young men to undertake these tasks.[146] In this way, the preferences of local members could influence women's roles in the JUNC.

Though the JUNC's encouragement of women's involvement in section life was ostensibly progressive, it was combined with a conservative emphasis on home life and the family. Motherhood had long been a concern for political forces of various colours. France's birth-rate had been in decline since the late eighteenth century. Only in the late nineteenth century though did demographers, prompted by France's defeat to Prussia in 1871, raise the alarm about the 'disappearance' of the French. In 1896, Jacques Bertillon established the Alliance nationale pour l'accroissement de la population française. Supported by prominent business interests and political figures, Bertillon succeeded in bringing to prominence the Alliance's agenda on pronatalism and family welfare.[147]

Veterans returned from the war to an unfamiliar world in which the gender divisions between man and woman were blurred. The entry of women into the workforce did much to upset traditional gender norms in French society.[148] Women who both continued to work and reject modest forms of dress and moral behaviour antagonised conservatives.[149] The *femme moderne* was a dangerous non-conformist who smoked, drank, indulged in promiscuous sex and was contemptuous of motherhood and marriage.[150] Faced with the prospect of career-minded, sexually liberated, childless women and the perceived virility of Germany and Italy (and the implications of this for the size of future armies), the right hoped to arrest the moral and demographic decline of the nation. Women would be returned to the home to fulfil their natural duty as wife and mother. Pronatalism was not confined to the right. Certainly, pronatalist policies were to be found in the programmes of groups such as the JP and the CF, but they were also supported by the radical and the socialist parties. The pronatalist campaign culminated in the Family Code, drawn up by radicals Daladier and Reynaud in 1939.

In the JUNC, female members were the guardians of French homesteads and tradition, the future wives of young French men and the feminine elite.[151] Though the association's female writers such as Paulette Chailleux and vice-president of the Courbevoie section Rocchesani claimed to support feminism, in agreeing with the UNC's definition of the family, they endorsed a patriarchal vision of society. Chailleux declared herself to be a feminist in so far as she supported women's 'application to all occupations suitable to her aptitudes and duties'.[152] A woman's 'aptitudes and duties' were best suited to motherhood. Youth groups were thus asked to direct women into activities in harmony with the 'delicateness of heart and morality' that was in 'woman's nature'.[153] The JUNC claimed that while laws granted women rights in the pursuit of jobs, they could not change the organic and physical difference between man and woman. This difference necessitated a natural division of labour. Woman's workplace was the home. She brought life into the world and it was her job to care for and educate this life. If a woman aspired to the professions, motherhood would teach her the skills of a psychologist, a teacher and a lawyer, in the natural setting of the home.[154] The JUNC permitted women to become nurses, a profession consistent with their feminine qualities. By November 1937, the Parisian group boasted thirty girls who had achieved the *diplômes d'auxillaire* and who then undertook work experience at a UNC health centre in Belleville.[155]

The JUNC deplored women who chose to work. If a woman's husband earned a salary sufficient for the family then she should be forced to give up her employment; a working mother could not care for her children.[156] Some women worked for selfish reasons. They enjoyed leaving each day for the office, well-dressed and 'all dolled up'. Others worked because they were bored with housework. Action féminine planned to combat this boredom not through encouraging women into careers but in educational courses that taught homemaking, cookery, sewing and clothes mending. By encouraging women to remain at home, Action féminine hoped to revive familial life and redress the moral situation in France.[157]

The JUF and the JUNC were no less concerned for young men than they were for young women. If family life and motherhood would correct the moral decline of young women, sport would reinforce the morality of young French men. Sport and physical recreation for men figured in the programmes of both groups. The groups' interest in sport was not unique. Sporting participation increased across France during the interwar years. By 1929, there were forty sporting federations with over 3.6 million members. Political movements took an interest in sport yet nonpolitical groups such as the Scouts de France and the Eclaireurs organised games based on a 'combative virility'. These groups concerned themselves with the 'soul, spirit and body' of members through games and exercise.[158] Influential at this time was the exercise doctrine of Lieutenant

Georges Hébert. Drawn up in 1906, Hébertisme emphasised 'natural' activities that encouraged precision, speed and form rather than allegedly useless sporting competition. It divided exercise into ten groups: walking, swimming, running, jumping, crawling, climbing, balancing, throwing, lifting and self-defence. Hébertisme was subsequently used in the army during the Great War and remained popular on the right throughout the 1920s and 1930s. Considered instrumental to the physical and moral regeneration of France, the Vichy government employed Hébert's techniques in the Compagnons de France and the Chantiers de la Jeunesse.[159] The JUNC also adopted Hébert's method.[160]

Political movements took an interest in sport for various reasons. Initially, the left dismissed physical recreation as the preserve of those wealthy enough to afford leisure time. However, once in government the Popular Front became concerned with improving the health of ordinary citizens. Blum's government founded the Conseil supérieur des sports in July 1936 to encourage physical recreation among the urban industrial classes. Minister of Sport and Leisure Léo Lagrange used public funds to improve physical education amenities. He introduced the Brevet sportif populaire in 1937, a certificate aimed at French people of various sporting ability. In 1937, 420,000 people obtained the Brevet.[161]

Right-wing groups were not interested solely in raising individual levels of health to a national standard. They linked the self-discipline and perfection of the body that exercise required to morality. The demands of sport would bring a physical and moral renovation of French men. Appearance took on a moral and patriotic value and the 'softness' of men was cited as proof of national decline.[162] A man should be muscular and steadfast in his convictions, a force for re-establishing virility and discipline in the nation. Regenerative in its effect, sport was comparable to the experience of war. It encouraged the development of masculine bodies essential for military service. The extreme right went further in its conception of sport. Elements in the CF and the PSF desired the complete moral, intellectual and physical renovation of French youth. Under the leadership of Gaëtan Maire and Jean Mierry, La Rocque's Société de préparation et d'éducation sportive worked to this end, though it stopped short of eugenicist and racial theories common to Nazism.[163]

Sport in the JUF and JUNC was confined to male members. In March 1937, the JUNC founded the Union Sportive Française (USF), under the impetus of André Magnier. By the first USF congress in September 1937, the association claimed to have twenty-eight affiliated sporting clubs. The USF aimed to improve the health of the nation's youth and prepare them for military service. It would contribute to the wider project for national renovation as the practice of sport would combat the 'decadent' lifestyle of French youth, epitomised in dancing, the cabaret and cinema.[164] Each club in the USF knew its mission: 'To make men, [who have] acquired through a suitable physical education, courage, strength, will and all the qualities necessary to confront life.'[165] Similar concerns informed the JUF's sporting programme. While the JUF acknowledged young people's 'right to pleasure', physical pursuits formed 'virile, loyal men' and prevented them from falling into debauchery.[166] The JUF asked that each UF departmental federation create a sporting groups oriented towards team competition. A national championship would be held each year at the UF's congress. Though different to the individualism of the JUNC's Hébertiste doctrine, the JUF believed that team sports would raise the physical and moral standards of youth.[167]

While sport was considered an effective means of raising young men's moral standards, it was nevertheless essential to train healthy, robust and dependable bodies.[168] The UF's Paul Patou specified that France had to be strengthened with numerous 'healthy and muscular sons'.[169] The JUNC wanted to remake French men.[170] Two factors informed this aim. Firstly, the JUNC felt it imperative to prepare young French men for military service. This comes as no surprise when one takes into account the JUNC's admiration of military values. J.R. Moustiers, president of the Marne JUNC, specified that the most important quality of the veterans was their military service. In order to be true sons of veterans, one had to act like a veteran and live by military values.[171] In January 1937, at a time when the UNC believed France to be under threat from a left-wing government and a resurgent Germany, Raudot demanded that the *jeunes* be trained and educated in military preparation. This preparation would facilitate the return of the notion of honour to the *patrie*, the cultivation of military virtues and the celebration of France's glorious and heroic past.[172] Secondly, the JUNC aimed to improve the moral and physical quality of the French race, for the two were connected. Sport would improve young men's bodies and imbue them with masculine values such as courage, strength and will power.[173] Sport, military preparation and the moral and physical renovation of the nation thus became intertwined.

Conclusion

To a certain extent, the veterans' 'youthful' challenge to 'aged' parliamentarians was a reformulation of the well-worn debate over competence in government. As the veterans understood it, politicians had tried and failed to solve the political and economic crisis in France. Their failure stemmed from the use of 'traditional' solutions when the situation called for 'modern' ideas. Paralysed by the mindsets and values of the previous generation, parliamentarians lacked the competence to face up to a uniquely 'modern' political and economic emergency. Similarly, the republic, whose constitution better suited the demands of the decade in which it was written, was in need of rejuvenation. Contained within the veterans' solution to the problem was an intrinsic authoritarianism. The UF and the UNC did not base their solution on raising the level of competence through technical and educational means. Their plan was to replace politicians with veterans, to replace the 'old' with the 'young' based on a non-technical and subjective definition of both terms. The associations' use of age as a political concept shored up their claim to historical legitimacy. 'Youthfulness' allowed the veterans to define a subjective national interest and then depict elected politicians and the regime as contrary to this. The UF's rhetoric displayed a moderation that UNC discourse lacked. The former did not explicitly attack the institutions of the Third Republic, even if it attacked the men that populated these institutions. The UNC's opposition targeted not only the content of the regime but at times included the institutions of the state.

The JUF and the JUNC extended the veterans' activities into the youthful milieu. This was thought necessary due to the miserable physical and moral state of young French citizens. Standing on the threshold of a new era, the veterans and their youth groups aimed to form a new generation of French. The JUF and the JUNC intended that organised sporting activities would raise the physical standard of young French men. Better physical health would engender improved moral health. The JUNC looked to improve the quality of the French race and make young men fit for military service. Regarding young women, Action féminine outlined a vision of woman's role as mother and homemaker in a future France and attempted to mobilise women in pursuit of this vision. Women members of the JUNC succeeded in establishing themselves within the wider movement. They faced opposition on the grounds of their sex yet, to some extent, they managed to overcome this and operate Action féminine semi-autonomously, if only for a short time. Female members exploited the division between the sexes to underscore their importance to the future of France. Moreover, Action féminine posited the 'natural' qualities of women and the return of women to the home as the solution to political corruption and national decline.

What motivated young French men and women to join these groups? Doubtless some considered the youth groups and their activities as little more than a means to make new friends. This was especially true for groups with a uniquely leisure-oriented and festive function. It would therefore be mistaken to assign all members, including those who joined politically motivated sections, the same political conviction. The JUF in particular championed social rather than political issues. Its associative life was relatively benign, where this term indicates a lack of explicit interest in the political conflicts that divided France at the time. The UF warned its youth members against becoming embroiled in revolutionary or reactionary leagues. The evidence available does not suggest that JUF members defied this warning.

The JUNC's associative life was as diverse as that of the JUF. Sections performed a variety of functions. Young men and women may have joined for any combination of reasons. Yet unlike the JUF, the JUNC had avowedly political aspirations. It denied neither its interest nor its intervention in politics, which it deemed essential. The JUNC supported corporatism, the organised profession and promoted the virtuous French peasant and family life. The JUNC never hid its endorsement of the leagues and their programmes. It encouraged its members to cooperate with extreme right-wing groups. Moreover, the reform plans of the JUNC cannot be reconciled with the republican centre. The JUNC desired an end to the Third Republic. Claiming that the form of the state was variable, it called for the destruction of French institutions and the subsequent creation of new ones. In this way the JUNC embodied an extremism that the UNC did not.

Notes

1   John Hellman, *The Knight-Monks of Vichy France: Uriage, 1940–1945* (Montreal: McGill-Queen's University Press, 1993), pp. 6–7; Kalman, *The Extreme Right*, p. 146.

2   Aline Coutrot, 'Youth movements in France in the 1930s', *Journal of Contemporary History*, 5 (1970), 26 and 32.

3   *Ibid.*, p. 29.

4   On youth movements in inter-war France see in particular Coutrot, 'Youth movements in France in the 1930s', 23–35; Rémi Fabre, 'Les mouvements de jeunesse dans la France de l'entre-deux-guerres', *Le Mouvement Social*, 168 (1994), 9–31; Wilfred D. Halls, *The Youth of Vichy France* (Oxford: Clarendon Press, 1981); Kalman, *The Extreme Right* pp. 145–85; Jean-Louis Loubet del Bayle, *Les Non-conformistes des années 30* (Paris: Editions du Seuil,

1969); Antoine Prost, 'Jeunesse et société dans la France de l'entre-deux-guerres', *Vingtième Siècle*, 13 (1987), 35–45; Susan B. Whitney, *Mobilizing Youth: Communists and Catholics in Inter-war France* (Durham, NC and London: Duke University Press, 2009).

5 Jon Savage, *Teenage: The Creation of Youth Culture* (London: Chatto and Windus, 2007), pp. 133–5.

6 On the concept of generations see Philippe Bénéton, 'La génération de 1912–1914: Image, mythe ou réalité?', *Revue française de science politique*, 21 (1971), 981–1009; Bessel, 'The "front generation"', pp. 121–2; Cabanes, '"Génération du feu"'; Peter Loewenberg, 'The psychoanalytical origins of the Nazi youth cohort', *American Historical Review*, 76 (1971), 1457–1502; Mark Roseman, 'Introduction: Generation conflict and German history', in Roseman (ed.), *Generations in Conflict*, pp. 1–47; Jean-François Sirinelli, 'Génération et histoire politique', *Vingtième Siècle*, 22 (1989), 67–80; Michel Winock, 'Les générations intellectuelles', *Vingtième Siècle*, 22 (1989), 17–38; Robert Wohl, *The Generation of 1914* (Cambridge: Harvard University Press, 1979).

7 Bessel, 'The "front generation"', pp. 121–2. In his work on Germany, Bessel concludes that the experiences of men at the front were diverse with the idea of a shared experience constructed after the end of the war. For Bessel, generations are 'imaginary concepts'.

8 Le Béguec, 'L'entrée au Palais-Bourbon', pp. 376–98.

9 Whitney, *Mobilizing Youth*, pp.16–50 and 137–208.

10 *Ibid.*, pp. 80–106.

11 Loubet del Bayle, *Les Non-conformistes*, p. 214.

12 For a discussion of the Faisceau and youth see Kalman, *The Extreme Right*, pp. 148–58.

13 *Ibid.*, pp. 145–85; Kennedy, *Reconciling France*, pp. 101–6 and 208–12.

14 Kalman, *The Extreme Right*, p. 165.

15 *Ibid.*, p. 160.

16 Irvine, *French Conservatism*, pp. 32–33.

17 'Jeunesses de l'Union Fédérale', *CUF* (1 June 1934).

18 L. Fontenaille, 'Des devoirs', *CUF* (1 March 1933).

19 'Le 9e Congrès nationale de l'UNC. Action Générale: La liaison avec les Jeunes,' *VC* (9 June 1928); A. Le Blanc, 'Les Jeunes: Leur psychologie, leurs tendances, leurs aspirations. Comment agir sur les Jeunes', *VC* (28 April 1934).

20 A. Nérisson, 'La liaison avec les Jeunes', *VC* (6 July 1929).

21 R. Schmitt, 'D'autres moyens de propagande', *VC* (23 June 1934).

22 A. Lesbordes, 'Allons les jeunes!', *VC* (7 January 1933).

23 'Centre permanent d'action: Séance du 3 mars', *VC* (10 March 1934).

24 'Notre Action', *VC* (6 November 1937); 'Conseil National', *VC* (1 April 1939).

25 J. Fourcade-Chourry, 'Jeunes et Anciens ont des obligations mutuelles', *VC* (25 February 1939).

26 'L'Assemblée générale des Jeunes de l'UNC', *VC* (9 November 1935).

27 Savage, *Teenage*, p. 183; Michael Ledeen, 'Italian fascism and youth', *Journal of Contemporary History*, 4 (1969), 137–54.

28 G. Berthau, 'A propos d'une enquête: Les Anciens Combattants à la conquête du pouvoir. Par qui ?', *VC* (3 August 1935).

29 'Jean Goy est élu président général de l'UNC en remplacement de Georges Lebecq démissionnaire', *VC* (14 December 1935).

30 R. Schmitt, 'Les Jeunes: Liaison avec les Jeunes', *VC* (28 April 1934).

31 'Au lendemain de notre magnifique congrès', *Le Combattant d'Ille-et-Vilaine* (March 1935).

32 H. Pichot, 'Nous voulons la France!' *CUF* (10 May 1938).

33 R. Grasset, 'Les Mutilés', *Journal des combattants et mutilés du Puy-de-Dôme* (January 1934).

34 P. Delore, 'Pensées d'automne', *Le Combattant du centre* (December 1933).

35 R. Etienne, 'Debout les Jeunes', *VC* (16 December 1933).

36 P. Vidal, 'Appel aux Jeunes par un Jeune', *L'Union fédérale du Gard* (December 1936).

37 'Sont jeunes ceux qui bâtissent, luttent, possèdent une foi …', *VC* (30 April 1938).

38 M. Ballot, 'Des Jeunes qui déjà sont vieux', *NF (Paris-Nord-Centre)* (October 1936).

39 A. Deprez, 'Des Jeunes', *VC* (11 February 1933); Bordachar, 'Plaidoyer pour les Jeunes … et contre nous', *VC* (21 January 1933).

40 H. Pichot, 'La maison en ordre', *CUF* (15 January 1933); H. Pichot, 'La Foi dans les Destinées Françaises', *CUF* (1 May 1935).

41 L. Viala, 'Réflexions d'un ancien poilu devant la jeunesse française', *CUF* (15 November 1933).

42 H. Pichot, 'La Foi dans les Destinées Françaises', *CUF* (1 May 1935); A. Belverge, 'De la critique à l'action', *Le Combattant creusois* (August-September 1935).

43 A. Guyot, 'Etre jeune, c'est aimer', *VC* (29 September 1934).

44 'Conseil National: Vue générale du mouvement', *VC* (26 March 1938).

45 H. Pichot, 'Cloches de Pâques', *CUF* (15 April 1935).

46 C. Hèline, 'Pour la jeunesse – Par la jeunesse', *CUF* (10 July 1936).

47 A. Costes, 'Les Jeunes d'Albi à l'action', *Le Poilu tarnais* (June 1934).

48 A. Guyot, 'Notre mystique', *VC* (5 May 1934); C. Gontemps, untitled, *VC* (30 October 1937); A. Guyot, 'Nous les Jeunes !', *VC* (15 September 1934).

49 C. Héline, 'A quand leur tour!', *CUF* (10 March 1936).

50 AN, 43 AS/8, H. Pichot, 'L'âme des jeunes', *La Revue des Vivants* (October 1927); H. Pichot, 'Cloches de Pâques', *CUF* (15 April 1935); H. Pichot, 'La Foi dans les Destinées Françaises', *CUF* (1 May 1935); H. Pichot, 'La vie

ardente', in André Gervais, André Jacques and Jean Mouraille (eds.), *Jeunesses* (Paris: Editions de l'Union fédérale, 1935), p. 6.

51 L. Fontenaille, 'Des devoirs', *CUF* (1 March 1933).

52 'La Jeunesse', *CUF* (15 June–1 July 1933); A. Jacques, 'Sortir de l'impasse: Pour aider les Jeunesses de l'UF', *CUF* (15 December 1933).

53 A. Jacques, 'Sortir de l'impasse: Pour aider les Jeunesses de l'UF', *CUF* (15 December 1933).

54 'Conseil d'Administration du 31 Mars 1935', *Le Combattant creusois* (March 1935).

55 H. Pichot, 'UF', *CUF* (1 June 1933).

56 C. Héline, 'Aux Jeunes de l'Union fédérale', *CUF* (1 March 1933).

57 H. Pichot, 'Cloches de Pâques', *CUF* (15 April 1935).

58 C. Héline, 'A quand leur tour!', *CUF* (10 March 1936); J. Mouraille, 'Jeunesses', *CUF* (15 April 1935); René Cassin, 'A l'oeuvre, les Jeunes', in Gervais *et al.*, *Jeunesses*, pp. 54 and 62–3.

59 A. Costes, 'Jeunesses italiennes, jeunesses françaises', *CUF* (1 March 1935).

60 C. Héline, 'Aux jeunes gens!', *CUF* (20 February 1936).

61 'Notre Référendum', *Le Front* (December 1931).

62 A. Gervais, 'Buts et doctrines', in Gervais *et al.*, *Jeunesses*, p. 16; AN, 43 AS/8, H. Pichot, 'L'âme des jeunes', *La Revue des Vivants* (October 1927).

63 C. Héline, 'A la jeunesse de France', *CUF* (20 December 1937).

64 'Comité fédéral du 11 mars 1934', *CUF* (15 March 1934); N. Lerat, 'Appel aux Jeunes,' *Après le combat* (November–December 1933); 'Quelques Réflexions,' *Après le combat* (October–November 1934).

65 A. Costes, 'L'éveil des Jeunes', *CUF* (15 June 1934).

66 J. Mouraille, 'Pourquoi et comment?' *NF (Paris)*, June 1936.

67 J. Mouraille, 'Formation et développement des associations de Jeunes', in Gervais *et al.*, *Jeunesses*, pp. 26–33.

68 'Le Congrès de Nice, du 4 au 7 juin 1938: Jeunesses de l'UF', *CUF* (10–20 June 1938); N. Lerat, 'Les Jeunes et les temps présents,' *Le Mutilé et combattant de la Haute-Loire* (February 1935).

69 C. Héline, 'L'action pour la paix', *CUF* (1 June 1933); C. Héline, 'Pour la jeunesses – Par la jeunesses', *CUF* (10 July 1936); C. Héline, 'Un programme d'Action pour la Jeunesse', *CUF* (1 May 1934); C. Héline, 'Aux jeunes gens!', *CUF* (20 February 1936)

70 Untitled, *Le Front* (April–October 1935).

71 J. Pintout, 'Bons camarades!' *Le Combattant creusois* (June 1936).

72 A. Costes, 'Jeunesses italiennes, jeunesses françaises', *CUF* (1 March 1935); L. Viala, 'Ayons confiance dans nos Jeunes', *CUF* (15 March 1935); C. Héline, 'A la jeunesse de France', *CUF* (20 December 1937).

73 'Les Voeux du congrès: Jeunesses de l'UF', *CUF* (1 May 1935).

74 F. Aubert, 'Rapport du Secrétaire Général', *VC* (31 May 1935).

75 J. Raudot, 'Aux anciens', *VC* (6 November 1937); 'Conseil National', *VC* (1 April 1939).

76 See, for example, the reports from the general assemblies of the Arcachon and Rugles youth groups in *VC* (10 March 1934; 21 April 1934).

77 UNC/EC, 24 November 1934.

78 J. Alaterre, 'Un appel aux Jeunes', *VC* (29 April 1939).

79 C. Galland, 'Le mal des jeunes ? C'est la médiocrité de l'Esprit français', *VC* (5 December 1936).

80 G. Berthau, 'A propos d'une enquête: Les Anciens Combattants à la conquête du pouvoir. Par qui ?', *VC* (3 August 1935). Rivollet (UNMR) and Cassin (UF) expressed this view on the ill-preparedness of French youth for government.

81 A. Guyot, 'L'Action des Jeunes', *VC* (5 August 1933).

82 R. Pinoteau, 'Pas d'assiette au beurre chez nous: Conseils aux Jeunes, Appel aux Anciens', *VC* (13 July 1935).

83 J. de Saint Louvent, 'La Relève', *VC* (2 December 1933); A. Guyot, 'L'Action Jeune', *VC* (5 August 1933).

84 L. De J., 'L'esprit combattant et les Jeunes', *VC* (6 May 1933); F. d'Hennezel, 'L'heure des jeunes', *VC* (3 March 1934).

85 H. Isaac, 'A nous les jeunes!', *VC* (17 November 1934).

86 P. Delore, 'La réforme primordiale: Celle de l'esprit public', *VC* (29 July 1933); P. Delore, 'Pensées d'automne', *VC* (11 November 1933).

87 G. de Cromières, 'Et Nos Jeunes', *VC* (30 October 1937).

88 'Que veut la Jeunesse?', *VC* (23 September 1933); A. Le Blanc, 'Les Jeunes: Leur psychologie, leur tendances, leurs aspirations. Comment agir sur les jeunes', *VC* (28 April 1934); J. Burger, 'Des moyens de propagande', *VC* (2 February 1935); J. Raudot, 'Aux anciens', *VC* (16 October 1938); A. Magnier, 'Union Sportive Française: Notre exemple à imiter', *VC* (12 February 1938).

89 R. Schmitt, 'Liaison avec les Jeunes', *VC* (28 April 1934); R. Marin, 'Avec ceux qui en sont revenus', *VC* (27 October 1934).

90 J. Raudot, 'En revenant de la revue', *VC* (11 June 1938); UNC/EC, 5 February 1938.

91 E. Veysset, 'Petite correspondance', *VC* (9 November 1935).

92 R. Pinoteau, 'Et demain?', *VC* (9 May 1936).

93 J. Fourcade-Chourry, 'Jeunes et Anciens ont des obligations mutuelles', *VC* (25 February 1939).

94 J. Dauguet, 'Appel aux Ainés', *VC* (17 March 1934); E. Veysset, 'Propagande pratique: L'activité minimum d'une section de JUNC', *VC* (4 July 1936).

95 R. Schmitt, 'Au travail de Suite!', *VC* (21 July 1934); R. Schmitt, 'Raymond Schmitt', *Inter-sections* (March 1936).

96 F. d'Hennezel, 'L'action', *VC* (14 April 1934).

97 E. Veysset, 'La propagande: Nous unissons, nous fédérons, nous ne démolissons pas', *VC* (7 September 1935).

98 E. Veysset, 'La Propagande: Conseils pour les Présidents de Sections', *VC* (6 July 1935).

99 'Centre permanent d'action: Séance du 9 août 1934', *VC* (25 August 1934).

100 E. Veysset, 'Action générale 1936: Pour la formation d'une élite des Jeunes de l'UNC', *VC* (18 January 1936).

101 R. Marin, 'Précisions nécessaires', *VC* (29 September 1934).

102 J. Mafaraud, 'La propagande', *VC*, 31 May 1935; C. Galland, 'Action Générale', *VC* (31 May 1935); M. Arnault, 'Mise au pas!', *VC* (1 April 1939).

103 E. Veysset, report from general assembly of the JUNC, *VC* (16 November 1935).

104 E. Veysset, 'La propagande: Les trois stades envisagées', *VC* (30 March 1935).

105 E. Veysset, 'Le sens profond de notre mouvement', *VC* (2 November 1935).

106 A. Guyot, 'Nous les Jeunes!', *VC* (15 September 1934).

107 Loubet, *Les Non-conformistes*, pp. 294–7, pp. 323–4.

108 E. Veysset, 'La Propagande: Pas de programme ?', *VC* (24 August 1935); Joublin, 'Etudes corporatives: Les méfaits du libéralisme', *VC* (10 September 1938).

109 R. Pinoteau, 'Notre politique: Violence? Inertie? Non! Révolution dirigée', *VC* (14 December 1935).

110 G. Merchiez, 'Les livres et nous … Les Jeunes face au monde politicien, Alphonso-Augustin Daulnois', *Inter-sections* (April 1936).

111 Monnet, *Refaire la République*, p. 311.

112 A. Guyot, 'Notre mystique', *VC* (5 May 1934).

113 R. Pinoteau, 'Notre politique: Violence? Inertie? Non! Révolution dirigée', *VC* (14 December 1935); F. Aubert, 'A propos d'une controverse', *VC* (16 May 1936).

114 'Action Générale', *VC* (28 April 1934).

115 E. Veysset, 'La Propagande: Pas de programme?', *VC* (24 August 1935).

116 'Voix de nos groupes: Un Appel des Jeunes de la Marne', *VC* (11 February 1939).

117 R. Schmitt, 'Grandes lignes de notre action sociale', *VC* (16 March 1935); 'Aux Français!', *VC* (26 June 1937); 'Rôle et fonctionnement de la Corporation', *VC* (17 September 1938); 'La corporation, c'est l'union organique des classes', *VC* (24 September 1938).

118 J. Vaujour, 'Appel à la jeunesse des campagnes', *VC* (14 December 1934); C. Galland, 'Action rurale: La Section rurale', *VC* (31 May 1935).

119 A. Debèvre, 'La décadence de la famille', *VC* (18 April 1936); 'La voie de salut', *VC* (4 February 1939).

120 A. Le Blanc, 'Rapport Moral', *VC* (31 May 1935).

121 E. Veysset, 'La Propagande: Pas de programme?', *VC* (24 August 1935).

122 Whitney, *Mobilizing Youth*.

123 John Horne, 'Masculinity in politics and war in the age of nation states and world wars, 1850–1950', in Stefan Dudink, Karen Hagemann and John Tosh (eds.), *Masculinities in Politics and War: Gendering Modern History* (Manchester: Manchester University Press, 2004), p. 32; Mosse, *Fallen Soldiers*, p. 167.

124 P. Brousmiche, 'Rapport moral', *CUF* (15 June–1 July 1935).

125 Whitney, *Mobilizing Youth*, pp. 73 and 197.

126 *Ibid.*, pp. 114–19

127 Kalman, *The Extreme Right*, p. 119.

128 *Ibid.*, pp. 123–5; Passmore, 'Planting the tricolour', 817. On women and the CF/PSF see Caroline Campbell's thesis 'Women and Men in French Authoritarianism: Gender in the Croix de Feu/Parti Social Français, 1927–1947'(Ph.D. dissertation, University of Iowa, 2009).

129 Report from the general assembly of the JUNC, *VC* (10 November 1934).

130 'Conseil National des Jeunes, 27–28 avril 1935', *VC* (4 May 1935).

131 'L'Assemblée générale des Jeunes de l'UNC', *VC* (9 November 1935).

132 'Les Jeunes: Arcachon', *VC* (21 April 1934).

133 Y. Boulet, 'Propagande féminine. Ce que dit un "Madelon" de 1935 à ses Jeunes Collègues de 1936', *VC* (21 December 1935); Y. Boulet, 'Petite correspondance de la propagande', *VC* (28 December 1935).

134 Y. Luzier, 'Rapport sur l'Action Féminine', *VC* (5 December 1936).

135 'IV Assemblée Générale des JUNC, 14 mars 1937', *VC* (20 March 1937); Y. Luzier, 'Action féminine', *VC* (26 June 1937).

136 'La réunion du Conseil National JUNC à Caen, le 25 mai 1938: Action féminine', *VC* (11 June 1938).

137 See the report featured in *VC* (2 February 1935). The JUNC's 7th section organised a meal for eighty children whose parents were unemployed.

138 Y. Luzier, 'Action féminine', *VC* (26 June 1937).

139 'La vie des Sections de Jeunes. Région parisienne: Les Lilas', *VC* (30 March 1935).

140 'La vie des Sections de Jeunes', *VC* (29 December 1934).

141 'L'Assemblée générale des jeunes de l'UNC 3–4 novembre 1934 fut une belle manifestation de l'activité', *VC* (10 November 1934).

142 Viala, 'Ayons confiance dans nos Jeunes', *CUF* (15 March 1935).

143 F. Aubert, 'Le coin des secrétaires', *VC* (1 September 1934); 'L'action féminine', *VC* (2 April 1938).

144 Y. Boulet, 'Petite correspondance … féminine', *VC* (23 November 1935).

145 'Propagande féminine', *VC* (7 March 1936).

146 Y. Boulet, 'Doit-il y avoir des limites à l'aide que nous apportions à ces "Messieurs" JUNC?', *VC* (18 April 1936).

147 Andrès Reggiani, 'Procreating France: The politics of demography, 1919–1945', *French Historical Studies*, 19 (3) (1996), 725–54; Richard Tomlinson,

'The "disappearance" of France, 1896–1940: French politics and the birth rate', *Historical Journal*, 28.2 (1985), 405–15.

148 Roberts, *Civilization Without Sexes*, pp. 9–10.

149 Kalman, *The Extreme Right*, p. 111; Cheryl Koos and Daniella Sarnoff, 'France' in Kevin Passmore (ed.), *Women, Gender and Fascism in Europe, 1919–1945* (Manchester: Manchester University Press, 2003), pp. 168–89.

150 Roberts, *Civilization without Sexes*, pp. 17–89.

151 F. Vivié, 'Les Jeunes', *Le Poilu basque*, April 1935; Y. Boulet, 'Notre féminisme', *VC*, 7 December 1935.

152 P. Chailleux, 'Sachons vouloir', *VC* (24 November 1934).

153 Report from the Commission des Jeunes, *VC* (20 January 1934).

154 A. Debèvre and M.-A. Schmitt, 'Réponse aux critiques contre le maintien de la femme au foyer', *VC* (28 March 1936).

155 Y. Luzier, 'Faisons le point', *VC* (27 November 1937).

156 Y. Luzier, 'Action sociale: Action féminine', *VC* (31 May 1935); A. Debèvre and M.-A. Schmitt, 'Pour défendre la Famille', *VC* (7 March 1936).

157 Y. Luzier, 'Action féminine: Faisons le point', *VC* (27 November 1937).

158 Laura Lee Downs, 'Comment faire appel à l'instinct viril du garçon'? La pédagogie du jeu et la formation de l'enfant au masculin: Les Scouts de France, 1920–1940', *Cahiers Masculin/Féminin de Lyon 2: L'éternel masculin* (2003), 55–62; Jean-Louis Gay-Lescot, *Sport et éducation sous Vichy* (Lyon: Presses universitaires de Lyon, 1991), p. 8.

159 Halls, *Youth of Vichy France*, p. 199.

160 D. Strohl, 'Le Sport et la Jeunesse: Comment créer des Centres d'éducation physique', *VC* (16 June 1934); R. Franconi, 'Le Devoir d'être fort', *VC* (19 November 1938).

161 Julian Jackson, *The Popular Front in France: Defending Democracy* (Cambridge: Cambridge University Press, 1988) pp. 131–8; Gay-Lescot, *Sport et Education*, p. 12.

162 André Rauch, *L'Identité masculine à l'ombre des femmes: De la Grande Guerre à la Gay Pride* (Paris: Hachette, 2004), p. 70.

163 Kalman, *The Extreme Right*, pp. 176–9.

164 A. Magnier, 'Actualité sportive', *VC* (10 April 1937).

165 A. Magnier, 'L'Union Sportive Française', *VC*, 30 April 1938.

166 C. Héline, 'L'action pour la paix', *CUF* (1 June 1933); C. Héline, 'Un programme d'Action pour la Jeunesse', *CUF* (1 May 1934).

167 'Les Jeunes de l'UF', *CUF* (20 April 1936).

168 'Le premier congrès de l'Union Sportive Française', *VC* (18 September 1937).

169 'XXIe Congrès de l'UF: Aix-les-Bains, 15–19 mai 1937: Motions adoptées. France saine, musclée et nombreuse', *CUF* (20 February 1937).

170 C. Galland, 'L'action des Jeunes: Action Générale', *VC* (31 May 1935); A. Magnier, 'L'Union Sportive Française', *VC* (30 April 1938).

171 J.R. Moustiers, 'Maintenant que vous êtes forts, soyez actifs', *VC* (25 September 1937).

172 J. Raudot, 'L'Allemagne en Armes', *VC* (23 January 1937).

173 A. Magnier, 'L'Union Sportive Française', *VC* (30 April 1938).

The veterans and the Popular Front

In June 1936, Léon Blum became the first socialist prime minister of France. For the first time, too, socialists took up ministerial posts alongside their radical coalition partners. Some things did not change. The communists refused ministerial participation, though they continued to support the coalition. The Popular Front took power at a tumultuous time. Since 6 February 1934, France had become increasingly divided between the combined forces of the left and the nationalist leagues. This division was increasingly expressed on the streets of France. More than 1,000 public ceremonies, gatherings and processions took place from February 1934 to May 1936. To have one's members in the street became more about a show of presence and strength than a protest over any particular policy. Violent clashes between members of rival groups resulted in injury and sometimes death.[1] Divisions deepened as a wave of strikes followed the left's election. In its negotiations to end the industrial action, the new government won immediate gains for workers. The Matignon agreements of 9 June 1936 established collective bargaining, granted workers an average pay rise of 12 per cent, the right to paid holidays, and reduced the working week to forty hours with no loss of pay. In spite of these concessions to labour the strikes continued.[2]

For the right the strike wave was a worrying occurrence and tensions heightened when Blum dissolved the leagues in June. The right's attacks on the left and its leading personalities were unprecedented in their malice. Anti-communism came to dominate right-wing discourse as conservatives increasingly perceived the hand of Moscow behind every action of the government. The FR, once a party of conservative republicanism, now counted hardliners Xavier Vallat and Philippe Henriot amongst its leading activists. Suspicion of communism was not unique to the right. From the beginning of the Popular Front neither right-wing radical deputies nor the party's middle-class supporters had been unanimously in favour of the coalition. The industrial unrest of summer 1936 planted further seeds of disquiet. Certain members of the radicals, socialists and trade unions began to question the wisdom of the alliance with communism.[3]

As discontent simmered beneath the surface, Blum's government confronted challenges that would prove insurmountable. Much to the anger of the communists, the government refused to engage France in the Spanish Civil War on behalf of the Frente Popular. Domestically, the left's election had frightened the markets and investors causing a flight of capital. Blum devalued the Franc in September 1936 in an attempt to shore up the economy but capital continued to desert France. Able to satisfy neither the left nor the right with his economic policy, the prime minister announced a pause in reform in February 1937. In June, he requested decree powers to force through legislation. His request denied by the conservative radical-controlled Senate, Blum resigned.

By 1938, divisions in the alliance seemed irreconcilable following the unsuccessful attempts of two governments to regain some momentum. Dissenting radical deputies found support among the largely conservative body of radical senators and the young radicals group. Sensitive to the concerns of the mass of the party's small property-owning supporters the right-wing radicals feared the effects of further social disorder and labour legislation as the Popular Front neared two years in office.[4] Blum's second tenure as prime minister, which began on 9 March 1938, lasted barely a month and sealed the coalition's failure. The succeeding administration under Edouard Daladier, though still technically a Popular Front government, saw the repeal of much of the coalition's legislation. In November 1938, Daladier successfully countered a CGT-led general strike. Two and a half years after the Popular Front's election, the labour movement lay crushed.

What was the attitude of the veterans' movement during this period? On 29 November 1936, the Confédération convened its members in Paris. The document which emerged from this meeting urged employers and workers to accept a compromise and end the threat of civil war. Distributed throughout the country, the veterans' appeal sought to avoid the division of France into antagonistic blocs. Calling on the country to return to its 'ancestral traditions and virtues' lest the democratic regime be undermined, it appeared that the confederated associations had achieved a remarkable degree of unity.[5]

Yet the platitudes contained within the document disguised political divisions. The responses of the UNC and the UF to the new government were perfectly in line with their politics. The UNC was resolutely hostile to the Popular Front government, as it had been to all previous leftist administrations. It believed that the coalition was a communist front controlled from Moscow. Indeed, the UNC continued to pursue familiar policies, such as the protection of veterans' benefits, yet anti-communism came to dominate its foreign and domestic agenda between 1936 and 1938. Like some conservatives, despite the growing threat from Germany following the remilitarisation of the Rhineland and the agreement of the Rome–Berlin axis, the UNC came to perceive domestic communism as the more immediate danger.[6] *La Voix du combattant* pilloried radical, socialist and communist deputies. It vilified the 'devilish' Blum, communist chief Maurice Thorez and condemned Popular Front deputies as Stalin's lieutenants and lackeys.[7] Even Blum's wife, Thérèse, was not spared from attack. She was portrayed as a *pétroleuse*, the violent feminine representation of the Paris Commune, much feared in conservative circles as a symbol of perverted gender roles.[8] When the Blum government dissolved the leagues in June 1936, the UNC expressed its anger. Why, it asked, should nationalist associations be dissolved while more threatening leftist formations continued to exist?[9] The UNC's anti-communist campaign went beyond hysterical rhetoric. In an attempt to fight the left-wing threat the UNC founded a nationalist coalition, the Rassemblement français.

None of this should give cause for surprise. The UNC had long opposed the left and its relations with the extreme right have been explored. Yet after May 1936 the UNC's attacks on the left were different. They were characterised by an unprecedented ferocity. Once again, the left was perceived to threaten the nation and the culture of war came to prominence in the association's discourse. The UNC drew on the culture's lexicon of terminology and structure of values to depict the government as un-French, un-Christian and contrary to the national interest. Furthermore, where once the UNC had encouraged informal relations with extremist groups, the Rassemblement concluded an official entente with La Rocque's PSF and Jacques Doriot's PPF among others.

The UF's relationship with the Popular Front was more complicated than that of its rival. Certainly, it did not react to Blum's government in as violent a manner as the UNC. The UF had always preferred centre-left radical administrations. Of course, during the election campaign, the UF repeated its well-worn call for veterans to replace the 'old men' of politics. Yet while its anti-parliamentarianism remained intact throughout the Popular Front's reign, the association nevertheless recognised that the parliamentary regime had found some stability under the new government. The UF hoped that the Popular Front represented the new men and ideas that France needed. It was impressed at the inclusion of the CGT in the government's plans. Pichot expressed a renewed optimism, stating in January 1937 that there was still life to be found in democracy.[10]

The UF's position changed in early 1938, influenced by developments in France and Germany. At home, the increasingly dire economic situation and the instability of parliamentary government underscored parliamentary incompetence. Abroad, French inaction over Hitler's desire for union with Austria drew condemnation from the UF.[11] In March 1938, the UF broke with the Popular Front government. This break was expressed in the association's call for a government of public safety. That same month the UNC endorsed the UF's plan. From then on, united in their campaign for state reform, both associations collaborated to an unprecedented extent.

The election of the Popular Front

Since February 1934, when street violence had deposed Daladier, successive governments had disappointed the UF. The promises and policies of parliamentarians had amounted to little. Reform of republican institutions and practices had not been forthcoming. The UF's plan for a 'combatants' republic' remained unrealised. Prior to the election of May 1936, Héline condemned all out-going and aspirant parliamentarians as sterile and stained by bad faith.[12] When advising its members on how to vote, the UF specified neither parties nor politicians. Instead it asked that UF veterans vote for 'honest people', qualified as men who wanted to put money, credit and the 'machine' at the service of French workers.[13] Members should not vote for advocates of the decree laws that had unfairly targeted veterans, 'apprentice dictators' or those who desired civil war. As for reform of the state, the UF advocated an 'organic' modification through the adaptation of existing institutions, though the association acknowledged the 'resistance and vitality' of these same institutions.[14]

The UF welcomed the Popular Front government as a new opportunity. It drew hope from the inclusion of men from the labour movement in the coalition. For the UF, the leaders of the CGT, like the veterans, were unblemished by politics. The association regretted the factory occupations but it recognised that the strikes were otherwise 'honest'. At a meeting of its federal committee on 11 October 1936 the UF approved the social gains made under the Popular Front but expressed concern that the industrial disturbances would threaten France's security at home and abroad.[15]

As the elections approached, the UNC was steadfastly unsympathetic to the Popular Front. In February 1936, its executive committee asked readers to reject candidates who did not repudiate the 'alliance of the Communist Party, the doctrines of hate and the enterprises of disorder'.[16] Nonetheless, following the election the association accepted the changes to labour legislation negotiated in the Matignon agreement. The UNC's calmness did not last long. When the concessions to labour failed to end the industrial disorder, fear of communism took hold of the UNC. Galland claimed that Blum had lost control of the labour movement to the profit of the communists. Aubert agreed. Factory occupations heralded the beginning of a revolution. Communists had infiltrated the Popular Front: the 'worm was in the fruit'. The UNC's attitude to the 'pure disorder' of the strikes hardened. Galland recommended a 'good [police] raid' on strikers as a solution.[17]

The success of the Popular Front as a mass movement brought about a change in the UNC's conception of the people. Left and right competed for leadership of 'the people' of France and the right to be recognised as the mouthpiece of the populace. To this end, traditional political boundaries were not fixed: the leagues and the right laid claim to the workers while the Popular Front appropriated previously nationalist rhetoric.[18] Political rivals waged a discursive and symbolic battle for the right to claim the nation. Since the inclusion of the radical party in July 1935, the Popular Front had moved from being a worker's movement to one of republican defence. To this end, the left sought to re-appropriate French national symbols from the right. The right reacted to this challenge and ridiculed the left's new-found patriotism. It alleged that the number of foreigners and Jews in the Popular Front represented a threat to French security. The government of France would only be truly national once these foreign elements were removed.[19]

The UNC had once lauded popular sovereignty over the mandate of the Chamber. Now it no longer regarded the masses as the repository of the 'true' national interest. The association accused the left of duping the 'reckless' masses.[20] It denied the premise of the left's claim to represent the national community. Drawing on the war experience, soon after the election the UNC levelled the charge of 'shirking' (*embusquage*) at left-wing deputies in order to compare the left with wartime shirkers and confirm their anti-national sentiment. During the war, the right had condemned factory workers and 'CGT shirkers' who were allegedly sheltered from the danger of the front and paid handsomely for the privilege.[21] *La Voix du combattant* published a cartoon that pictured a disabled veteran opposite communist luminaries Maurice Thorez and Jacques Duclos. In response to the latter's pronouncement on the need for a 'French front' to bring liberty to France, the veteran replies: 'You weren't there in 1914 to teach us this!'[22]

The UNC joined the battle to appropriate national symbols and discourse. Its veterans dearly prized the national icons of French culture such as the national flag, anthem and commemorative days. When the UNC perceived that these symbols were under threat from the left, it reacted furiously. In December 1933, Lebecq had condemned the communist commemoration of the armistice the previous month.[23] In June 1934, at the inauguration of a war memorial, the UNC had decried the government's decision to allow a communist ceremony to take place where attendees stood under the flag of the Soviet Union and sang the Internationale.[24] Consequently, in July 1936 the association denounced left-wing agitation and public demonstrations held under the red flag. Strikers, it claimed, undermined the freedom to work while agitators had practically abolished the 'freedom of the street'.[25] The UNC's answer was to ask the people of France to display the tricolour in every window. With each town and village decorated in the national colours, the UNC hoped to take back French public space and the symbols of France.

This tactic was apparently not without risk. Aubert reported an incident in which three coal deliverymen attacked a veteran for wearing a tricolour cockade. When the veteran in question informed police, officers responded that they could take no action. Aubert cited this story as proof of the subversion of the police force.[26] Goy concurred, alleging that the police treated French 'patriots' who dared to display the national symbols as criminals. Such offences were punished with arrest or a beating, such as that of 'grand mutilé' Joseph Magne, founder of the UNC's Nîmes section and holder of the *légion d'honneur* and the *croix de guerre*. Allegedly assailed by communists upon his exit from a section meeting, his crime was to display a tricolour on a medal awarded in recognition of his thirty-two years' service as a miner.[27] Similar incidents provided further 'proof' of communist depravity. The UNC depicted communists as uncivilised brutes who attacked women and the war disabled. These reports, like wartime atrocity propaganda, demonstrated the enemy's alleged inhumanity and provided a means by which to re-legitimise the anti-communist crusade. In September 1936, *La Voix du combattants* reported that a group of 'about one hundred yobs', which included 'Armenians, Arabs and Spaniards', had attacked UNC veterans and their wives. Under the 'benevolent gaze' of the police, the attack targeted the most vulnerable people at the meeting. The young rowdies spat on women, insulted the elderly and beat the war-disabled with coshes. The crowd, reportedly under the orders of a CGT member, then marched down the street, fist in the air, singing the Internationale and breaking windows with impunity.[28]

The UNC's Rassemblement français

Believing themselves engaged in a fight for the future of France, the UNC's leadership resolved to act. With much bitterness, the executive committee recognised that the French public had rejected its civic action programme. Action combattante had not taken root. Provincial members had failed to take up the much vaunted Wagram manifesto of October 1933. Rival groups had hijacked the UNC's ideas and presented them as their own. Yet the UNC was not beaten. Executive committee members decided to launch a new initiative open to all French, veterans and non-veterans.[29] In July 1936, 6,000 veterans attended a meeting in the Salle Wagram that officially launched the Rassemblement. Goy announced to the audience that the executive committee, the policy-making committee and the national congress had decided it was time to take action beyond the scope of veterans' rights. The UNC would no longer languish in political neutrality.[30]

Ostensibly, the Rassemblement was intended to encourage national reconciliation at a time of conflict and division in France. However, the proposed alliance rejected groups deemed contrary to a national interest as defined by the UNC. It 'exclude[d] from the French family those who fetch their watchword from abroad and prepare the ruin of society through economic anarchy and civil war': the revolutionary left and its allies.[31] Those French who favoured 'demolition' over 'construction' would be 'eliminated'. Members of the Rassemblement were ultimately united by one aim: 'That communism be combated and hunted down.'[32]

Led from Paris, the Rassemblement found support among some provincial veterans. While one must rely on *La Voix du combattant* for reports of support for the Rassemblement, one should not dismiss them out of hand. Though partisan, the newspaper reported that several provincial groups were reluctant to support the campaign. It did not claim that enthusiasm was widespread. This apparent transparency surrounding issues of consent lends some authenticity to the reports. The UNC held meetings across France to promote the Rassemblement. Speaking before 450 members at Saint-Malo, Alexis Thomas of the UNC's Lorraine group denounced Stalin's control of French domestic policy by means of the CGT. Thomas warned provincial members that the time had come to stop communism. It was reported that attendees 'literally drank his words'. His call to stand up to the invader received an ovation.[33] A meeting of the *poitevin* group attended by 1,500 members issued a communication that approved the Rassemblement.[34] In Lyon, 2,500 members agreed that the UNC should aid all groups in favour of order against bolshevism.[35] In December 1936, the Vaucluse group also lent its support to the national campaign.[36] A meeting of twenty-eight section presidents and one youth section in the Calais region chastised the Parisian leadership for a lack of clarity in the launch of the Rassemblement yet nevertheless voiced its confidence in the new initiative.[37] The groups of the Bas- and Haut-Rhin approved too.[38] Expressions of support came from the general assembly of the Ille-et-Vilaine group, the departmental group of the Sarthe, a meeting of 2,500 members in Nancy, the Ardèche group, the Limoges group and the seventeenth departmental congress of the Maine-et-Loire which spoke for 282 sections and 30 JUNC groups.[39]

Goy intended the JUNC to be the 'apostles' of the new Rassemblement.[40] Like its parent organisation, the JUNC was unequivocal in its opposition to communism. In June 1934, d'Hennezel had lamented that his hometown of Saint-Quentin was subjected to the tyranny of the Internationale.[41] In March 1935, the JUNC section in Angevillers had vowed to combat the forces of socialism and communism by all means available.[42] After the election of the Popular Front, the JUNC vowed not only to fight but to destroy the 'crime' and 'treason' of the left. It supported the Rassemblement. Indeed, the Jeunes du Nord linked the success of the UNC's campaign to the very success of the JUNC itself.[43]

On one occasion a meeting of the Rassemblement resembled the organisation and logistical arrangements more familiar to the CF than previous UNC gatherings. The meeting took place in the Drôme in September 1936. *La Voix du combattant* claimed that the Popular Front had tried to ban the gathering. As a result, a field was found at short notice near Malissart, four kilometres from Valence. The decision to hold the meeting there was kept secret until midday. At this time, members of the UNC and associated groups were notified. One thousand vehicles were reported to have descended upon Malissart so quickly that the meeting was able to begin at 3.30 p.m. Goy and Isaac both addressed the audience and in response to vociferous demands from the crowd, Xavier Vallat gave an impromptu speech against the 'Muscovite extremists' who had attempted to ban the event.[44]

The Rassemblement once again revealed the diversity of opinion in the UNC's leadership and membership. Among provincial groups, the president of the Berry group and four others were reported to have simply preferred to follow an action independent of the UNC.[45] Section president in the Marne, the Saône-et-Loire, the Indre-et-Loire and Berry voiced their opposition.[46] In the Orne, the UNC's collaboration with the PSF prompted the resignation of the president of the Mortagne section and drew reprobation from the sections in Flers and Alençon.[47] Moreover, given the political diversity of the UNC, each section's endorsement or rejection of the Rassemblement was subjective and often ambiguous. Groups rarely elaborated upon their understanding of the campaign. For some, the Rassemblement was a political campaign in which the collaboration of the former leagues was desirable. For others, it was a moral movement, designed more to influence French opinion than engagement in political activism. Whichever interpretation provincial sections subscribed to, there can be little doubt that they understood the Rassemblement as an anti-communist project, so explicit was the UNC about this fact.

In the executive committee, some members were unconvinced about a campaign against the left even before the founding of the Rassemblement. Goudaert expressed concern that in the Nord any campaign against the Popular Front would alienate the 10,000 socialists and communists in his group. Nationally, he feared that the association may lose one-third of its members.[48] Meanwhile, according to UNC section president Morizot, an anti-communist campaign may displease some members but the association should be prepared to accept a 'thinning out' of its ranks as long as those who were 'to march' remained committed to the cause.[49]

The culture of war revived

Developments in the Spanish civil war added an element of urgency to the UNC's anti-communist campaign. From the beginning of hostilities in Spain, the French right-wing press argued for non-intervention. Conservatives feared that French intervention against Franco would be just the first campaign in a global battle against fascism. Goy himself argued that a war against Hitler would likely result in communist revolution in Germany.[50] War abroad would then be followed by revolution at home, especially given the increased strength of the communists in French politics. Consequently, the threat from foreign fascism was diminished in right-wing opinion. In this context, once hard-line anti-German conservatives could vacillate over opposing Hitler.

The press campaign was so fierce that Blum's government adopted the policy of neutrality.[51] The UNC advocated a firm and absolute neutrality in the Spanish conflict. The Parisian leadership criticised the French government for not presenting a unified policy, wavering as it did between the non-interventionism of Blum and the 'bellicosity' of CGT leader Léon Jouhaux who, the UNC alleged, had 'forgotten' to do his duty in the last war.[52] As August 1936 progressed and the communist campaign for intervention intensified, UNC policy on Spain became concerned with Moscow's designs on France. It claimed that French participation in the war would lead only to revolution and civil war. This would benefit only Moscow and Berlin, the former preparing to launch a revolution and the latter ready to invade in just that event.[53] Conversely, although the UF did not advocate intervention, it feared encirclement by fascist powers.[54]

Events in Spain combined with the UNC's hostility to the domestic left to bring about the re-emergence of the culture of war in conservative veterans' discourse. During the war, the culture had targeted the German as a militaristic barbarian. Following the conflict, the culture encompassed the revolutionary left during the industrial unrest of 1919 and 1920. Under the first Cartel des gauches government in 1924, the right had added the radical and socialist government to its list of national enemies. Briand's foreign policy had drawn the Germans back into the western community. Together France and Germany confronted the enemy of civilisation: war. The cultural demobilisation of the mid-1920s had not affected the right's anticommunism though it receded once conservative government was re-established. In 1936, with the left once again in power and the communist party's campaigning for war in Spain, the language and concepts of the culture of war revived in UNC discourse. For the association, communism now meant war, and war was the enemy of humanity.

Using the example of Spain, the UNC sought to demonstrate communism's incompatibility with Western civilisation: 'The civil war which bloodies Spain … is in reality nothing other than the clash of the national doctrine of order and the international doctrine of upheaval and disorder propagated by muscovite Soviets. It is a localised episode in the global fight between civilisation and barbarism.'[55] Stories of atrocities committed by the 'Reds' in Spain concerned religious symbols and the clergy, and thus reinforced the image of the barbaric left. Comparable only to the brutality of the Turks under Suliman and the pagan Roman emperors, Spanish communists allegedly tortured bishops and priests, raped and molested nuns, destroyed churches, displayed profane images and prevented citizens from practising their religion.[56] Firmly behind

Franco's bid to rid Spain of communism, the UNC was unequivocal in its condemnation of the Spanish Popular Front: 'Civil war broke out in Spain because the dictatorship of the Popular Front (*Frente Popular*), led by the Soviets, had become intolerable for the country … Communism = Tyranny + Murder … The responsibility for the civil war lies completely with the Popular Front.' Communist savages and brutes recruited among the purported defenders of liberty while Franco only allowed indigenous and strictly disciplined men to join his cause.[57]

The UNC did not miss the opportunity to attack the French left. It linked the 'revolutionary' actions and laws of the Spanish Popular Front with the 'crimes' of the French incarnation, such as the dissolution of the right-wing leagues. The association condemned the CGT and Jouhaux for supporting men who slit the throats of nuns and burned down churches.[58] The desire to avoid a fate similar to Spain's reinvigorated the UNC's commitment to the Rassemblement. Asian barbarism would not triumph.[59] In the Limoges, the UNC vowed to prevent France from slipping into the 'primitive barbarity' practised by the Popular Front in Spain.[60] Executive member Desroches underlined the atrocities 'worthy of the worst Asian torture' committed against women and children in Spain. If Moscow continued to govern France, then the French could expect the same. The solution lay in the Rassemblement.[61]

In October 1936, the UNC's anti-communist hysteria hit fever pitch. The association, still fearing that Blum would intervene in Spain, was alarmed at the economic crisis that had prompted the devaluation of the franc. The UNC claimed that its members were more anxious now about the future of France than at Verdun in 1916.[62] Goy had warned previously that the French republic was ceding ground, little by little, to a republic of Soviets.[63] His association now depicted the new government as a *de facto* soviet regime.[64] Isaac warned against the perils of allowing the 'Bolshevik virus' to survive in France.[65] Goy wrote: 'The Popular Front means revolution, bankruptcy and war! … More than ever action is essential, we must make the RASSEMBLEMENT FRANCAIS!'[66] In the provincial *Le Combattant du centre*, de Cromières expressed a similar assessment of France's predicament:

> France, betrayed and sold-out by its leaders, itself submits to slavery … at the present time, it is Moscow who rules in Paris. France of our forbears, of 1914 … heir to all the civic and national virtues, no longer exists. The defence of our borders is an illusion. The Maginot line cannot stop our most dogged and cruel enemy. He is already among us. It is he who governs,

commands, enforces. International Jewish Bolshevik high finance has conquered the people of France with [its] lies and moral poison.[67]

UNC discourse could be violent. Former UNC president Lebecq appealed to members to 'use the same means' as the communists and promised that the UNC would take to the street to 'shoot down' communism.[68] UNC member Georges Merchiez called on his comrades to be vigilant, as in the event of the Popular Front's failure, the 'scum' on the left would continue the battle in the streets. Murder and rape would follow and blood would flow.[69] Arnault of the JUNC vowed that the veterans would 'have [communism's] skin. The *anciens* and the *jeunes* would come together to fight 'ferociously' against the 'crime' and 'treason' of communism.[70]

Old allies: The UNC and the extreme right

The Rassemblement demonstrates that the UNC continued to pursue political intervention. However, the association's fundamental rejection of political participation meant that it could not be an electoral alliance. The Rassemblement aimed to form local ententes against communist action that would attract support from the veterans' movement and beyond. These local coalitions attracted ex-leaguers to the Rassemblement, a fact that caused consternation among some veterans of the UNC and other veterans' associations too.

In late October 1936, the UNC announced the adhesion of political parties to the Rassemblement.[71] This represented a significant change in the nature of the UNC's relations with political groups. For the first time, links with sympathetic political associations were formalised rather than tacitly endorsed. The Rassemblement provided a framework for continued cooperation with political groups from the centre to the extreme right.[72]

Colonel de La Rocque formally endorsed the UNC's national alliance to which he declared his new party's adhesion. Following the Blum government's dissolution of the leagues, the colonel founded a political party, the PSF. While it is difficult to believe that La Rocque came to embrace electoral politics overnight, it is equally mistaken to judge the PSF as identical to its predecessor. The most recent scholarship on the PSF demonstrates that the party publicly accepted electoralism and became less violent. However, rather than simply accepting the republican status quo, it sought to transform fundamentally French society based on an exclusionary vision of national identity. The PSF remained steadfastly authoritarian.[73]

La Rocque and Goy released a joint statement outlining their plans to form local ententes oriented toward anti-communist action and the 'disarmament' of those propagating civil war.[74] *Le Flambeau* reported that the agreement established the principle of cooperation in the groups' relations, a course of action long recommended by La Rocque.[75] Cooperation between the UNC leadership and the PSF stretched as far as electoral agreements. In 1937, Goy ran for election in Falaise (Calvados). To facilitate Goy's election, the PSF agreed to withdraw its candidate and asked followers to vote for Goy. Endorsed by the PSF's executive committee and parliamentary group, La Rocque's party hailed this anti-communist inspired act of unity.[76]

Both leaders were keen to maintain their organisational independence and stressed that neither group would be subordinated to the other. Veterans still presented an attractive constituency to La Rocque.[77] Yet instances of co-opted membership did not always favour the colonel's party. In November 1936, after the PSF joined the Rassemblement, La Rocque sent a memo to all local officials denying rumours that he had advised members to join the UNC *en masse* after the dissolution of the league. Accusing traitors, provocateurs and police officers of spreading this rumour, he feared that the influx of ex-CF into the UNC would threaten the veteran association's existence, lest it be perceived as the league reconstituted.[78] It is likely that La Rocque was concerned too about the integrity of his own association.

Collaboration with La Rocque gave rise to familiar concerns from some UNC members. Members of the executive committee, including Goy, believed that the PSF was attempting to infiltrate the UNC. Maillard of the Manche and Desroches from the Finistère stated that this was the case in their departments. Maillard had been in conflict with the PSF in his department. In the Mortain by-election, he had proposed Goy as a candidate as a means of combating the PSF in the area.[79] *Le Flambeau* subsequently complained that the UNC and PSF were allies against communism and they should not therefore compete with each other.[80] Another executive member stated that he had encountered little trouble from any political party *except* the PSF. Some members blamed the public accord between Goy and La Rocque for this situation. Their provincial comrades were still confused about the relationship between the two groups with some believing that UNC and PSF members were now 'marching together'.[81] Goudaert claimed that links with the PSF were having a deleterious effect on the UNC. Radicals, socialists and members of the FOP and FNCR were now adversaries of the association.[82]

Doriot's PPF also endorsed the Rassemblement.[83] Founded in June 1936 by former communist Doriot, the PPF had moved sharply to the right by the end of the year. Doriot denounced parliament and looked to establish an authoritarian 'Popular French state'. For the UNC, the PPF was a 'national' group, ready to combat communism. *La Voix du combattant* publicised Doriot's support for the anti-communist Rassemblement in October 1936.[84] In 1937, the JUNC encouraged its members to liaise with the PSF and PPF within the structure of the alliance.[85] Was this the first instance of collaboration between Doriot and the UNC? Perhaps not. In April 1935, Grancoin, a communist in Saint-Denis, told a meeting that if Doriot was re-elected he could thank the UNC.[86] In the Côtes du Nord, UNC departmental president Rual advised members to read Doriot's *La France ne sera pas un pays d'esclaves*. After doing so, he claimed, they would no longer doubt that communist revolution was under way.[87] In January 1937, a provincial PPF newspaper attested to the 'unity of thought' between the UNC and Doriot's party. PPF members attended a local UNC meeting, at which they heard veteran Alexis Thomas denounce the Popular Front's 'communist dictatorship'.[88] The following month, Lebecq spoke at a PPF meeting in Paris.[89]

The UNC's cooperation with the extreme right proceeded. At Cholet (Maine-et-Loire) in August 1936, 25,000 attendees, including local UNC members, heard guest of honour Philippe Henriot vigorously attack communism.[90] The same month, Lebecq, Henriot and the Peasant Front held a meeting at Saint-Mars-la-Jaille (Loire-Inférieure).[91] In October 1936, Saut, president of the Béarn UNC section, presided over a meeting with Jean Ybarnégaray, Jean Chiappe, former JP president Clapier and La Rocque in attendance.[92] In December, the UNC's Jeunes de Somain urged members to group nationalists from the extreme right to the 'patriotic' left. Whether the head of the local group was an ex-member of the CF, the JP, the SF or the AF was of little import. Communism had to be confronted.[93] In January 1937, Colonel Bertin, president of the Angers UNC section, spoke at a meeting with delegates of Taittinger's Parti républicain national et social (PRNS).[94] The following month, under the auspices of the UNC's ninth Parisian section representatives of the AF, the PSF, the Ligue des Chefs de Sections, the PRNS and the Association Catholique des pères de famille met. Anti-communist diatribes tinged with anti-Semitism were delivered. Lebecq drew on the themes of the war culture in his speech as he called communism a 'barbarism' contrary to civilisation.[95] At the fourth JUNC general assembly in March 1937, Raudot announced the death of the vice-president of a provincial group and the injury of the president of the Ardennes section, both alleged victims of communist activists as they left a PSF meeting.[96]

Veterans in the wider movement watched the UNC's activity with unease. Leftist associations took direct action. Goudaert claimed that members of the FOP and the FNCR were attempting to destroy UNC sections. In these cases, left-wing veterans infiltrated UNC sections and subsequently instigated a leadership contest. Ensuring that their candidates were selected, the newly elected committee declared the section independent of the UNC. After a short time the section joined another veterans' association.[97] The UF continued to express concern at the UNC's contact with the extreme right. In July 1936, the relationship between the two great veterans' associations hit a new low. At this time, Pichot demanded that the UNC leave the Confédération. He argued that the UNC should declare itself a political association, a political league even, as its actions in the recent elections had shown this to be the case.[98] He repeated the accusation a month later despite Goy's response in defence of the UNC.[99] However, some UF veterans were sympathetic to the UNC. In one instance, a group of UF veterans (who were also members of the PSF) expressed a desire to defect to the rival veterans' association.[100]

Designed to coalesce all 'national' movements, the Rassemblement was not limited to political groups. In depicting communism as a threat to French spirituality, the UNC hoped to establish an ecumenical alliance against the left. The war culture had used religious language and themes to emphasise further the humanity (or inhumanity) of protagonists and thus help define the threat from Germany to both the nation and the West. Doubtless the threat to Christian civilisation from communism seemed real for the numerous Catholics in the leadership of the UNC. For more pragmatic members, religious rhetoric was an expedient medium in the anti-communist campaign. In January 1937, Goy, a man who according to Prost 'owed nothing to the Catholic tradition' presided over a conference entitled 'French civilisation: Bolshevik materialism against spirituality'. The meeting, convened in association with the Union patriotique des français israélites, united Catholics, Protestants and Jews to discuss Bolshevism's attack on spirituality. For men such as Goy, the appeal to a common spiritual identity facilitated the construction of a unifying moral and national interest for France. Speakers at the conference emphasised the anti-religious quality of communism. Pastor Wautier d'Aygallier claimed that there was an absolute opposition between Christianity and Bolshevism, which allied 'the barbarism of the Asian mind to the troubled soul of the Tartar'. Father Ferrand recalled the union of the trench fraternity in his appeal for a new battle against barbarism while Bloch of the AGMG compared the current battle against communism to the wartime campaign against Germany. The communist, as a godless barbarian, replaced the Boche in his opposition to French civilisation. The motion voted at the meeting called on France's 'great spiritual families' to combat the 'rising forces of this barbarism'.[101]

Ultimately, the UNC was disappointed with its members' response to the Rassemblement. In May, the executive committee decided that the initiative would become a 'campaign of ideas' rather than a political action. Maillard demanded that the UNC renounce all politics and concentrate solely on the veterans' material demands. He attributed the Rassemblement's failure to the division that it had caused among provincial groups.[102] For the activists in the UNC, this change of tactic amounted to a defeat. The reluctance and relative moderation of some UNC members had reined in the political ambitions of their activist counterparts. As in the past, the moderates and activists had come into conflict over the meaning and practice of the UNC's civic action. In this case, the moderates prevailed.

Confronting the Popular Front: Xenophobia and anti-Semitism

The failure of the Rassemblement did not temper the UNC's violent attacks on the Popular Front. Consistent with the association's depiction of the government as an anti-French coalition, its diatribes usually made reference to the influence of foreign elements. These attacks were in tune with a broader atmosphere of intolerance in France.[103] Given the country's declining birth-rate and high levels of unemployment after the onset of the Depression, scare stories abounded about the disappearance of the French race and the pollution of national blood by freeloading foreigners. Anxiety over foreign workers in French industry stretched back at least as far as the war, when Russians and Poles were singled out as foreign *embusqués*.[104] Such concerns were shared by workers and professionals alike and resulted in legislation restricting foreigners' freedom to work as the 1930s progressed.[105]

Though the increasing number of Jewish refugees from Germany hardly appeased racist sentiment, the anti-Semitic tradition stretched back to the earliest decades of the Third Republic. Since the 1880s, extreme right-wing groups, intellectuals and authors such as Edouard Drumont had denounced the deleterious presence of Jews. The flawed conviction of Jewish army captain Alfred Dreyfus deeply divided France.

Dreyfusards furiously criticised the establishment and the army's cover-up. Anti-Dreyfusards argued that nothing, least of all an inconvenient truth, should be allowed to compromise the standing of the army. Right-wing thinkers such as La Tour du Pin and Barrès denied Jews the right to be French. From the turn of the century, the AF and the Ligue des Patriotes regularly protested against the residence of Jews and foreigners in France.

During the 1920s, though tolerance characterised French attitudes to Jews following their service in the war, the AF and the Faisceau kept anti-Semitism alive. Jewish immigration during the 1930s exposed the limits of French tolerance. Nationalist leagues took up the crusade to save France from Jewish influence. Extreme right-wing personalities and newspapers enjoyed great success with little censure from contemporaries.[106] On the left, the CGT protested against the influx of German Jewish refugees and the effect this would have on the French job market. The victory of Blum, France's first Jewish prime minister in May 1936, reignited anti-Semitism as never before. Jews had long been associated with Marxism and the left in anti-Semitic propaganda, which alleged that Jews had founded communism and sought to bring the entire world under their authority.[107] Even Paul Faure of the socialist party complained that Jews wanted war with Hitler to protect their families in Germany.[108]

In some measure, the UNC's xenophobia stemmed from the economic crisis. Its polemics accused foreigners of taking French jobs while millions of Frenchmen, many of them veterans, remained unemployed. Activist Georges Heldet argued that the *poilus* had not fought for four years to lose their jobs to foreigners.[109] The association supported a bill to exclude foreign labour from public works. In 1936, when this bill was defeated, the newspaper printed the names of all 328 deputies who had voted against the proposal.[110]

Aside from economic concerns, the UNC was anxious about the threat that foreigners allegedly posed to the physical and metaphorical health of the French race. In August 1936, Berthau combined the fear of the invasion of the workplace with that of the body. He compared French reliance on foreign labour to a blood transfusion. Berthau demanded that undesirable immigrants be denied the right to naturalisation. 'Healthy' immigrants were fathers with families abroad or foreign women who married Frenchmen.[111] His exclusion of single men revealed a deeper concern that male immigrants should not have access to Frenchwomen. The UNC considered the foetus of a Frenchman and his foreign wife to be French while the foetus of a Frenchwoman and her foreign husband was not. The situation would be dire indeed if, in women, foreign foetuses developed in French wombs, while in men foreign cancers ate away French bodies. Limitations alone would preserve the national and ethnic substance of the French race.[112]

The UF's Pichot expressed concerns similar to those of the UNC. In February 1937, he wrote that the gradual decline in births would lead to 'national suicide'. Instead of 'collective cowardice' France needed men who would fulfil their first and most important duty: procreation. The Frenchman was in danger of becoming a 'rare object', especially when France was housing and feeding too many foreigners. The association's national congress in Aix-les-Bains that year passed a motion demanding the protection of the race and measures conducive to raising the birthrate.[113]

The UNC connected the deleterious effect of immigration and the declining birth-rate with the left and the Popular Front. It alleged that immigration was nurturing corruption and political agitation in seedy communist-controlled suburbs.[114] Employing the language of pathology to describe the threat from both foreigners and communism, the UNC attributed the poor health of the French to '[i]nnumerable microbes at work in the national and social body [of which the] most virulent have been imported from outside France'.[115] André Vital, writing in *L'UNC de Paris*, claimed that despite the fact that foreigners allegedly insulted French traditions and spat on the French flag, the government continued to allow the carriers of 'physically and morally morbid germs' to poison the French race. French hospitals, 'cluttered with the dregs of humanity', proved this 'fact'.[116] As for the birth-rate, the UNC linked the left's desire for equality in the workplace with a levelling of living standards between large families and single men and women, which the UNC judged unfair.[117] It offered the family as the only remedy to the communism in charge of France. Activists urged youth members to have children soon and thus banish the *métèques* from France.[118]

Anti-Semitism was not widespread in UNC publications. True enough, Aubert expressed surprise that six Jews were present in the Popular Front cabinet. Surely, he stated, this number was disproportionate when one considered the number of Jews in France.[119] In the provincial sections, expressions of anti-Semitism depended on individual members. The JUNC in Somain (Nord) denounced the Popular Front government as being in the pay of Jews.[120] Yet nowhere was anti-Semitism more common or more venomous than in the writings of Gérard de Cromières, UNC section president in the Limoges. In his group's newspaper, *Le*

Combattant du centre, de Cromières' monthly editorials relentlessly harangued Jews. His anti-Semitism was based on race. A Jew's physical appearance marked him out as a barbarian: 'Their oily skin, the shape of their nose and their jaws, their look, their odour, the profile of their shoulders, distinguish them as Barbarians.' Consequently, de Cromières rejected the notion of assimilation: whether M. Blum changed his name to M. Fleur, or M. Lévy became M. Lefèvre, he would remain a Jew.[121] According to de Cromières, communism was a tool of Jewish invasion. The communist takeover of France, embodied in the victory of the Popular Front, was a fine victory for the Jew.[122] De Cromières contended that the Popular Front 'government of Jews' was conspiring to bring about the destruction of France.[123] In this event, the men of the 'Jewish Front' in alliance with bolshevism would feed on the blood of Frenchmen.[124] In spite of the vile and ubiquitous racism of de Cromières, his was an isolated case. The UNC was not an anti-Semitic association.

'And they claim that we are still a republic!'

By February 1937, cracks in the Popular Front alliance had begun to appear. Able to satisfy neither the left nor the right in his attempts to shore up the French economy, Blum announced a pause in reform, much to the anger of the CGT. The following month, the government's refusal to ban a PSF meeting in the Parisian working-class district of Clichy led to violent clashes between police and counter-demonstrators. Fighting left five protesters dead and two hundred injured. The left condemned the PSF's 'provocation' and called for it to be banned. The CGT declared a half-day strike. On the right, the Popular Front came in for intense criticism not least because the socialist mayor, the communist deputy for Clichy and a communist councillor had sanctioned the counter-protest.[125]

For the UNC, the violence at Clichy was a harbinger of a coming revolution. Galland voiced his association's fear of the masses under the direction of Jouhaux while Aubert questioned whether freedom of expression in France still existed if one could not criticise the left without the fear of an officially licensed counter-demonstration. He concluded: 'To suppress all liberty, that's the characteristic of dictatorship. We are already there.'[126] In May 1937, Jean Redondin of the Limoges JUNC section expressed a similar concern that the government was now a dictatorship.[127] Redondin's counterpart in the Ille-et-Vilaine youth section, Lagrée, reminded his readers that in the face of oppression, insurrection was not only a right but also a duty.[128]

In the wake of the incident at Clichy, Doriot launched the Liberty Front, an alliance intended to coalesce nationalist forces. The UNC's executive committee considered joining the Front. At a meeting in May 1937, certain executive members reacted strongly against joining Doriot. De Pontalba declared himself hostile to both the Popular Front and the Liberty Front. Toutain, Isaac and Charron refused to allow the UNC to make the mistakes of the past in collaborating with political groups. The UNC did not join Doriot's alliance.[129] Some provincial members were more receptive to the PPF. In June 1937, the Antibes section of the UNC sent a telegram to Doriot. The signatories of the telegram included Dr Ulm, UNC vice-president and PPF member plus six other UNC veterans. They proposed a new National Front, which would fuse the UNC's Rassemblement and Doriot's Front. The telegram ended with a call for militant and perhaps violent action against the government: 'With the banner of Joan of Arc and Saint Denis forward march on Paris, to kick the foreign out of France …'[130]

In June, Blum resigned when the Senate, controlled by conservative radicals, refused his request for decree powers. Chautemps took over the premiership. His government extended the pause but did little else. With the government apparently immobile, disenchantment gripped the UF. In August Pichot condemned the 'total and absolute' impotence of governments since the end of the war. Though he did not question the social gains made under the Popular Front, his sweeping denunciation of the many political combinations that had governed since the war included the incumbent left-wing coalition. The Popular Front 'spoke' and 'thought' like the governments of the pre-war era. Pichot saw little hope for France in the current situation. Parliament and public were as blind as each other in searching for a solution to the economic crisis. The UF demanded a 'new economy' run by planners who possessed the economic expertise that politicians lacked.[131]

Meanwhile, the UNC's offensive against the government continued. The Cagoule plot, in which right-wing conspirators conspired to overthrow the regime, supplied further grist to the mill. In certain sections of the press the UNC stood accused of involvement in the planned coup. Among the more radical elements of the UNC's provincial press, the Cagoule affair aroused anger and racism. Published in the JUNC's *Entre Nous*, the article 'Le Cagoulard' left the reader in little doubt about the cagoulard's foreign origins: 'If one manages to tear back his hood, one would no doubt find the slanting eyes of the Asian, the hooked nose of the Ghetto-dweller, the thick lips of an untrustworthy foreigner and in his pockets money from every country … Bleurgh!'[132] De Cromières alleged that the 'vampires' of the Jewish Front had framed the veterans in question for the crime of terrorism.[133] The mainstream UNC, though certainly not racist in its reporting of the Cagoule affair, was no less alarmed. *La Voix du combattant* concluded: 'Well, this country is ripe for dictatorship … These are Bolshevik methods that have been installed in France … And they claim that we are still a republic!'[134] The JUNC condemned the harassment of veterans while the police turned a blind eye to communist arms dumps. The *jeunes* compared the current situation to that of living under a dictatorship: 'it is unacceptable that the accused should remain any longer in prison [for they] are ignorant of what they have been accused; or then let's admit straight away that it is as if we are in Russia or Germany, where citizens are only free to the extent that the government allows them to be.' This perceived injustice led the JUNC to question whether France was now a police state. If the government was prepared to arrest and imprison citizens arbitrarily then it would soon execute them without trial. Frenchmen, the JUNC claimed, were faced with a choice: react now or suffer revolution, dictatorship and war.[135]

As 1937 came to an end, the UNC believed that a communist dictatorship would likely be installed. To prevent this, it positioned itself as defender of the republic and suggested that armed insurrection in defence of individual liberties was not out of the question. How can this be reconciled with the association's past condemnation of the parliamentary regime? Firstly, the UNC's conception of the national interest was subjective. Embodied in its veterans, the national interest was based on conservative values and was, in the eyes of the UNC at least, thoroughly French. The Popular Front, a left-wing coalition under the influence of the 'foreign' communist doctrine, did not fulfil these requirements. It could not therefore represent the French national interest. Secondly, the UNC's conception of the republic was also subjective: a right-wing authoritarian regime with limited political pluralism under a military leader. In this sense alone the UNC was 'republican'. But its 'republican' regime would, it must be stressed, bear little resemblance to the Third Republic and especially the Popular Front administration. The UNC could therefore assume the position of moral defender of the 'republic'.

1938: the campaign for public safety

When Chautemps's government fell on 14 January 1938, first Georges Bonnet and then Blum attempted and failed to form a viable administration.

Consequently Chautemps formed a second ministry on 18 January 1938, which was widely recognised as a temporary measure.[136] Divisions in the Popular Front seemed permanent. The UNC remained hostile to the government and the UF was rapidly becoming disillusioned. Exasperated, Pichot claimed that what France needed was a government of fifteen 'good men' not thirty-six ministers.[137] Still, nothing at that point suggested that the associations' discontent would converge. After all, the UF had denounced the UNC's cooperation with political groups and it did not share its rival's violent anti-leftist sentiment.

In March 1938, when Germany annexed Austria, the international crisis brought the associations together as never before. In the late 1930s, France's position in relation to the fascist powers in Europe dominated the veterans' international concerns. Developments in Germany gave particular cause for anxiety. In February 1938, Hitler placed the armed forces under his supreme command. The appointment of Joachim von Ribbentrop to the Reich's foreign ministry promised a more radical direction in foreign affairs. Meanwhile, in eastern Europe, new Romanian leader and anti-Semite Octavian Goga threatened to undermine France's alliance system.[138]

Despite these worrying developments, the UF retained its faith in collective security. It had maintained this position throughout the 1920s and 1930s in tandem with the stipulation that France should remain strong enough militarily to defend itself.[139] As Hitler's efforts to undermine the 1918 peace settlement multiplied, a split occurred in the UF's foreign policy. Cassin supported a tough line against the fascist powers, a stance which, he claimed in 1962, saw him accused of warmongering by some of his UF comrades.[140] Pichot was more conciliatory to Germany.[141] In 1935, Hitler had reassured the UF president of his peaceful intentions towards France. Consequently, despite Hitler's dissolution of the German republican veterans' associations (which had been members of the CIAMAC) Pichot maintained the UF's relations with Nazi veterans through the France-Germany Committee. Established in 1935 with Pichot and Goy of the UNC as founding members, the Committee organised regular meetings between French and German ex-servicemen.[142] In 1938, Pichot continued to support rapprochement with Hitler. He blamed the Germanophobia of the French left and nationalist right for obstructing an accord between the two peoples, both of whom, Pichot claimed, desired peace.[143]

The UNC was traditionally more strident than its rival in emphasising the need for a largely unilateral and strong defence policy.[144] Throughout

1933 and 1934 Hitler's ostensibly peaceful declarations did not appear to have fooled the association.[145] Nevertheless, some UNC veterans sought to open a dialogue with Hitler. On 2 November 1934, Jean Goy met the German chancellor in Berlin. Otto Abetz had set up the conference, to which Pichot declined an invitation to attend. His meeting would take place the following month. The subsequent publication of the Goy interview, in which Hitler attempted to mollify French concerns, caused a sensation in France and the combatant world.[146] UNC veteran Louis Dejean reminded his comrades of Hitler's description of France in *Mein Kampf* as the pitiless, most infamous and mortal enemy of the German people.[147] But Goy's interview with Hitler spoke to a section of the UNC that desired rapprochement with the former enemy. The executive committee authorised relations with German veterans though it advised that caution remain paramount.[148] Aubert continued to denounce Germany's incessant infringements upon the peace treaty. One could not reason, he alleged, with a people who did not know how.[149]

Reservations aside, the UNC's cautious rapprochement proceeded. During 1937, *La Voix du combattant* featured a series of interviews on the subject of Franco-German relations with veteran and author Pierre Drieu La Rochelle, senator Henri-Haye and deputy Victor Bataille, all of whom endorsed closer cooperation with Germany.[150] In August, the JUNC leadership met with the heads of German youth organisations in Paris. Early the following year, twenty-five youth members visited Munich in response to an invitation from the Hitler Youth.[151] On returning from Germany in February 1938, Goy informed UNC readers that German re-armament was merely a reasonable response to the Franco-Soviet pact. The majority of Germans desired peace and the rearmament programme would end once the country had regained the ability to defend itself.[152]

Hitler's claim on ethnic Germans beyond his country's borders tested both associations' commitment to rapprochement. At the outset of 1938, the prospect of a unified Austrian-German state looked real. Mussolini had opposed Germany's previous attempt on Austria in 1934 but was unlikely to resist a second time; both countries had cooperated during the Spanish Civil War. True enough, Italy did not intervene when Germany annexed Austria. In February 1938, Austrian chancellor Kurt von Schuschnigg met Hitler at Berchtesgaden. Bullied and harassed by Hitler throughout the day, Schuschnigg felt constrained to agree to military and economic 'co-ordination' between Austria and Germany, or face invasion. Confronted with pro-Nazi demonstrations in several cities upon his return home, Schuschnigg announced a plebiscite for 13 March in an attempt to safeguard his nation's independence. A furious Hitler mobilised troops along the border. Schuschnigg agreed to abandon the plebiscite and promptly resigned. The new government under Nazi sympathiser Arthur Seyss-Inquart formally requested German troops cross the border, ostensibly to keep the peace. Shortly after, Hitler announced to a rapturous Viennese crowd that following the Anschluss, Austria was the newest bastion of greater Germany.

The Austrian crisis unfolded at an inopportune moment for France. Chautemps had resigned as prime minister two days prior to Hitler's ultimatum to Vienna. After much political wrangling Blum was able to form a government on 13 March but the damage had been done. France would not be able to arrest Germany's march into Austria. Worse still, few in France were under the illusion that Blum's government was anything other than a transitional administration.[153]

The international and domestic crises dismayed the veterans. Germany had annexed a sovereign state and committed its biggest violation of the Versailles treaty to date while a ministerial imbroglio had paralysed France. The UF and the UNC knew where to lay the blame. The fascist states were undoubtedly ruthless, the former admitted, but French errors and weakness had facilitated, if not encouraged, their advances. France, 'the mother of democracies', had capitulated to the dictators. Goy attacked France's 'disastrous' foreign policy from which the veterans had been excluded.[154]

A week after Blum formed his government, a meeting between Pichot and president of the republic Albert Lebrun revealed the depths of the UF leader's exasperation. Pichot urged Lebrun to appoint Marshal Pétain as head of government. According to Pichot, the Marshal was the only man who could unite the French. This idea had been mooted too in press and right-wing circles.[155] Aware of his constitutional obligations, Lebrun refused.[156] On 17 March, the day after Pichot's meeting with the president, the UF issued a motion to the president and the leaders of the Chamber and the Senate calling for a public safety government.[157] On 26 March, the UNC met at the Salle Wagram in Paris and endorsed the UF's campaign.[158] The veterans were not alone in their preference for a public safety government. Similar ideas were expressed on the left and the right.[159] Worrying commentaries accompanied the veterans' announcement. The UF's Paul Patou lamented that democracy had momentarily 'exhausted its virtue' and would need to 'take its medicine' if it was not to become defunct. If the parties refused to accept the truce outlined in the plan then they would find the country ranged against them.[160] JUNC leader Raudot refused to see an answer in parliamentary democracy. He argued that legality lay with the people of France; they alone, not the political parties, could save the country.[161]

The veterans' initiative took the form of a public pressure campaign. The plan relied upon the willingness of Lebrun to appoint a new government. The UNC circulated petitions of support for the veterans' plan, which would then be presented to the president of the republic. Outside direct action this was the only means available. The associations were not political parties and so could not effect change from within the Chamber. Their only course of action was extra-parliamentary. In any case, the UF and the UNC were well-practised as pressure groups and they had found this method successful in the past, notably during the second battle for pensions.

The public safety government would be a temporary measure.[162] It would implement the reforms necessary for France to recover and regain its former greatness. In March 1938, neither the UF nor the UNC predicted how long this process would take. As for parliament, the new administration would be allowed to operate without deputies' persistent obstructions. Pichot recommended that the parties 'suspend themselves' (*se mettre en vacances*) and that parliament do likewise.[163] Patou required that the parties be 'put on ice' (*mise en sommeil*).[164]

The UF and the UNC did not call for their presidents to become head of the new government. Neither Pichot nor Goy would be dictator of France. Around the leader would be a small team of 'honest' men. During a speech to the Fédération des mutilés et anciens combattants de Saone-et-Loire, at Chalon-sur-Saone on 20 March, Pichot condemned the 'democratic hesitations' and the 'demagogic depravity' of the preceding days. The new men of government would be those who had proved their worth in the combatants' movement and not the 'ministerial rabble' and 'harlequin gatherings' of governments past.[165] However, there was tension between Pichot's prescription for the new ruling team and the ideas of his colleagues in the UF leadership. When sketching out the composition of the future governing team, Patou favoured a distinctly political and leftist coloration: Blum, Daladier, Herriot and Reynaud. Pichot would join the team as the voice of the generation of fire.[166] This decidedly parliamentary team sat uncomfortably with Pichot's preference for Pétain and ministers drawn from beyond the parliamentary milieu. Given the UNC's hatred of the left and its distrust of the radicals, it is unlikely the association would have accepted Patou's proposal. The UNC excluded from its plan anyone who had participated in 'recent [political] battles'.[167] Goy preferred to give the government a more apolitical patina. If Pétain would not lead France, then the armed forces comprised many other capable leaders.[168]

Conclusion

According to the UF, the election of the Popular Front presented a unique opportunity. New men, including those ostensibly exterior to the political classes, had taken power. In spite of the association's traditional anti-parliamentarianism, the UF expressed confidence in the administration and its revitalisation of institutions. Pichot continued to express concern over the UNC's cooperation with the extreme right and the apparently political path that it had taken. The UF's enthusiasm for the Popular Front came to an end in mid-1937. Following the fall of Blum's government, the reform project seemed to have ground to a halt. Party politics and squabbling had resurfaced. Pichot complained that little had changed in parliament. His frustration peaked during the Austrian crisis of 1938. The French had failed to stop Hitler dictating his demands to Austria. The UF put this failure down to the weakness that beset the French regime. In March 1938, Pichot resolved to end this lamentable instability once and for all. France needed a strong government. The UF's plan for the public safety administration would provide this.

For the UNC, the election of the Popular Front had brought France to the brink of revolution. The coalition was a cover for the soviet infiltration of France, evidence of which lay in the replacement of French national symbols, the influx of foreigners and the destruction of the family. These beliefs, coupled with the hostility to the alleged bellicosity of the communists over Spain saw the culture of war revive in the UNC's campaign. The association's discourse at this time revealed an authoritarianism that pitted a single national interest, embodied in the veterans and the nationalist right, against the anti-national forces of the left. Though the UNC appeared to show concern for the republic, this concern rested on its own conception of the regime. As in the past, when the political content of the government moved to the left, the UNC alleged that the republic had been corrupted. After the violence at Clichy and the exposure of the Cagoule plot, the UNC went further in its accusations: it claimed that France was practically a dictatorship.

The UNC's solution was to preach a form of national reconciliation that entailed a union of forces deemed 'national' against those considered to be 'anti-national'. What end would this coalition serve? It was not an electoral coalition. Electoral involvement was anathema to the veterans. An anti-communist campaign of ideas remained an option, and this was in fact what the Rassemblement became. Though some in the association may have preferred militant and possibly violent action against the left, in alliance with the extreme right, the moderates in the UNC's leadership and provincial sections prevented the Rassemblement from becoming anything more than a propaganda campaign.

By 1938, the UF and the UNC's dissatisfaction with the Popular Front and the worsening international situation prompted them to resort to an authoritarian plan for French government. An exasperated UF finally lost patience with the ailing coalition. Though the domestic political impasse and the Anschluss worried the UNC, it needed little excuse to join a campaign for the restoration of governmental authority, especially at the expense of the left. Once again, the importance of immediate circumstance weighed upon the associations' decisions.

In finding common ground with the UF, the UNC did not move to the centre. Though elements of the associations' vision of the future government may have differed, the UF moved away from the centre and toward the right. The veterans' reform plan did not allow for the political pluralism familiar to the Third Republic. It espoused reformist themes familiar to the UNC's previous campaigns. Reform would not emanate from within parliament but though an extra-parliamentary coterie of veterans and national personalities. Though the UNC did not call for a constituent assembly, the public safety government would perform the same function. During the parliamentary hiatus, the government would draw up and implement the 'necessary' reforms while administering the country. Given the association's discourse during the 1930s, it is safe to assume that the UNC planned to exclude once and for all the radicals and the left from power. In launching the campaign, the UF, too, supported extra-parliamentary reform. It had done so before in 1934 when it perceived the parliamentary regime to have irremediably broken down following the February riot. The UF's conception of the new government was similar to the UNC's in so far as it envisaged a temporary reformist government of public figures and veterans, possibly under Pétain. Considering Pichot had believed democracy was full of life in January 1937, this represented a significant volte-face for the UF. As in 1934, the launch of the public safety campaign and the plans that accompanied it underscored the UF and the UNC's conditional support for the parliamentary republic and their tenuous attachment to its inherent democratic processes.

Notes

1 Tartakowsky, 'Stratégies de la rue', pp. 32 and 55.
2 Jackson, *The Popular Front*, pp. 1–17 and 96.
3 Jackson, *France: The Dark Years*, pp. 79–80; Kevin Passmore, 'Catholicism and nationalism: The Fédération républicaine, 1927–1939', in Kay Chadwick (ed.), *Catholicism, Politics and Society in Twentieth-Century France* (Liverpool: Liverpool University Press, 2000), p. 52.
4 Serge Berstein, 'Le Parti radical, enjeu des affrontements politiques, et les incertitudes d'Edouard Daladier', in René Rémond and Janine Bourdin (eds), *La France et les français, 1938 en 1939* (Paris: Presses de la Fondation Nationale des Sciences Politiques, 1978), p. 278.
5 'Au Pays', *JM* (6 December 1936).
6 'Le XVIII Congrès National de l'UNC fut une impcsante manifestation de force et d'union. 2e Assemblée plénière: Relations internationales: Relations avec la Russie', *VC* (26 June 1937).
7 'L'Affût', *VC* (4 July 1936); J. Goy, 'Sommes-nous encore en république?', *VC* (11 July 1936); P. Galland, 'Le Temps des Paradoxes: Révolutionnaires en peau de Scapin' and 'L'Affût', *VC* (12 September 1936).
8 'L'Affût', *VC* (6 June 1936).
9 H. Aubert, 'De mon observatoire: Le bâton pour faire se battre', *VC* (27 June 1936); P. Galland, 'L'épuration nécessaire', *VC* (4 July 1936). Galland expressed similar views a year previous in 'Les ligues, les fronts de l'Etat', *VC* (13 July 1935).
10 H. Pichot, 'La grande alerte', *NF (Paris)* (March 1936); C. Héline, 'Du problème d'aujourd'hui à celui de demain', *CUF* (20 May 1936); 'Emploi des forces morales de ce pays', *CUF* (10 June 1936); A. Belverge, 'La tâche urgente', *NF (Paris)* (June 1936); C. Héline, 'Oui, l'expérience est à faire', *CUF* (10 October 1937); L. Viala, 'Quelques rayons sur le proche avenir', *CUF* (10 January 1938); H. Pichot, 'Démocratie', *CUF* (20 January 1938).
11 H. Pichot, 'Austerlitz, Iéna. 1815–1843–1871. Février 1938'; R. Cassin, 'Nouveaux pas vers l'abîme', *CUF* (20 February 1938).
12 C. Héline, 'A quand leur tour!', *CUF* (10 March 1936).
13 'Homme UF 100%. Comment vas-tu voter?', *CUF* (20 March 1936).
14 'Pour une France vivante', *CUF* (20 April 1936).
15 Prost, *Les Anciens Combattants*, I, p. 188; H. Pichot, 'Les urnes ou le plan. Et après les urnes, le plan. Des idées neuves et des hommes neufs', *CUF* (10 January 1936); C. Héline, 'Emploi des forces morales de ce pays', *CUF* (10 June 1936); 'Le Comité fédéral de l'Union fédérale', *JM* (18 October 1936).
16 'L'UNC et les élections législatives', *VC* (7 March 1936).
17 P. Galland, 'La révolution spontanée', *VC* (13 June 1936); H. Aubert, 'Dépassement', *VC* (13 June 1936); P. Galland, 'L'épuration nécessaire', *VC* (4 July 1936).
18 Wardhaugh, *In Pursuit of the People*, pp. 231–2.

19 Jessica Wardhaugh, 'Fighting for the Unknown Soldier: The contested territory of the French nation, 1934–1938', *Modern and Contemporary France*, 15 (2007), 192–5; Philippe Burrin, 'Poings levés et bras tendus. La contagion des symboles au temps du Front populaire', *Vingtième Siècle*, 11 (1986), 5–20.

20 A. Partiot, 'La nécessité de l'action sociale', *VC* (11 January 1936).

21 Charles Ridel, *Les Embusqués* (Paris: A. Colin, 2007), pp. 45–6.

22 'La leçon de patriotisme', *VC* (22 August 1936).

23 G. Lebecq, 'A propos d'une manifestation déplacée', *VC* (2 December 1933).

24 'Un monument profané', *VC* (23 June 1934).

25 'Au Peuple Français!', *VC* (4 July 1936).

26 H. Aubert, 'Pourquoi les Français pavoisent', *VC* (4 July 1936).

27 'Pour protester contre le drapeau rouge: Un meeting à Nîmes organisé par l'UNC', *VC* (11 July 1936); J. Goy, 'Sommes-nous encore en république ?', *VC* (11 July 1936).

28 'Le Rassemblement français: Le triomphal meeting de la Drôme. Après la réunion', *VC* (12 September 1936).

29 UNC/EC, 28 May 1936.

30 'Au Meeting de Wagram organisé par l'UNC, le rassemblement des Français est réclamé par tous', *VC* (25 July 1936).

31 'L'Union Nationale des Combattants opère le Rassemblement français', *VC* (24 October 1936).

32 J. Goy, 'Le Rassemblement français est en marche', *VC* (1 August 1936); H. Aubert, 'Les yeux qui s'ouvrent', *VC* (31 July 1937).

33 'Vie du groupe: Saint-Malo', *Le Combattant d'Ille-et-Vilaine* (February 1937).

34 'Une grande manifestation d'union. Le 16e Congrès Départemental du Groupe Poitevin à Lussac les Chateaux', *VC* (10 October 1936).

35 'Pour la renaissance française', *VC* (21 November 1936).

36 'Dans l'Action', *VC* (19 December 1936).

37 'Réunion des Présidents de Section du 13 décembre 1936', *Le Créneau* (January–February 1937).

38 A. Soubiran, 'Réunion des Présidents du Groupe', *L'Ancien Combattant du Berry* (November 1936).

39 'Dans l'Action: Le XVII Congrès du groupe départemental Maine-et-Loire à Angers, 7 mars 1937', *VC* (6 December 1936); 'Assemblée générale du groupe d'Ille-et-Vilaine à Rennes, 20 décembre 1936', *VC* (26 December 1936); 'Congrès départemental du groupe de la Sarthe à Vibraye, 6 décembre 1937' and a report from a meeting of 2500 veterans in Nancy, *VC* (2 January 1937); 'L'Ardèche donne son adhésion au Rassemblement français', *VC* (9 January 1937); 'Chronique de l'UNC du Limousin: Section de Limoges, Réunion des Présidents de Section', *Le Combattant du centre* (September 1936).

40 'Congrès départemental du groupe de la Sarthe à Vibraye, 6 décembre 1937', *VC* (2 January 1937).

41 F. D'Hennezel, 'France d'abord! De Saint-Quentin à Metz', *VC* (16 June 1934).

42 'La vie des Sections de Jeunes', *VC* (9 March 1935).

43 'Documentation: Bien les connaître pour mieux les combattre', *VC* (26 September 1936); M. Arnault, 'Le communisme nous aurons sa peau', *VC* (5 December 1936). 'Les Jeunes et l'Action de l'UNC', *L'UNC de Normandie* (December 1936).

44 'Le Rassemblement français: Le triomphal meeting de la Drôme', *VC* (12 September 1936). Compare this to the tactics of the Croix de Feu as described in Passmore, *From Liberalism to Fascism*, p. 232 and Tartakowsky, 'Stratégies de la rue', 40.

45 'Réunion des Présidents de Section du 7 novembre 1936', *L'Ancien Combattant du Berry* (December 1936).

46 A. Soubiran, 'Réunion des Présidents du Groupe', *L'Ancien Combattant du Berry* (November 1936).

47 AN, F7/13039, 'Le Préfet de l'Orne à Monsieur le Minsitre de l'Intérieur', 27 November 1936.

48 UNC/EC, 29 February 1936.

49 UNC/EC, 28 May 1936.

50 Eugen Weber, *Action française: Royalism and Reaction in Twentieth-Century France* (Stanford, CA: Stanford University Press, 1962), p. 285, note.

51 Jackson, *The Popular Front*, p. 258.

52 H. Aubert, 'Oui ou non, veut-on la paix ?', *VC* (15 August 1936).

53 P. Galland, 'Neutralité … Neutralité', *VC* (22 August 1936); H. Roure, 'La comédie de la neutralité'; R. Angot, 'Pour la paix … pour la neutralité; P. Galland, 'Silence aux embusqués !', *VC* (29 August 1936).

54 L. Viala, 'Y a-t-il complot contre la paix?' *NF (Paris-Nord)* (August–September 1936).

55 H. Roure, 'La comédie de la neutralité', *VC* (29 August 1936).

56 A. Albaret, 'L'Espagne ruinée: Ruines matérielles et ruines spirituelles', *VC* (6 February 1937).

57 A. Goudaert, 'Français, Restez Français !', *VC* (11 November 1936).

58 H. Roure, 'La comédie de la neutralité', *VC* (29 August 1936).

59 A. Albaret, 'L'Espagne ruinée: Ruines matérielles et ruines spirituelles', *VC* (6 February 1937).

60 'Réunion des Présidents de Sections', *Le Combattant du centre* (September 1936).

61 D. Desroches, 'La Patrie en Danger !', *Le Cri du poilu* (1 October 1936).

62 'Comment s'est fait le Rassemblement', *VC* (31 October 1936).

63 J. Goy, 'Sommes-nous encore en république?', *VC* (11 July 1936).

64 'Comment s'est fait le Rassemblement', *VC* (31 October 1936).

65 H. Isaac, 'Ni communisme, ni fascisme', *VC* (10 October 1936).

66 J. Goy, 'Le Front populaire vient de commettre sa première escroquerie!', *VC* (3 October 1936) (capitals in original).

67 G. De Cromières, 'Pays d'esclaves', *Le Combattant du centre* (October 1936).

68 AN, F7/12966, 'Réunion dite de "Rassemblement français" organisée par les groupements nationaux du IXe arrondissement, Salle du Petit Journal, 21 rue Cadet, le 25 février', 26 February 1937.

69 G. Merchiez, 'Vers la … Cassure', *VC* (10 October 1936).

70 M. Arnault, 'Le communisme, nous aurons sa peau', *VC* (5 December 1936).

71 'L'Union Nationale des Combattants opéra le Rassemblement français', *VC* (24 October 1936).

72 The following groups expressed their support for the UNC's Rassemblement: the Parti nationale, the PSF, the FR, the Parti démocrate populaire, the Parti populaire, the Parti socialiste de France, the Groupement des radicaux indépendants, the Parti républicain radical et radical-socialiste, the AGMG Paris, the Association des officiers combattants, Taittinger's Parti républicain national et social, the Ligue des patriotes and the Comité d'entente des grandes Associations pour l'Essor national. The following newspapers also expressed their support: *République*, *Le Jour*, *L'Ami du peuple*, *L'Echo de Paris*, *Le Petit Parisien*, *Le Temps*, *Action Française*, *L'Intransigeant*, *Le Matin*, *Le Figaro*, *Le Journal*, *Paris-Soir*, *Ere Nouvelle* and *Débats*. This list was published in *L'Action combattante (Bures-sur-Yvette, Gometz-le-Châtel et Gometz-la-Ville)* (January 1937).

73 Kennedy, *Reconciling France*, p. 11.

74 AN, AP 451/121, 'Coopération', undated.

75 'Entre d'autres: L'adhésion du Parti Social Français', *VC* (31 October 1936).

76 *Le Flambeau*, 17 April 1937; 'Précisions', *VC* (24 April 1937).

77 Kennedy, *Reconciling France*, p. 130.

78 AN, AP 451/108, circular from La Rocque to local presidents, 3 November 1936.

79 AN, AP 317/72, Guiter to Marin, 29 January 1937.

80 'Le PSF devant les électeurs: L'élection de Mortain', *Le Flambeau* (10 April 1937).

81 UNC/EC, 16 January 1937.

82 UNC/EC, 5 February 1938.

83 AN, F7/12966, 'Réunion dite de "Rassemblement français" organisée par les groupements nationaux du IXe arrondissement, Salle du Petit Journal, 21 rue Cadet, le 25 février', 26 February 1937; 'Assemblée générale du 31 Janvier 1937: Compte rendu de la séance', *Le Combattant des Côtes-du-Nord* (February 1937).

84 'L'Union Nationale des Combattants opéra le Rassemblement français', *VC*

(24 October 1936).

85 'IV Assemblée Générale des JUNC, 14 mars 1937', *VC* (20 March 1937).

86 AN, F7/13320, 'Meeting organisé par le Parti Communiste, Cinéma Ivry Palace rue de Paris à Ivry', April 1935.

87 Rual, 'Soyons unis …', *Combattant des Côtes-du-Nord* (September 1936).

88 E. Beauquter, 'Les idées de l'Union Nationale des Combattants. Des vérités qui sont en marche', *Libérateur du Sud-Ouest* (14 January 1937).

89 Soucy, *The Second Wave*, p. 230.

90 CAC, 19 940500/237, meeting report in 'Le Rassemblement National de Cholet', *Le Jour*, 3 August 1936.

91 Philippet, *Le Temps des Ligues*, I, p. 633.

92 CAC, 19 940500/237, 'Le péfet des Basses-Pyrénées à Monsieur le Ministre de l'Intérieur', 26 October 1936.

93 Gydé, 'Rassemblement de toutes les bonnes volontés!', *Entre nous* (December 1936).

94 CAC, 19 940500/237, 'Le préfet du département de la Vienne à Monsieur le Ministre de l'Intérieur', 9 January 1937.

95 AN, F7/12966, 'Réunion dite de "Rassemblement français" organisée par les groupements nationaux du IXe arrondissement, Salle du Petit Journal, 21 rue Cadet, le 25 février', 26 February 1937.

96 'IV Assemblée Générale des JUNC, 14 mars 1937', *VC* (20 March 1937); AN, F7/13208, 'Le Commissaire Divisionnaire, chef de la 12 Brigade Régionale à Reims à Monsieur le contrôleur général des services de police à Paris', 28 February 1937.

97 UNC/EC, 5 February 1938.

98 H. Pichot, 'Etre ce qu'on est … L'UNC doit quitter la Confédération', *CUF* (20 July 1936).

99 'Etre ce qu'on est et dire ce qu'on veut. UNC et mouvement combattant. La réponse de Jean Goy', *CUF* (15 August 1936).

100 UNC/EC, 16 January 1937.

101 'La civilisation française en péril: Le matérialisme bolchevique contre la spiritualité', *VC* (30 January 1937).

102 UNC/EC, 23 October 1937.

103 On xenophobia and anti-Semitism in France at this time see Winock, *Nationalisme, antisémitisme et fascisme en France*, pp. 79–195, especially pp. 115–41 on Edouard Drumont, author of *La France juive*.

104 Ridel, *Les Embusqués*, p. 176.

105 Recent research on immigration and legislation concerning foreign residents includes Vicki Caron, *Uneasy Asylum: France and the Jewish Refugee Crisis, 1933–1942* (Stanford, CA: Stanford University Press, 1999); Mary Dewhurst Lewis, *The Boundaries of the Republic: Migrant Rights and the Limits of Universalism in France, 1918–1940* (Stanford, CA: Stanford University Press, 2007); Daniel A. Gordon, 'The back door of the nation state:

Expulsions of foreigners and continuity in twentieth-century France', *Past and Present*, 186 (2005), 201–33; Paul Lawrence, 'Un flot d'agitateurs politiques, de fauteurs de désordre et de criminels': Adverse perceptions of immigrants in France between the wars', *French History*, 14 (2000), 201–22; Gérard Noiriel, *The French Melting Pot* (Minneapolis: University of Minnesota Press, 1996).

106 Gérard Noiriel, *Les Origines républicaines de Vichy* (Paris: Hachette littératures, 1999), explores the roots of Vichy's racial legislation in the era of the Third Republic.

107 J.- J. Becker & S. Berstein, *Histoire de l'anticommunisme. Tome 1: 1917–1940* (Paris: O. Orban, 1987), p. 307.

108 Kalman, *The Extreme Right*, p. 199.

109 G. Heldet, 'Les étrangers chez nous', *VC* (25 August 1934).

110 G. Berthau, 'On aura tout vu: Comme "ILS" défendent les ouvriers de France', *VC* (1 August 1936).

111 G. Berthau, 'Naturaliser, oui, mais qui?', *VC* (22 August 1936).

112 H. Laferrière, 'Le Sang Français', *VC* (31 July 1937); 'Voix de nos groupes: Un Appel des Jeunes de la Marne', *VC* (11 February 1939).

113 H. Pichot, 'Pour que vive la France, il faut d'abord qu'il y ait des Français', *CUF* (20 February 1937); 'XXIe Congrès de l'UF: Aix-les-Bains, 15–19 mai 1937. Motions adoptées: France saine, musclée et nombreuse', *CUF* (15–19 May 1937).

114 A. Loez, 'L'invasion étrangère', *VC* (11 September 1937).

115 P. Galland, '"National" et "International"', *VC* (22 January 1938).

116 A. Vital, 'Métèques', *L'UNC de Paris* (January 1938).

117 Langlois, 'Allocations familiales', *VC* (26 June 1937).

118 A. Loez, 'Politique nataliste ou politique familiale', *VC* (29 August 1936); Le Dur-Caillou, 'Un ancien parle aux Jeunes', *VC* (18 December 1937).

119 H. Aubert, 'Dedans et Dehors', *VC* (19 March 1938).

120 'La juiverie internationale déclare …', *Entre nous* (May 1937).

121 G. de Cromières, 'On va voler nos noms', *Le Combattant du centre* (December 1937). De Cromières's anti-Semitism was typical of the time. See Pierre Birnbaum, *Anti-Semitism in France: A Political History from Léon Blum to the Present* (Oxford: Blackwell, 1992).

122 G. de Cromières, 'La France juive', *Le Combattant du centre* (September 1938).

123 G. de Cromières, 'Le vrai complot', *Le Combattant du centre* (April 1938).

124 G. de Cromières, 'Et la France !', *Le Combattant du centre* (July 1938).

125 Kennedy, *Reconciling France*, pp. 128–9.

126 H. Aubert, 'Le Deuil de la Liberté', *VC* (27 March 1937); P. Galland, 'La dictature de l'anonymat', *VC* (8 May 1937).

127 J. Redondin, 'Réflexions d'un Jeune', *Le Combattant du centre* (May 1937).

128 J. Lagrée, 'Liberté', *Le Combattant d'Ille-et-Vilaine* (15 April 1937).

129 UNC/EC, 8 May 1937.
130 CAC, 19 940500/229, 'A Doriot Député Maire, Saint-Denis-sur-Seine', 20 June 1937.
131 H. Pichot, 'Lettre aux responsables', *CUF* (August-September 1937).
132 'Le Cagoulard', *Entre nous* (April 1938).
133 G. de Cromières, 'Et la France !', *Le Combattant du centre* (July 1938).
134 'La dictature de la CGT', *VC* (18 December 1937).
135 'La justice et la liberté: Mauvais exemple', *VC* (25 December 1937).
136 Jackson, *The Popular Front*, p. 244.
137 H. Pichot, 'Salut Public', *NF (Paris-Nord)* (February 1938).
138 R. Cassin, 'Concentrations et réservations', *CUF* (10 February 1938).
139 'Le Comité Fédéral de l'Union fédérale s'est réuni, à Paris, le 9 janvier 1938', *CUF* (20 January 1938); Fagerberg, *The 'Anciens Combattants' and French Foreign Policy*, p. 71.
140 *Ibid.*, p. 160.
141 See for example H. Pichot, 'Un peuple à la recherche de lui-même', *CUF* (1 June 1933).
142 Fagerberg, *The 'Anciens Combattants' and French Foreign Policy*, p. 161.
143 H. Pichot, '1938. Paix franco-allemande', *CUF* (10 January 1938).
144 Fagerberg, *The 'Anciens Combattants' and French Foreign Policy*, p. 73.
145 P. Galland, 'Où sont les pacifiques?', *VC* (8 April 1933); W. d'Ormesson, 'Grandes manoeuvres ou Congrès?', *VC* (15 September 1934).
146 'France-Allemagne: Un interview de Hitler avec Jean Goy', *VC* (24 November 1934); 'L'incident entre M. Jean Goy et M. Franklin-Bouillon ne donnera pas lieu à rencontre', *Le Matin* (28 November 1934).
147 L. Dejean, 'La propaganda allemande', *VC* (24 November 1934).
148 UNC/EC, 22 December 1934.
149 H. Aubert, 'Nous ne pouvons pas nous comprendre', *VC* (23 March 1935).
150 'Le rapprochement Franco-Allemand, interview de M. Drieu-La Rochelle', *VC* (3 April 1937); 'Le rapprochement Franco-Allemand, interview de Henri-Haye, Sénateur de Seine-et-Oise, Maire de Versailles', *VC* (1 May 1937); 'Le rapprochement Franco-Allemand, interview de Victor Bataille', *VC* (15 May 1937).
151 'Les chefs des organisations allemandes de la Jeunesse en visite à Paris sont reçues par les Jeunes de l'UNC, 25–27 août 1937', *VC* (4 September 1937); J. Maire, 'Impressions de voyage: La Jeunesse hitlérienne et le rapprochement Franco-allemand', *VC* (22 January 1938).
152 C. Inargues, 'Retour d'Allemagne: Jean Goy nous dit … ', *VC* (19 February 1938).
153 W. d'Ormesson, 'Non-sens', *Le Figaro* (14 March 1938); L.-A. Pagès, 'Un gouvernement de transition', *L'Ouest-Eclair* (15 March 1938); 'Le cabinet Blum devant la Chambre', *L'Intransigeant* (18 March 1938).
154 H. Pichot, 'Toute force française est dans l'union', *CUF* (20 March 1938); L.

Viala, 'Pronostics', *CUF* (20 March 1938); Y. Fouéré, 'La fin des traités', *CUF* (20 May 1938); R. Cassin, 'Pour sauver la liberté', *CUF* (10 March 1938); 'Jean Goy remet sollenellement le drapeau à sa section', *VC* (26 March 1938).

155 'Le Cabinet Léon Blum devant les Chambres'; Saint-Pourçain, 'De plus en plus, on parle du ministère d'union', *L'Intransigeant* (18 March 1938).

156 Cointet, *La Légion française des combattants*, p. 22.

157 H. Pichot, 'Salut Public: La nation est une et solidaire', *CUF* (10 March 1938). 'Pour le salut de la nation', *CUF* (20 March 1938).

158 'A l'appel de l'UNC, plus de 10,000 anciens combattants réclament un ministère de salut public et la non-intervention dans les affaires de l'Espagne, Salle Wagram, 26 mars 1938', *VC* (2 April 1938).

159 'Journée de tractations entre M. Léon Blum et les radicaux-socialistes', *L'Ouest-Eclair* (12 March 1938); P. Simon, 'Salut Public', *L'Ouest-Eclair* (13 March 1938); 'La CGT insiste pour la formation d'un gouvernement de salut public autour du Rassemblement populaire', *L'Ouest-Eclair* (13 March 1938); 'Un manifeste du parti démocrate populaire en faveur d'un gouvernement de salut public', *L'Ouest-Eclair* (13 March 1938); W. d'Ormesson, 'Non-sens', *Le Figaro* (14 March 1938); J. Fabry, 'Gouvernement de "salut public"', *L'Intransigeant* (19 March 1938); 'La Confédération nationale des anciens combattants demande l'institution d'un gouvernement de salut national', *Le Matin* (23 March 1938).

160 P. Patou., 'Le noyau d'une solide équipe', *CUF* (10 April 1938); H. Pichot, 'Salut Public. Combattants au gouvernement', *CUF* (20 April 1938).

161 J. Raudot, 'Gargarisme à l'usage du Français moyen', *VC* (26 March 1938).

162 H. Pichot, 'Combattants au gouvernement?', *NF* (May 1938).

163 H. Pichot, 'Salut Public. Combattants au gouvernement', *CUF* (20 April 1938).

164 P. Patou, 'Le noyau d'une solide équipe', *CUF* (10 April 1938).

165 L. Viala, 'Lettre ouverte au chef de gouvernement … de demain', *NF* (April 1938); 'De l'union en paroles au salut national', *CUF* (20 March 1938); H. Pichot, 'Salut Public. Combattants au gouvernement', *CUF* (20 April 1938); 'Les anciens combattants et la situation politique', *Le Figaro* (21 March 1938); 'Le dimanche politique: Appels à l'union', *La Croix* (22 March 1938).

166 P. Patou, 'Le noyau d'une solide équipe', *CUF* (10 April 1938).

167 'Les anciens combattants et la situation politique', *Le Figaro* (21 March 1934).

168 'Réunis à la Salle Wagram les anciens combattants réclament un gouvernement de salut public', *Le Figaro* (27 March 1938).

Conclusion

Toward Vichy

On 10 April 1938, radical deputy Edouard Daladier became prime minister. He would remain in the post until 20 March 1940 and thus led France into the Second World War. Daladier's government, like its predecessors, was formed under the Popular Front banner despite dissent within the coalition. The growing influence of the right wing of the radical party had ensured an ever more precarious existence for the alliance even before Daladier took up the premiership. By 1938, conservative radicals were pushing for the party to abandon the coalition and defend their middle-class supporters.[1] It initially appeared that the government would leave intact the Popular Front's legislation. Daladier dispelled these illusions on 21 August 1938 when he announced that France would be put back to work. His tenure as premier allayed the fears of conservatives who since June 1936 had lived in terror at the prospect of revolution. The support of provincial radical federations and committees for Daladier's increasingly conservative policy further strengthened the right of the party.[2] As the government's policy moved progressively rightward, the Popular Front cracked.

Daladier's style grew increasingly authoritarian. The premier's reliance on decree powers allowed him to dispense with the particulars of parliamentary government. In July 1939, he postponed the session until 1942. The abdication of parliament was complete.[3] Few publicly opposed Daladier's restoration of authority to government. Soon after the failed general strike the conservative press rallied to the prime minister, as did the centrist AD. The radical party's conservatism had advanced far enough to place it in competition for the same middle-class electoral constituency as La Rocque's PSF. On the left, with war looming, the socialists were factionalised between Blum's policy of anti-fascist resistance and pacifists around Paul Faure.[4]

The veterans' public safety campaign continued throughout spring and summer 1938. Cooperation between the provincial sections of both groups got under way though old suspicions remained. Some UNC veterans were guarded about the alliance with the UF. Executive members were hesitant about their rival's sudden change of heart. Accepting that Pichot seemed to be moving closer to the UNC's position, they were unsure whether the UF president truly spoke for his association or solely for himself, particularly after an unnamed section of the UF had attacked the UNC as a subversive organisation. Goudaert complained further that in the Nord he had made every effort to cooperate with the UF without success. Moreover, certain UF members had attempted to entice UNC veterans away from their sections.[5]

The Czech crisis in September 1938 provided the backdrop to an intensification of the public safety campaign. Czechoslovakia had been an ally of France since 1925. During the summer and autumn of 1938 the French and British governments both pressed the Czechs to concede to Hitler's demands for the incorporation of the ethnically German Sudetenland into the Third Reich. Matters reached a head in September 1938. On 10 September, the Soviet Union promised to protect Czechoslovakia if France upheld its commitment to the 1925 treaty with the Czechs. When Hitler further added to his list of wishes, France declared a partial mobilisation on 24 September. The Soviet government signalled its readiness for war the following day. As the threat of conflict loomed, the appeasement campaign in France intensified. Under pressure to avoid a conflict, Daladier agreed to Germany's demands at the international meeting at Munich. On 2 October the Chamber approved the Munich agreement. Only the communists, a lone socialist and Henri de Kérillis opposed. Communist opposition to the agreement sounded the death knell of the Popular Front. On 12 October the radicals declared the alliance over.

The veterans' movement was divided on Munich. Unsurprisingly, the diversity of groups made a unified response impossible. The FNCR and the ARAC opposed the capitulation to Germany. The Confédération's reaction was cautious. It did not identify with Daladier's policy as wholeheartedly as the UF and the UNC.[6] The UF approved of the Munich agreement for it had avoided a more general war.[7] Yet it was unlikely that the UF would condemn the agreement. After all, Pichot and Randoux (with the endorsement of the UNC and the SDC) had accompanied the French delegation to Germany. The UNC's Galland regretted the difficult choice that faced the Czechs but he advised them to make the necessary concessions.[8] Following the conference, Galland unabashedly hailed Munich a victory.[9] Even within the two largest associations some expressed reservations. Cassin did not share Pichot's optimism. He bemoaned the successive failures of Britain and France as well as of the League of Nations, which had culminated in the 'diplomatic Sedan' at Munich. He recommended that France begin to rearm in earnest, to 'over arm' even.[10]

In spite of the UF and the UNC's relief that war had been averted, Munich gave the associations a start. Having come close to a general European war, French unity was a higher priority than ever. Consequently, in October 1938, the UF and the UNC renewed their plea for a public safety government.[11] The second call cited parliament's 'state of resignation' and the need for 'exceptional measures' to save the country. The government's use of decree powers had not been sufficient and Aubert noted that politicians had returned to their usual 'vomiting'.[12] Parliament had granted special powers to Daladier for forty-five days but Pichot was aghast: this would not be long enough. These powers were needed for one year at least and preferably until the elections in 1940. During the parliamentary hiatus, the government should formulate plans for institutional reform.[13]

There were new implications to what the veterans now demanded. The plan of March 1938 had called for the suspension of the parties. In October, though this idea was repeated, it was accompanied with a new belligerence from sections of both associations. Pichot insisted that if parliament refused to submit to the new government it should be dissolved, at which point the veterans would 'throw themselves into the fight'. He threatened that if it came to this, the majority of parliamentarians would see their political careers terminated.[14] Once elections were again held, Pichot claimed he would lead the veterans into the electoral battle in order to effect the 'cleaning'.[15] JUNC president Raudot stated that all parties should disband and, if they refused, the government should forcibly dissolve them. During the period of reform, parties should not be allowed to operate. The government would 'adopt parliamentary methods, without parliament', 'liberated' from the encumbrance of elections.[16]

Neither the UF nor the UNC now mentioned Pétain. Instead, both associations suggested Daladier as head of the public safety government.[17] Since Daladier's arrival in power, his extensive use of decree powers had progressively sidelined parliament. Rule by decree had become the principal recourse of government. After November 1938, with the communists in opposition and the socialists no longer in government, the discrepancy between the electoral majority and the government was glaring.[18] Nonetheless, Daladier was popular with the French public. The veterans' associations may be taken as a measure of this popularity. According to the UNC, Daladier was once again worthy of the veteran title, his involvement in the 'murderers' government' of February 1934 apparently forgotten.[19] However, their endorsement of the premier rested to some extent on his willingness to implement the veterans' plan. As for the public safety government's ministers, they would be a group of honest and sincere republicans, without 'labels' and as such presumably not from political parties.[20]

The public safety government would not be a permanent dictatorship. Its work done, the government would abdicate. However, the resultant regime would be quite different to the parliamentary Third Republic. Indeed, Pichot admitted that the 'republic' of 1938 was not the one for which the veterans had fought.[21] Although the UF and the UNC had different ideas about the regime that would emerge, it is likely that an authoritarian government would be formed. Both associations were, after all, united in demanding authority, order and discipline. The veterans would make the regime more 'efficient' but only according to their own definition of efficient government: an authoritarian government that would restore and maintain 'order' and prioritise the public role of the veterans at the expense of the parties and parliament.

Besides the veterans' campaign of spring 1934, the UF had maintained faith in parliament's ability to reform and improve the quality and function of republican institutions. Upon the election of the Popular Front it had expressed optimism in the future of government. On the other hand, the UNC had always favoured extra-parliamentary reform. From March 1938 both associations once again became close. Yet the UNC tempered neither its anti-parliamentary discourse nor its extra-parliamentary and authoritarian reform programme. It was the UF that moved closer to the position of its right-wing rival. The public safety campaign therefore reveals more about the veterans' associations in 1938 than simply their authoritarian ambitions. It is worth examining the UF's shift rightward within the context of the radicals' turn to conservatism. Prost's investigation of the sociology of the combatant movement's leaders found that the socio-economic profile of the UF's leadership accounted for its radical sympathies.[22] As for the UF's membership, while it is impossible to generalise about the political loyalties of nearly a million veterans, the association did not hide its radical preference, which influenced its discourse and policies throughout the inter-war years. It is difficult to assess whether the UF's conservative turn instigated the radicals' move to the right. Radical policies did not depend solely on UF veterans and were subject to all the influences that weighed on a political party at that time. It is true, though, that voices on the left and the right of the radical party appealed for the formation of a public safety government following the Anschluss.[23] These calls coincided with the launch of the veterans' campaign. However, one should bear in mind that in 1936 the UF had publicly supported the Popular Front whereas right-wing radicals, who so came to dominate the party, had long held misgivings.

It is possible that the UF simply reflected the radicals' growing conservatism. Yet given the association's proximity to the party and the radical preferences of many of its leaders and members, it is plausible that the UF's conservative turn reinforced that of the radicals. It was the conservatism of provincial radical federations and committees that shored up the party's conservative transformation and Daladier's authoritarian policy.[24] The UF was a federation of influential veterans' associations. This structure gave the association a strong provincial presence and there is evidence that provincial UF veterans were moving closer to the right. In May 1938, president of the UNC's Corrèze group Lacoste informed his colleagues that, in his area at least, the vast majority of UF 'troops' were '100 per cent UNC'.[25] Furthermore, though the UNC had initially been unsure of the UF's politics, by February 1939 its suspicions had eased. In fact, UNC executive members noted that Pichot's association had consulted the UNC on everything since the public safety campaign. Isaac perceived little divergence between the two groups' doctrines.[26] Goy, too, was sure of the support of the UF's provincial associations, while Berthier noted that the UF had come closer to the UNC rather than the reverse.[27] The two largest veterans' associations were now to be found on the right.

Taking into account the growing authoritarianism of the Daladier government, historians often characterise the final radical administration of the inter-war years as a prelude to the Vichy regime. On issues such as immigration and family policy the continuities between the late Third Republic and the Vichy state are evident. Though it may seem that from March 1938 republican institutions were revitalised, with the government finally able to act decisively and with authority, Daladier's disregard for parliament seemed to prefigure Vichy's authoritarian rule. The UF and the UNC's politics during 1938 and 1939 were in line with the climate of growing authoritarianism. If we are to consider the veterans' associations, with their large and diverse memberships, as barometers of public opinion then the movement's rightward shift points to a similar shift in French society and politics.

Becoming the Marshal's men

The Anschluss and the Munich agreement forced the UF and the UNC to confront a harsh reality: Hitler's territorial ambitions would be an insurmountable obstacle to Franco-German rapprochement. This did not undermine completely the confidence of men such as Pichot and Goy, who continued to meet with German veterans in the France-Germany Committee. In 1938, the UF's national congress expressed its continued faith in collective security, even if the League of Nations looked to have failed.[28] In December 1938, Pichot welcomed the non-aggression accord concluded in Paris by foreign minister Georges Bonnet and Ribbentrop.[29] Shortly after this, Pichot and Goy were praised for their role on the France-Germany Committee at a dinner held in honour of the German foreign minister.[30] Such warm relations were not to last for much longer. With the threat of armed conflict hanging over Europe, veteran support for rapprochement was already in decline.[31] Neither the UF nor the UNC were intransigently pacifist. Both associations called on Daladier to maximise arms production. Their attitude was closer to what Prost has called 'patriotic pacifism' and what recent research has termed 'war anxiety'.[32] The veterans' committee in charge of the 20th Armistice celebrations decided to donate the 700,000 francs left over to the Caisse autonome de la Défense Nationale with the intention of '[stimulating] the zeal of the French'.[33]

The veterans' fading confidence in rapprochement mirrored a growing desire for assertiveness in French political and public circles. Italy's claims on French metropolitan and colonial territories infuriated France and Daladier refused to give ground to Mussolini. The premier's visit to North Africa in January 1939 sent a public statement of France's determination to hold onto its colonial possession. Animosity between the two nations was echoed in the veterans' movement. The Union of French and Italian Veterans, founded in 1935 as homologue of the France-Germany Committee, was suspended in December 1938. Daladier's African visit chimed, too, with a growing popular enthusiasm for the empire, a visible symbol of French grandeur. The veterans' associations reflected this enthusiasm. The UF emphasised the value of French colonies in its press and its national congress that year. Overseas territories and especially the Maghreb offered a reservoir of men and valuable resources and were thus essential to France.[34] Likewise, the UNC stressed the importance of France's imperial enterprise of which the veterans were the best representatives for they had fought in an army of 'all colours'.[35] The UNC's congress in 1939 was dedicated to celebrating the Empire and representatives from the colonies spoke at the closing ceremony.[36]

As for Germany, Hitler's occupation of the remaining parts of Czechoslovakia on 15 March 1939 dashed remaining French hopes for a lasting peace. Now that the fall of the Popular Front had diminished the threat of social revolution at home, the right, which had once so supported concessions to Hitler, backed a strong foreign policy. The veterans, too, gave up hope of an accommodation with Hitler. The France-Germany Committee was wound up in March 1939.[37] The UNC warned that it was when Germans spoke of peace that they were planning something else.[38] The UF for the first time implied that force would be needed to stop Hitler. Pichot lamented that if France had had a government of public safety, Hitler would not have been in Prague. He continued to draw a distinction between the sovereignty of the people (and the veterans) and that of parliament. France needed a 'man of iron' to take the helm of government. Pichot did not name this man, but specified that he should be equal to other men of iron, namely Clemenceau, Hitler and Mussolini.[39]

Given their preference for strong government, it comes as little surprise that both the UF and the UNC supported the granting of full powers to Daladier and the prorogation of the Chamber in July 1939.[40] The UNC qualified the latter as a measure of 'good sense'.[41] The associations' support was for a government that had sidelined parliament and whose politics was becoming ever more right wing. Some veterans envisaged collaboration with, if not participation in, the state apparatus. An undated and unsigned document in the archives of the UF's Cassin specified that during a general mobilisation police and security service auxiliaries should be recruited from among those men who were not mobilised: veterans. The author counted upon collaboration between the UF and the authorities for the maintenance of internal security.[42] The *Cahiers de l'UF* echoed these sentiments in May 1939.[43] The UF was not alone in espousing such an idea. In October 1938, Aubert, under the pseudonym François Malval, described a new role for the veterans if war should break out: with the army and the police otherwise occupied, the veterans would keep a watchful eye on potentially subversive elements in France, namely foreigners and factory workers. Though these plans appeared to outline a French-style Home Guard, they were not limited to times of war. In fact, 'Malval' wrote: 'Already in some communes where foreign elements were starting to agitate in recent days, all that was needed was for some veterans to act as police (*faire la police*) so that things returned to order.'[44] These remarks offered a chilling harbinger of Vichy's combatants' Legion.

Throughout 1939, relations between the UF and the UNC continued to be warm. The policy-making committees of both associations dined together on several occasions. Provincial groups had close relations: the UNC's Lacquièze reported that in his department UF and UNC veterans desired collaboration. Yet the UNC's executive committee recognised that there was hostility to the veterans' plan within the association too. Goudaert spoke in particular of the deputies affiliated to the UNC who, despite having been activists in the past, were now hostile to the UNC's plan. He gave the example of André Parmentier who, in the Nord, had suspended the groups in his district until further notice.[45]

Cooperation was institutionalised soon after the outbreak of the Second World War. On 12 November 1939, the UF and the UNC founded the Légion des combattants français (LCF). High-level UF and UNC members filled the leadership of the LCF. They included UF and UNC presidents Pichot and Goy as well as Jacques Delahoche and Léon Berthier, who were representatives of the CIAMAC and the FIDAC respectively.[46] Each association continued to preserve its national and provincial structures; the LCF merely provided a formal framework for cooperation. Much depended on local circumstances and the particular arrangements made between provincial sections. In the Puy-de-Dôme, for example, the provincial newspapers of both associations were fused into one.[47] For its part, the Confédération founded its own 'legion' on the initiative of smaller combatants' groups who feared the dominance of the two largest associations. Tension existed between the two blocs, which led some local associations to remain independent of both.[48]

Genuine fusion of the veterans' associations happened only after the defeat of France in May 1940. On 10 May, German forces invaded France through the Ardennes and not via Belgium, as the French believed they would. The Battle of France was short. Six days later the Germans enjoyed an unhindered advance to Paris. On 14 June, German troops entered the capital. Within two days Pétain succeeded Paul Reynaud as head of government and an armistice was signed on 22 June. France was divided into a northern Occupied Zone and a southern Unoccupied Zone. The army was demobilised and reduced to a rump of 100,000 men, while the navy was disarmed. Occupation costs were placed on the French government.

On 1 July, the final administration of the Third Republic took up residence in the Unoccupied Zone at Vichy. Pétain quickly sought to consolidate his position. Deputy premier Pierre Laval formulated a plan that would see parliament grant the Marshal powers to revise the constitution.

Already approved by the cabinet, parliament met in Vichy to discuss the plan on 9 July. The next day, Pétain, empowered by parliament, put an end to the Third Republic and became head of the *Etat français*. Installed by legal means, Pétain immediately dropped the pretence of legality. The Marshal soon dispensed with the republican apparatus, his first acts on 11 July placing power in his hands alone.

There was no veterans' revolution yet in his first address to the nation on 17 June 1940, Pétain mentioned the support of the veterans. Cointet suggests that in light of Pichot's meeting with Lebrun in March 1938, it is possible that the UF president was in contact with the Marshal when he delivered his speech. When deputies and senators invested Pétain with full powers and the authority to design a new constitution, the circumstances of defeat had prompted parliament to act in a way that the veterans had previously considered unthinkable. The veterans had not believed that parliamentarians would 'commit suicide' in the way they did in 1940. Traditionally, the UF placed its faith in the parliament's ability to reform itself. The UNC had favoured a constituent assembly. From 1938, both hoped that the president would appoint a public safety government. Though the method may have differed, with Pétain as head of state, the result may have pleased a good proportion of veterans.

On 28 August 1940, Vichy's council of ministers merged all veterans' associations into the Légion française des combattants. Pichot was instrumental in drafting the statutes of the Légion, thanks to his close relations with Vichy's secretary general for veterans Xavier Vallat. Members of the defunct UNC joined the leadership of the movement. Jacques Péricard became vice president representing the army. Lebecq was chosen as president of the occupied zone, although the Légion was soon prohibited in the north.[49] The *directoire* of the Légion contained fifteen members, of which Aze, du Plessis de Grenédan, Emile Goudaert and Vimal de Fléchac were former UNC members. From the UF, Blanchard, Lhospied, Maupoil and Mercier had all been members of their association's executive committee in 1940.[50] In the choice of departmental presidents, where the candidate had belonged to an association before the war former UNC members held the lion's share, with thirteen out of forty-five seats compared to the UF's seven.[51]

Though its role was to support the public powers, the Légion was not intended to fulfil the role of a single party so common to dictatorships. With Pétain as the Légion's president, veterans of both wars would be his trusted representatives in communes throughout France. They would spread the values of the National Revolution at the grass roots level. Yet their primary function was to act as the 'eyes and the ears' of the Marshal in order to maintain a close surveillance over public opinion.[52] Whether 'puritanical zealots' or 'vigilantes', the Légion gave the veterans a chance to put into practice twenty years of verbose moralising.[53]

Assessments

The history of the UF and the UNC between the two world wars is complex. Each association identified with a particular politics. Though the UF and the UNC were certainly not political parties or leagues, they were political entities. They commented regularly on the political situation and made interventions through their press, meetings, congresses and demonstrations. The veterans' discourse was not disconnected from reality, nor was it confined to generalisations about unnamed parties and anonymous politicians. Their political involvement was serious and considered. The UF leant toward the radicals thanks to the socio-economic profile of its leadership and members. The association did not hide its political preferences and it is reasonable to assume that UF veterans were aware of these sympathies. The UNC was stridently right wing. It hid neither its rejection of radicalism and the left nor its preference for conservatism and, at times, the extreme right. Indeed, some UNC veterans came to perceive a blurring of boundaries between their associations and the paramilitary leagues. Indeed, these political positions accounted for each association's basic orientation yet, in explaining the UF and the UNC's history, they offer little more than a starting point.

In practice there was not a simple division between the associations. Cooperation occurred in several circumstances. Firstly, and most commonly, veterans from groups across the movement met regularly at meetings of the Confédération and entente committees. Rival associations produced united statements such as the list of demands sent to candidates prior to elections. Secondly, the whole combatants' movement could unite in a campaign to put pressure on the incumbent government when it believed that its veterans' direct interests were under threat. Usually these campaigns involved the defence of material rights. This was the case in 1932 during the second battle for pensions, when even the UNC and the ARAC were prepared to share meetings for the veterans' cause. Unity of action could also occur in instances when the veterans perceived a threat to their moral rights and heritage. Such a situation arose in 1926 when combatants feared that the Washington Accords would undermine the gains of their hard-won victory. Thirdly, associations collaborated at times of perceived national crisis. For the UF and the UNC, this took place on two occasions: between February and July 1934, and during the campaign for the public safety government after March 1938. The two associations undertook united action at this time, though their aims and motivations differed to an extent.

How could the UF and the UNC, who were so bitterly opposed on some issues, collaborate so closely? For one thing, any political group's programme is subject to myriad internal and external influences. Policies may be retained, changed, suspended or abandoned completely. Policies are often contested and, once formulated, continue to be the site of struggles and negotiations. Much can depend too on the personalities and agendas of actors within a group. The hardcore of conservatives on the UNC's executive committee often seemed to have the upper hand in the association, particularly after Henri Rossignol assumed the leadership in 1926. Henceforth, conservative activists retained their grip on the presidency. Georges Lebecq led the association into the February riot and publicly sympathised with the leagues. Jean Goy, like his predecessor, continued to take the UNC in a political direction. Yet despite the dominance of this faction, it did not succeed in wresting control completely from moderate members of the executive committee who were able to arrest the political move of the association on several occasions. Even when an action or policy was agreed upon, its success depended on the motives of high and mid-level officials and their interpretation of policy. While it is difficult to assess the importance of provincial influence on national decisions, the implementation of a programme depended on local idiosyncrasies. Implementation became all the more unreliable due to the sometimes diverse opinions and priorities of grass-roots members.

Factors external to each association could influence policy decisions, too. One of the best examples of this is the UF's decision to campaign for state reform after February 1934. In what amounted to a complete about-turn in policy, the UF embraced extra-parliamentary reform and at the Confédération's 8 July meeting effectively voted to topple Doumergue. One could argue that the UF's change of policy in 1934 lay ultimately in its preference for centre-left government. Yet its reformist campaign did not simply aim to bring the radicals back to power; it targeted a wholesale transformation of the regime. Immediate political circumstance could thus cause profound policy reversals.

Given the multitude of influences on association policy, it is unwise to explain the processes behind each association's actions and behaviour with reference to an inherent 'nature' or 'essence'. We know today that the

French veterans' associations did not launch a coup against the regime. In spite of their threats that the day of reckoning, 'H hour', was close the veterans did not act. Yet a variety of outcomes was possible. We should not seek therefore to discern and ultimately privilege the particular historical path that led to this outcome. In doing so, one is forced to identify aspects of behaviour and discourse as revelatory of a group's 'true' nature and dismiss all words contrary to this nature. When veterans violently attacked the regime, we cannot claim that these words were simply hyperbole, designed purely to arouse enthusiasm and little else, for it is difficult to 'know' how these words were received, internalised and acted upon. Conversely, not all attacks on the regime implied a desire for a non-republican government. A commitment to republicanism existed in the UF and the UNC alongside preferences for other forms of government. These loyalties were not constant and could be modified.

The discourse of the veterans' world questioned the legitimacy of parliamentarians. In practice, not all politicians were unacceptable to the UF and the UNC. The UF preferred radical deputies and could support them in power. The UNC desired conservative government. Under Doumergue in 1934, the association blocked the Confédération's attempt to topple the government because it believed that Doumergue would implement reform. Parliament could therefore be useful in certain situations. Nonetheless, the UF and the UNC sought to undermine parliamentarians' claim to represent the national interest, while posing the veterans as the sole alternative. Whether it claimed to be more patriotic or more youthful, this discourse portrayed the veterans as more competent than the leaders of France. For conservative veterans, the culture of war offered another means to attack left-wing governments and portray them as the antithesis to French national interests. With the war culture's conceptual framework and terminology attached to the revolutionary left, the UNC used it as a weapon against the cartel governments and the Popular Front. However, to argue that the persistence of the war culture in UNC discourse points to a more general brutalisation of right-wing politics would be a step too far. The UNC drew on the culture only in particular circumstances.

Following from these attacks, the veterans held a subjective view of what deserved to be called the republic. Neither the UF not the UNC explicitly condemned the republic as a regime. The UF had more faith in the institutions of the Third Republic than its rival. It rejected reform until 1934. It found again its optimism in the republic after May 1936 but this disappeared with the public safety campaign. The UNC preferred extra-parliamentary reform and pursued campaigns to this end. At times the UF and the UNC, in particular, targeted republican institutions such as parliament. More generally though, in attacking their content, the institutions themselves were called into question. Moreover, when the veterans perceived a deficiency in the regime, their subjective definition of the 'republic' allowed them to claim to be republican, the only 'true' republicans, while advancing opinions and plans that were some way removed from the institutions of the Third Republic. This discourse must be placed within the context of a more general disconnection between 'republicanism' and parliamentary democracy.[54] While identification with this point of view was not as strong in the veterans' associations as in the nationalist leagues (for genuine republicanism existed in the combatants' world without a doubt), one cannot claim that the UF and the UNC reinforced the French commitment to the parliamentary Third Republic.

To what extent did the veterans prefer a non-republican regime? Examining the associations' plans for reform, following a period of temporary dictatorship, the regime to emerge would be authoritarian while retaining institutions such as parliament and elections. These institutions would be very different though. Both associations would likely limit political pluralism and the power of parliamentarians. The government would be powerful and able to act according to the veterans' definition of strong government. It is mistaken to argue that these plans foreshadowed the executive authority of the Fifth Republic. This line of argument is teleological as it posits the current regime as the culmination of efficient government to which the veterans were, and all French *should* have been, working. Reform plans were politically motivated and were neither technical nor disinterested. Elements of the veterans' programme may be common to the later regime, but others are not. Under the Fifth Republic, the socialist and centre parties are excluded neither from government nor parliament. The Communist Party is not outlawed. Parliamentarians of earlier regimes were not forced into retirement. These were components of either the UF or the UNC's plan.

It is tempting to conclude that with the founding of Vichy, the veterans finally had the regime that they desired: a strong (read authoritarian), moral and national government under a French war hero. However, it would be a mistake to judge Vichy as the culmination of the veterans' authoritarian designs and discourse. Pétain's regime arose from the circumstances of the defeat and the armistice. Yet one cannot deny the long-term origins of Vichy in inter-war politics. Of course, one cannot argue that the veterans paved the way for the worst excesses of Vichy, such as the deportation of French Jews and the gradual evolution toward a police state. Likewise, support for the veterans' Légion in 1940 did not imply support for its extreme offspring, the Service d'ordre legionnaire. Nor were the veterans alone in their support for Vichy. In the wake of the defeat, with the republic discredited, few in number were the French who did not lend their support to Pétain's project for national and moral renovation.[55] It was not yet clear what Vichy would become. It is plausible that the UF and the UNC believed Pétain's administration would act in the manner of the public safety regime that they so desired. Once the Marshal had restored order to France and the country had recovered from defeat, he would abdicate and leave in his wake the strong regime for which the associations had campaigned. It was not possible to say when this would happen due to the uncertainty of the occupation and the circumstances of war.

Nevertheless, since 1918, veterans' associations had warned the French about impending disaster if the republic was not 'put in order'. The UF and the UNC exposed their followers to authoritarian ideas and their warnings became ever more shrill during the 1930s. The importance of the veterans, therefore, lies in the fact that when disaster struck, they had prepared their members for the solution that was proposed. While it is not true that the veterans were solely responsible for the French acceptance of Vichy (for the shock of the defeat was one of several important factors), after twenty years of moralising and authoritarian discourse their part should not be downplayed. More broadly, the UF's move to the right during 1938–39 hints at a general move to conservatism in French public opinion. The popularity of the leagues further demonstrates ample support for right-wing authoritarianism in French society. The growing authoritarianism of the UF and the UNC's politics was symptomatic of France's incremental move to authoritarianism.[56] Following the defeat, the French were ready to accept the end of the republic, whose decadence had allegedly caused the defeat. Nonetheless, the history of the veterans demonstrates, too, that French society's move to authoritarianism was not a linear and ineluctable process. Analysis of the two largest veterans' associations reveals an intricate story of political fluctuations that defies simple explanation. The responses of the UF and the UNC to the events of the 1930s were not fixed. In the politics of the late Third Republic, classifications were unclear. An essential nature neither governed the veterans' associations nor France.

Conclusion

Notes

1   Serge Berstein, *Histoire du parti radical* (Paris: Presse de la Fondation Na-
    tionale des Sciences politiques, 1982), 2 vols, II, pp. 514–19.

2   *Ibid.*, p. 544.

3   Sandro Guerrieri, 'L'affaiblissement du Parlement français dans la dernière
    législature de la Troisième République (1936–1940)', *Parliaments, Estates
    and Representation*, 23 (2003), 200–3.

4   Jackson, *France: The Dark Years*, p. 103; Passmore, *From Liberalism to
    Fascism*, p. 261; Rosemonde Sanson, 'L'Alliance démocratique', in Rémond
    and Bourdin (eds), *La France et les français*, p. 331.

5   UNC/EC, 23 May 1938.

6   Gorman, 'The anciens combattants and appeasement', 80.

7   'Le comité fédéral de l'Union fédérale', *CUF* (10 October 1938).

8   P. Galland, 'Ca n'est pas fini', *VC* (24 September 1938).

9   P. Galland, 'La plebisicite de la Paix', *VC* (8 October 1938).

10 R. Cassin, 'L'effondrement d'une politique', *CUF* (10 October 1938).

11 M. Randoux, 'La vraie force nouvelle: Tous les Anciens Combattants unis au
    service de la Nation', *VC* (22 October 1938). The second call found support
    from within and without the veterans' movement. *La Voix du combattant*
    listed as in support of the UNC and the UF: the AGMG, the UNMR, SDC,
    the Association des ecrivains combattants, the Ligue des droits du religieux
    ancien combattant (DRAC), and the Association des prisonniers de guerre.
    Support in the non-combatant world came from the Confédération géné-
    rale des classes moyennes, the Confédération nationale des syndicats agri-
    coles and the Comité du plan. See A. Gervais, 'Notre dernière bataille', *VC*
    (29 October 1938).

12 H. Aubert, 'Et maintenant?', *VC* (15 October 1938).

13 'Les Anciens Combattants exigent ...', *Le Matin* (12 October 1938); 'L'Union
    fédérale et l'avenir français', *CUF* (10 October 1938); 'L'UNC réclame un
    gouvernement de Salut Public'; F. Malval, 'L'UNC d'accord avec l'UF pour
    proclamer un Gouvernement de Salut Public', *VC* (22 October 1938); A.
    Thomas, 'Refaire un pays fort: Interview d'Alexis Thomas, Président du
    Groupe de Lorraine', *VC* (5 November 1938); 'L'union pour le Salut Public',
    NF (Paris) (November 1938).

14 'L'heure des combinaisons est finie déclare M. Pichot qui, au nom des an-
    ciens combattants demandent la constitution d'un gouvernement de salut
    public', *Le Figaro* (12 October 1938); 'Les anciens combattants demandent
    un gouvernement de salut public', *Le Figaro* (13 October 1938); 'Au nom des
    anciens combattants M. Pichot président de l'UF réclame un gouvernement
    de salut public', *L'Ouest-Eclair* (12 October 1938).

15 'Les Anciens Combattants exigent ...', *Le Matin* (12 October 1938).

16 J. Raudot, 'Les Jeunes avec les Combattants', *VC* (22 October 1938).

17 'Les anciens combattants demandent un gouvernment de salut public', *Le*

Figaro (13 October 1938).

18 Guerrieri, 'L'affaiblissement du Parlement français dans la dernière législature de la Troisième République', 203.

19 P. Galland, 'Le levain dans la pâte', *VC* (14 January 1939).

20 'Au nom des anciens combattants M. Pichot president de l'UF réclame un gouvernement de salut public', *L'Ouest-Eclair* (12 October 1938); 'Les anciens combattants demande un gouvernement de salut public', *Le Figaro* (13 October 1938); 'Les Anciens Combattants exigent ...', *Le Matin* (12 October 1938).

21 'Les Anciens Combattants exigent ...', *Le Matin* (12 October 1938).

22 Prost, *Les Anciens Combattants*, II, pp. 162–4.

23 Berstein, *Histoire du Parti radical*, II, pp. 532–40.

24 *Ibid.*, p. 564; Serge Berstein, 'Le Parti radical', p. 295.

25 UNC/EC, 23 May 1938.

26 P. Galland, 'Pour l'union', *CUF* (25 July 1939).

27 UNC/EC, 18 February 1939.

28 'Motion générale', *CUF* (10–20 June 1938); 'Rapports internationaux', *CUF* (10–20 June 1938).

29 H. Pichot, 'L'accord franco-allemand', *CUF* (10 December 1938).

30 'Un déjeuner au Comité France-Allemagne', *CUF* (10 December 1938).

31 Gorman, 'The anciens combattants', 85.

32 Prost, *Les Anciens Combattants*, III, 72–124; Daniel Hucker, 'French Public Attitudes towards the Prospect of War in 1938–1939: "Pacifism" or "War Anxiety"?', *French History*, 21 (2007), 431–449.

33 'Réliquat du 20e anniversaire de l'Armistice: Les anciens combattants remettent 700,000 fr à la Caisse Autonome de la Défense Nationale', *VC* (21 January 1939).

34 'Importance de l'Afrique du Nord dans l'Empire français', *CUF* (10 February 1939); G. Castel, 'Marseille, Capitale d'Empire', *CUF* (25 February 1939); 'Respect à l'Empire', *NF (Paris-Nord)* (February 1939); H. Pichot, 'France impériale', *NF (Paris-Nord)* (February 1939).

35 P. Galland, 'Le levain dans la pâte', *VC* (14 January 1939).

36 'La grandeur de l'empire française', *VC* (20–27 May 1939).

37 'A l'unanimité le Comité France-Allemagne décide de cesser son activité', *CUF* (15 March 1939).

38 H. Aubert, 'Et après Prague?', *VC* (18 March 1939).

39 H. Pichot, 'Juillet 1914-mars 1939', *CUF* (25 March 1939); H. Pichot, 'Des Hommes de Fer!', *NF (Paris)* (May 1939); 'Une belle journée pour l'UF du Gard', *L'Union fédérale du Gard* (December 1938).

40 H. Pichot, 'Juillet 1914-Mars 1939', *CUF* (25 March 1939).

41 P. Galland, 'Cette RP n'est pas intégrale', *VC* (1 July 1939); Roux-Desbreaux, 'La prorogation de la Chambre', *VC* (5 August 1938).

42 AN, AP 382/11, anonymous and undated document.

43 M. Randoux, 'Suggestions sur le rôle des Ancie ns Combattants si une guerre était imposée à la France', *CUF* (10 May 1939).

44 F. Malval, 'Pour la défense intérieure du Pays afin que ceux de l'avant aient toute tranquillité', *VC* (1 October 1938). See also C. Inargues, 'En cas de mobilisation, chacun à sa place', *VC* (15 April 1939).

45 UNC/EC, 18 February 1939.

46 'Comités de la Légion', *NF* (December 1939).

47 See *Journal des combattants et mutilés de Puy-de-Dôme* (November 1939).

48 Prost, *Les Anciens Combattants*, I, p. 199–200.

49 Cointet, *La Légion française des combattants*, p. 92.

50 *Ibid.*, p. 74.

51 *Ibid.*, pp. 314–16. There were forty-five departmental presidents of which fifteen had no previous affiliation to a veterans' association. The thirteen former UNC members were from the Ardèche (former group president), the Corrèze (former member of the national council and the policy-making committee), the Dordogne (former group president), the Drôme (former group president), the Hérault, the Haute Loire, the Basses-Pyrénées (former departmental president), the Hautes-Pyrénées (former departmental president), the Rhône (former section president), the Vienne and the Haute Vienne. The number of departmental presidents drawn from other associations were as follows: UF, seven; UNP, one; Fédération Bourbonnaise des AC, one; the SDC, one; the Fédération Maginot, three; the AGMG, one; the UMAC, one; the Fédération des Poilus de la Loire, one; the Gueules Cassées, one.

52 *Ibid.*, pp. 54–9

53 Paxton, *Vichy France*, pp. 147; 190–1; Jackson, *France: The Dark Years*, p. 304.

54 Passmore, 'Boy-scouting', 536.

55 Jackson, *France: The Dark Years*, pp. 289–90.

56 Jenkins, 'The *six février*', 346.

Select bibliography

Archival sources
Archives départementales du Rhône
4M, 33

Archives d'histoire contemporaine de la Fondation nationale des Sciences politiques, Paris
Papiers La Rocque: Carton LR 56 II B4

Archives nationales, Paris
F[7] Police générale: 12952, 12954, 12960, 12963, 12966, 12990, 13006, 13015, 13024, 13025, 13026, 13027, 13028, 13029, 13032, 13033, 13038, 13039, 13040, 13228, 13231, 13232, 13233, 13234, 13305, 13308, 13316, 13317, 13320, 14608
C Archives de l'Assemblée nationale – III République : 15092, 15094
Fonds Louis Marin AP 317: 72
Fonds René Cassin AP 382 : 10, 11
Fonds Henri Pichot 43 AS: 1, 6, 7, 8 (43 AS 6 and 7 comprise *Les Cahiers de l'UF*)
Fonds La Rocque 451 AP: 81, 83, 108, 121

Archives de la Préfecture de Police (APP), Paris
BA 1852, 1853, 1854, 1901

Archives de l'UNC, 18 rue Vézelay, Paris
La Voix du combattant
La Voix du combattant (regional edition). *Seine-et-Marne.*
Minutes of the National Executive Committee, 18 June 1932–18 February 1939
Lebecq dossier: letter from G. Lebecq to the executive committee, undated.

Select bibliography

Rossignol dossier: Jean Goy, 'Quelques constatations', undated.

Centre des Archives contemporaines, Fontainebleau

19 940459: 130
19 940500: 229, 237, 238

Newspapers

Bibliothèque Nationale, Paris

Combatant press

Journal des mutilés et réformés (non-affiliated)
Le Poilu républicain (FNCR)

General press

Action française
L'Ami du peuple
La Croix
L'Echo de Paris
Excelsior
Le Figaro
Le Flambeau
L'Humanité
L'Intransigeant
Le Jour
Le Journal
Le Matin
Le National
L'Ouest-Eclair
Le Peuple
Le Populaire
Le Temps
La Victoire

UF (name of publication and location, where not stated in the publication's title)

Après le combat (Loire-Inférieure)
Le Béquillard meusienne
Le Combattant creusois
Le Combattant mutualiste (Pas-de-Calais)
La France mutilée (national publication)
Le Front (Nord)

Select bibliography

Journal des combattants du Puy-de-Dôme
La Liaison (Deux-Sèvres)
Le Mutilé et combattant de la Haute-Loire
Notre France (national publication)
Le Poilu tarnais
Le Retour au foyer
L'Union fédérale du Gard
Servir (Loiret)

UNC (name of publication and location, where not stated in the publication's title)

L'Action combattante (Bures-sur-Yvette, Gometz-le-Châtel and Gometz-la-Ville [Essone])
L'Ancien Combattant du Berry (Cher-et-Indre)
Le Combattant du IXe (Paris)
Le Combattant du Cantal
Le Combattant du centre (Limoges)
Le Combattant des Côtes-du-Nord
Le Combattant des Deux-Sèvres
Le Combattant de la Drôme
Le Combattant d'Ille-et-Vilaine
Le Combattant landais
Le Combattant du Poitou
Le Combattant du Sud-Est (Ain, Drôme, Isère, Loire, Rhône, Haute-Savoie)
Le Créneau (Calais)
Le Cri du poilu (Morbihan)
L'Echo montmartrois
Entre nous (Somain [Nord])
Inter-sections (national JUNC)
Le Poilu (Finistère)
Le Poilu basque
Le Trait d'union (Oise)
L'UNC de Normandie
L'UNC de Paris et du département de la Seine

Combatant publications

Gervais, André, André Jacques and Jean Mouraille (eds), *Jeunesses* (Paris: Editions de l'Union fédérale, 1935).

Goy, Jean, Victor Beauregard and Léon Berthier, *Le programme d'action civique des anciens combattants* (Paris: Edition de l'Action combattante, 1935).

Isaac, Humbert, *La Route de salut: Pensées, espoirs, volontés des anciens combattants et des jeunes* (Paris: Union nationale des combattants, 1935).

Select bibliography

Les Anciens Combattants et la confédération générale du travail (Paris: Edition de l'Action combattante, 1934).

Pichot, Henri, *Les Combattants avaient raison* ... (Montluçon: Editions de la Maison du combattant, 1940).

Vilain, Charles, *Les Combattants exigent* ... *Du manifeste de la salle Wagram au congrès de l'UNC à Metz* (Rouen: Imprimerie commerciale du Journal de Rouen, 1934).

XVe congrès national de l'UNC: Rapports, discussions, discours (Paris: Editions Voix du Combattant, 1934).

General bibliography

Audoin-Rouzeau, Stéphane, 'Le parti communiste et la violence, 1929–1931', *Revue historique*, CCLXIX/2 (1983), 365–83.

—— *Men at War 1914–1918: National Sentiment and Trench Journalism in France during the First World War* (Oxford and Providence: Berg, 1992).

—— and Annette Becker, *14–18: Understanding the Great War* (London: Profile, 2002).

—— and Christophe Prochasson (eds), *Sortir de la grande guerre. Le monde et l'après 1918* (Paris: Tallandier, 2008).

Becker, Annette, 'From war to war: A few myths, 1914–1942', in Valerie Holman and Debra Kelly (eds), *France at War in the Twentieth Century: Propaganda, Myth and Metaphor* (Oxford: Berghahn, 2000), pp. 15–27.

Bénéton, Philippe, 'La génération de 1912–1914: Image, mythe ou réalité?', *Revue française de science politique*, 21 (1971), 981–1009.

Bensoussan, David, *Combats pour une Bretagne catholique et rurale. Les droites bretonnes dans l'entre-deux-guerres* (Paris: Fayard, 2006).

Berger, Suzanne, *Peasants against Politics: Rural Organization in Brittany 1911–1967* (Cambridge, MA: Harvard University Press, 1972).

Berstein, Serge, *Le 6 février* (Paris: Gallimard, 1975).

—— *Histoire du Parti radical*, 2 vols (Paris: Presse de la Fondation nationale des Sciences politiques, 1980–82).

—— 'La France des années trente allergique au fascisme', *Vingtième Siècle*, 2 (1984), 83–94.

Bonnevay, Laurent, *Les Journées sanglantes de février 1934* (Paris: Flammarion, 1935).

Burrin, Philippe, 'Poings levés et bras tendus. La contagion des symboles au temps du Front populaire', *Vingtième Siècle*, 11 (1986), 5–20.

Cabanes, Bruno, *La Victoire endeuillée. La sortie de guerre des soldats français 1918–1920* (Paris: Seuil, 2004).

—— '"Génération du feu": Aux origines d'une notion', *Revue historique*, 641 (2007), 139–50.

Campbell, Caroline, 'Women and Men in French Authoritarianism: Gender in the Croix de Feu/Parti Social Français, 1927-1947'(Ph.D. dissertation, University of Iowa, 2009).

Cazals, Rémy, '1914-1918: Chercher encore', *Le Mouvement Social*, 199 (2002), 107-13.

Chavardès, Maurice, *Le 6 février: La République en danger* (Paris: Calmann-Lévy, 1966).

—— *Une campagne de presse: La droite francaise et le 6 février 1934* (Paris: Flammarion, 1970).

Chopine, Paul, *Six ans chez les Croix de Feu* (Paris: Gallimard, 1935).

Cointet, Jean-Paul, *La Légion française des combattants: La tentation du fascisme* (Paris: Albin Michel, 1995).

Coutrot, Aline, 'Youth movements in France in the 1930s', *Journal of Contemporary History*, 5 (1970), 23-35.

Delaporte, Sophie, *Gueules cassées de la Grande Guerre* (Paris: Viénot, 2004).

Dobry, Michel, 'Février 1934 et la découverte de l'allergie de la société francaise à la "Révolution fasciste"', *Revue francaise de sociologie*, XXX (1989), 511-33.

—— (ed.) *Le Mythe de l'allergie française au fascisme* (Paris: Albin Michel, 2003).

Douglas, Allen, 'Violence and Fascism: The case of the Faisceau', *Journal of Contemporary History*, 4 (1984), 689-712.

Fabre, Rémi, 'Les mouvements de jeunesse dans la France de l'entre-deux-guerres', *Le Mouvement Social*, 168 (1994), 9-31.

Fagerberg, Elliott Pennell, *The 'Anciens Combattants' and French Foreign Policy* (Geneva: Graduate Institute of International Studies, 1966).

Gibelli, Antonio, 'Le refus, la distance, le consentement', *Le Mouvement Social*, 199 (2002), 113-19.

Gorman, Lyn, 'The anciens combattants and appeasement: From Munich to war', *War and Society*, 10 (1992), 73-89.

Guerrieri, Sandro, 'L'affaiblissement du Parlement français dans la dernière législature de la Troisième République (1936-1940)', *Parliaments, Estates and Representation*, 23 (2003), 195-207.

Halls, Wilfred D., *The Youth of Vichy France* (Oxford: Clarendon Press, 1981).

Hellman, John, *The Knight-Monks of Vichy France: Uriage, 1940-1945* (Montreal: McGill-Queen's University Press, 1993).

Henriot, Philippe, *Le 6 février* (Paris: Flammarion, 1934).

Horne, John (ed.), *14-18 Aujourd'hui-Today-Heute: Démobilisation culturelle aprés la Grande guerre* (Paris: Editions Noesis, 2002).

—— 'Demobilizing the mind: France and legacy of the Great War, 1919-1939', *French History and Civilization*, 2 (2009), 101-7.

—— (ed.), *State, society and mobilization in Europe during the First World War* (Cambridge and New York: Cambridge University Press, 1997).

—— and Alan Kramer, 'German "atrocities" and Franco-German opinion, 1914: The evidence of German soldiers' diaries', *Journal of Modern History*, 66 (1994), 1-33.

Howlett, Gareth Adrian, 'The Croix de Feu, Parti Social Français and Colonel de

La Rocque' (Ph.D. dissertation, Nuffield College, Oxford University, 1986).

Hurcombe, Martin, 'Raising the dead: Visual representations of the combatant's body in interwar France', *Journal of War and Culture Studies* 1 (2008), 159–74.

Irvine, William, *French Conservatism in Crisis: The Republican Federation in the 1930s* (Baton Rouge, LA: Louisiana State University Press, 1979).

—— 'Fascism in France: The strange case of the Croix de Feu', *Journal of Modern History,* 63 (1991), 271–95.

Jackson, Julian, *The Popular Front in France: Defending Democracy* (Cambridge: Cambridge University Press, 1988).

—— *France: The Dark Years, 1940–1944* (Oxford: Oxford University Press, 2001).

—— *The Fall of France: The Nazi Invasion of 1940* (Oxford: Oxford University Press, 2003).

Jeanneney, Jean-Noël, 'Les anciens combattants: Fascistes ou démocrates?' *Histoire,* 1 (1978), 86–8.

Jenkins, Brian, 'The Paris Riots of February 1934: The Crisis of the Third French Republic' (Ph.D. dissertation, London School of Economics, 1979).

—— (ed.), *France in the Era of Fascism* (New York: Berghahn, 2005).

—— 'The *six février* 1934 and the "survival" of the French Republic', *French History,* 20 (2006), 333–51.

Kalman, Samuel, *The Extreme Right in Interwar France: The Faisceau and the Croix de Feu* (Aldershot: Ashgate, 2008).

Kéchichian, Albert, *Les Croix de Feu à l'âge des fascismes* (Seyssel: Champ Vallon, 2006).

Kennedy, Sean, *Reconciling France Against Democracy: The Croix de Feu and the Parti Social Français, 1929–45* (Montreal and London: McGill-Queen's University Press, 2007).

Koos, Cheryl, 'Fascism, fatherhood, and the family in interwar France: The case of Antoine Rédier and the Légion', *Journal of Family History,* 24 (1999), 317–29.

—— and Danielle Sarnoff, 'France', in Kevin Passmore (ed.), *Women, Gender and Fascism in Europe, 1919–1945* (Manchester: Manchester University Press, 2003), pp. 168–89.

Kramer, Alan, *Dynamic of Destruction: Culture and Mass Killing in the First World War* (Oxford: Oxford University Press, 2007).

Le Clère, Marcel, *Le 6 Février* (Paris: Hachette, 1967).

Le Béguec, Gilles, 'L'entrée au Palais Bourbon: Les filières privilégiés d'accès à la fonction parlementaire 1919–1939' (Ph.D. dissertation, Université de Paris X-Nanterre, 1989).

Loubet del Bayle, Jean-Louis, *Les Non-conformistes des années 30* (Paris: Editions du Seuil, 1969).

Machefer, Philippe, 'Les Croix de Feu (1927–1936)', *L'information historique,* 34 (1972), 28–34.

——, 'Le Parti Social Français', in René Rémond and Janine Bourdin (eds), *La France et les Français, 1938 en 1939* (Paris: Presses de la Fondation nationale des Sciences politiques, 1978), pp. 307–27.

Martinez, Gilles, 'Joseph Bartélemy et la crise de la démocratie libérale', *Vingtième Siècle*, 59 (1998), 28–47.

Milza, Pierre, *Fascisme français* (Paris: Flammarion, 1987).

Monnet, Francois, *Refaire la République: André Tardieu, une dérive réactionnaire, 1876–1945* (Paris: Fayard, 1993).

Mosse, George L., *Fallen Soldiers: Reshaping the Memory of the World Wars* (Oxford: Oxford University Press, 1990).

Nobécourt, Jacques, *Le Colonel de La Rocque, 1885–1946 ou les pièges du nationalisme chrétien* (Paris: Fayard, 1996).

Noiriel, Gérard, *Les Origines républicaines de Vichy* (Paris: Hachette littératures, 1999).

Passmore, Kevin, 'Boy scouting for grown-ups? Paramilitarism in the Croix de Feu and the Parti social français', *French Historical Studies*, 19 (1995), 527–57.

—— 'The Croix de Feu: Bonapartism, national populism or fascism?' *French History*, 9 (1995), 93–123.

—— *From Liberalism to Fascism: The Right in a French Province, 1928–1939* (Cambridge: Cambridge University Press, 1997).

—— '"Planting the tricolour in the citadels of communism": Women's social action in the Croix de Feu and Parti Social Français', *Journal of Modern History*, 71 (1999), 814–52.

—— 'The construction of crisis in interwar France', in Brian Jenkins (ed.), *France in the Era of Fascism* (New York: Berghahn, 2005), pp. 151–99.

Paxton, Robert O., *Vichy France: Old Guard and New Order* (New York: Knopf and Random House, 1972).

—— *French Peasant Fascism: Henry Dorgères's Greenshirts and the Crisis of French Agriculture, 1929–39* (New York and Oxford: Oxford University Press, 1997).

—— 'The five stages of fascism', *Journal of Modern History*, 70 (1998), 1–23.

Pellissier, Pierre, *6 Février 1934: La République en flammes* (Paris: Perrin, 2000).

Philippet, Jean, *Le Temps des Ligues: Pierre Taittinger et les Jeunesses Patriotes*, 5 vols (Lille: Atelier national de reproduction des thèses, 2000).

Prost, Antoine, *Les Anciens Combattants et la société française, 1914–1939*, 3 vols (Paris: Presses de la Fondation nationale des Sciences politiques, 1977).

—— 'Jeunesse et société dans la France de l'entre-deux-guerres', *Vingtième Siècle*, 13 (1987), 35–45.

—— 'La guerre de 1914 n'est pas perdue', *Le Mouvement Social*, 199 (2002), 95–102.

—— 'Les limites de la brutalisation: Tuer sur le front occidental, 1914–1918', *Vingtième Siècle*, 81 (2004), 5–20.

Ridel, Charles, *Les Embusqués* (Paris: A. Colin, 2007).

Roberts, Mary Louise, *Civilization Without Sexes: Reconstructing Gender in Post-war France, 1917–1927* (Chicago: University of Chicago Press, 1994).

Roseman, Mark (ed.), *Generations in Conflict: Youth Revolt and Generation Formation in Germany, 1770–1968* (Cambridge and New York: Cambridge University Press, 1995).

Rymell, John, 'Militants and Militancy in the Croix de Feu and Parti Social Français: Patterns of Political Experience on the French Far Right (1933–1939)' (Ph.D. dissertation, University of East Anglia, 1990).

Savage, Jon, *Teenage: The Creation of Youth Culture* (London: Chatto & Windus, 2007).

Scales, Rebecca, 'Radio broadcasting, disabled veterans, and the politics of national recovery in interwar France', *French Historical Studies*, 31 (2008), 643–78.

Shaw, Lynette, 'The anciens combattants and the events of February 1934', *European Studies Review*, 5 (1975), 299–311.

Sirinelli, Jean-Francois, 'Génération et histoire politique', *Vingtième Siècle*, 22 (1989), 67–80.

Smith, Leonard, *The Embattled Self: French Soldiers' Testimony of the Great War* (Ithaca, NY: Cornell University Press, 2007).

Soucy, Robert, 'France: Veteran politics between the wars', in Stephen R. Ward (ed.), *The War Generation: Veterans of the First World War* (Port Washington and London: Kennikat Press, 1975), pp. 59–103.

—— *French Fascism: The First Wave* (New Haven, CT and London: Yale University Press, 1986).

—— 'French fascism and the Croix de Feu: A dissenting interpretation', *Journal of Contemporary History*, 26 (1991), 159–88.

—— *French Fascism: The Second Wave* (New Haven, CT and London: Yale University Press, 1995).

Sternhell, Zeev, *La Droite révolutionnaire 1885–1914: Les origines françaises du fascisme* (Paris: Editions du Seuil, 1978).

—— *Ni droite ni gauche: L'idéologie fasciste en France* (Paris: Editions du Seuil, 1983).

Taithe, Bertrand, *Defeated Flesh: Welfare, Warfare and the Making of Modern France* (Manchester: Manchester University Press, 1999).

Tartakowsky, Danielle, 'Stratégies de la rue. 1934–1936', *Le Mouvement Social*, 135 (1986), 31–62.

——, 'La construction sociale de l'espace politique: Les usages politiques de la place de la Concorde des années 1880 à nos nos jours', *French Historical Studies*, 27 (2004), 145–73.

Tellier, Thibaut, 'Paul Reynaud et la réforme de l'Etat en 1933–1934', *Vingtième Siècle*, 78 (2004), 59–73.

Varley, Karine, *Under the Shadow of Defeat: The War of 1870–1871 in French Memory* (Basingstoke and New York: Palgrave Macmillan, 2008).

Wardhaugh, Jessica, *In Pursuit of the People: Political Culture in France, 1934–1939* (Basingstoke: Palgrave Macmillan, 2009).

Whitney, Susan B., *Mobilizing Youth: Communists and Catholics in Interwar France* (Durham, NC and London: Duke University Press, 2009).

Winock, Michel, 'Fascisme à la française ou fascisme introuvable?' *Le Débat*, 25 (1983), 35–44.

—— 'Les générations intellectuelles', *Vingtième Siècle*, 22 (1989), 17–38.

—— *Nationalisme, antisémitisme et fascisme en France* (Paris: Editions du Seuil, 2004).

—— *La Fièvre hexagonale: Les grandes crises politiques, 1871–1968* (Paris: Seuil, 4th edn, 2009).

Winter, Jay (ed.), *The Legacy of the Great War: Ninety Years On* (Columbia, MO and London: University of Missouri Press, 2009).

Wirsching, Andreas, 'Political violence in France and Italy after 1918', *Journal of Modern European History*, 1 (2003), 60–79.

Index

(Note: 'n.' after a page reference indicates the number of a note on that page)

Index

EU authorised representative for GPSR:
Easy Access System Europe, Mustamäe tee 50,
10621 Tallinn, Estonia
gpsr.requests@easproject.com

www.ingramcontent.com/pod-product-compliance
Lightning Source LLC
Chambersburg PA
CBHW031126270326
41929CB00011B/1510